Advising and Supporting Teachers

CAMBRIDGE TEACHER TRAINING AND DEVELOPMENT

Series Editors: Marion Williams and Tony Wright

This series is designed for all those involved in language teacher training and development: teachers in training, trainers, directors of studies, advisers, teachers of in-service courses and seminars. Its aim is to provide a comprehensive, organised and authoritative resource for language teacher training and development.

Teach English – A training course for teachers
by Adrian Doff

Training Foreign Language Teachers – A reflective approach
by Michael J. Wallace

Literature and Language Teaching – A guide for teachers and trainers*
by Gillian Lazar

Classroom Observation Tasks – A resource book for language teachers and trainers*
by Ruth Wajnryb

Tasks for Language Teachers – A resource book for training and development*
by Martin Parrott

English for the Teacher – A language development course*
by Mary Spratt

Teaching Children English – A training course for teachers of English to children*
by David Vale with Anne Feunteun

A Course in Language Teaching – Practice and theory
by Penny Ur

Looking at Language Classrooms
A teacher development video package

About Language – Tasks for teachers of English
by Scott Thornbury

Action Research for Language Teachers
by Michael J. Wallace

Mentor Courses – A resource book for trainer-trainers
by Angi Malderez and Caroline Bodóczky

Alive to Language – Perspectives on language awareness for English language teachers
by Valerie Arndt, Paul Harvey and John Nuttall

Teachers in Action – Tasks for language teacher education and development
by Peter James

Advising and Supporting Teachers
by Mick Randall with Barbara Thornton

* Original Series Editors: Ruth Gairns and Marion Williams

Advising and Supporting Teachers

Mick Randall with
Barbara Thornton

CAMBRIDGE
UNIVERSITY PRESS

CAMBRIDGE UNIVERSITY PRESS
Cambridge, New York, Melbourne, Madrid, Cape Town, Singapore, São Paulo

Cambridge University Press
The Edinburgh Building, Cambridge CB2 2RU, UK

www.cambridge.org
Information on this title: www.cambridge.org/9780521630856

First published 2001
3rd printing 2005

A catalogue record for this publication is available from the British Library

Library of Congress Cataloguing in Publication data

Advising and supporting teachers / edited by Mick Randall with Barbara Thornton.
  p.   cm. – (Cambridge teacher training and development)
Includes bibliographical references and index.
ISBN 0 521 63085 1 – ISBN 0 521 63896 8 (pb.)
1. English language–Study and teaching–Foreign speakers.
2. English teachers–Training of.
I. Randall, Mick, 1946– .   II. Thornton, Barbara, 1953– .   III. Series.
PE1128.A2 A329 2001
428′0071–dc21   2001035344

ISBN-13 978-0-521-63085-6 hardback
ISBN-10 0-521-63085-1 hardback

ISBN-13 978-0-521-63896-8 paperback
ISBN-10 0-521-63896-8 paperback

Transferred to digital printing 2005

Contents

Thanks and acknowledgements

Dedication: to Lynn, Sean, Luke, Wanda and Basil Lesowiec.

The authors would like to thank all the students, teachers and inspectors who have worked with us on many courses in Oman, Egypt, Poland, the Czech Republic, Brazil and on Mentor and MA programmes in the UK at University College Chichester and Leicester University. Many of their ideas and perspectives from the basis of the interpretations we offer.

For help in the process of publishing this book we are indebted to both series editors, Marion Williams and in particular to Tony Wright for his painstakingly detailed editing and useful comments on the different drafts. We would also like to thank Alison Sharpe, Frances Amrani and Bernie Hayden for helping to see the project through to completion.

The authors and publishers are grateful to the following for permission to reproduce copyright material. It has not been possible to identify the sources of all the material used and in such cases the publishers would welcome information from copyright owners.

Categories for Comment by the University of Cambridge Local Examinations Syndicate, DTEFLA/DELTA on p. 37; *Notes for Guidance on Newly Qualified Teachers* by the British Teacher Training Agency (DfEE, London), 1997 on p. 37; *Teacher's Professional Learning* edited by J. Calderhood, 97–115 Cassell, 1987 on p. 215; *Mentoring in the Effective School* by P. Smith and J. West Burnham, Longman, 1993 on p. 220; *Working with your Student Teacher* by Calvert and Fletcher, Nelson Thornes, 1994 on p. 221; 'Exam cheat role play' from *A Handbook of Commercial and Industrial Education*, by the British Association of Commercial and Industrial Education, 1978 on p. 233; *Body Language* by A. Pease, Sheldon Press, 1981 on pp. 243–244; Figure 4.1 'Cultural barriers to communication' in *Race, Culture and Counselling* by Colin Lago and Joyce Thompson, Open University Press, 1996 on pp. 210–11.

Introduction

This book is a handbook for those involved in teacher education in ELT (English Language Teaching). It explores the way that language teachers can best be advised and supported in their teaching situations. Such advisory encounters happen in a wide variety of contexts and involve a wide variety of different advisors and teachers. In-service seminars, pre-service training programmes, and workplace appraisal meetings all contribute to providing advice and support for teachers. However, we believe that a very important element in all of these situations is the discussion of teaching which takes place between the advisor and the teacher, i.e. the provision of feedback. It is this aspect of providing advice which we examine here. Thus, the book looks at the way that advisors operate within the classical teaching practice cycle as defined by Turney *et al.* (1982). They divide supervision into 3 stages: the Pre-observation Conference, the Lesson and the Debriefing:

PRE-OBSERVATION ——▶ LESSON ——▶ DEBRIEFING
   CONFERENCE

It is specifically the support and advice given to teachers and trainees within this cycle which we shall be examining in this book.

The book explores this aspect of teacher education in two ways. Part 1 provides a discussion of the processes of giving advice and Part 2 provides a series of activities and tasks which allow the reader to reflect upon the processes described in Part 1.

Who is the book for?

The book is designed for those who are involved in advising teachers in the widest sense of the term. The provision of effective feedback is an important part of the job of:

- college teaching practice supervisors and school-based mentors working with teachers at pre-service level
- tutors involved in observing teachers as part of INSET (in-service training) programmes
- inspectors in state education systems who are involved in both assessing the teacher and helping that teacher to develop

- Directors of Studies, headteachers and other promoted teachers conducting teacher appraisal or providing induction programmes for new teachers
- teachers working together collaboratively and acting as 'critical friends' to one another, either as part of informal teacher development programmes or more structured action research projects

All the above personnel will be involved in providing advice and giving feedback of one type or another – on a lesson, a lesson plan, or some other aspect of teaching and learning. We believe that this feedback is centrally important to the way that teachers learn and develop. It is the purpose of this book to provide an opportunity for all of those involved in providing feedback to reflect on the methods which can be used to maximise the effectiveness of this learning encounter.

The philosophy of the book

The model of the teacher

We believe that a fully professional teacher is one who is able to reflect critically on their own practice. Although the model of the teacher as the Reflective Practitioner (Schön 1983, 1987, Wallace 1991 and Chapter 2) is an expression of an ideal which often fails to be realised in the hectic day-to-day business of the real classroom, it is a central tenet of this book that effective teachers should be prepared to question and evaluate their teaching seriously with a view to understanding the processes of teaching and learning and in developing their own professional conduct. This means that teachers should be more than programmed automata delivering pre-selected material; they should be actively engaged in critically examining what they do in classrooms. Thus, the ultimate aim of providing advice is to produce a teacher or trainee capable of such independence of thought and action.

Counselling theories

Much of what has been written about helping others to develop in ELT education has its roots in theories of counselling. The models of counselling we use assume that the most effective development and change spring from within the individual themselves. Effective advice has to be 'owned' by the teacher and not merely imposed from the outside. Although this does not preclude prescriptive advice in certain circumstances, the model of counselling which is assumed is 'client-centred' in the sense that the ultimate goal is to encourage the teacher to explore personal experience and to arrive at personally-derived plans for action.

The model of learning

The approach to learning which underlies the tasks in the book is one of experiential enquiry, of working from data outwards towards abstract concepts. Thus, the tasks provided in Part 2 are designed to provide the 'raw experience' which will allow the reader to reflect on their own preferences and feelings about the procedures involved. From this reflection, it is believed that new ways of viewing the process will emerge, which can then be compared with the explanations and discussion provided in Part 1 of the book.

The humanist 'paradigm'

There is a clear relationship between the views of counselling, teaching and learning expressed above. Each rests on the importance of the individual as the main actor in the process. This is not surprising. Ideas within different areas of activity such as education, training and psychology interact with each other and this interaction produces an amplifying effect. The net result of such interactions is the production of an interlocking system of thought: a general 'paradigm', which apparently offers a total view of the world and within which most thinkers and practitioners of a period work. The relationship between the Experiential Learning movement in learning theories, the Reflective Practitioner concept in education and the client-centred or humanistic approach in counselling represents just such an interlocking paradigm.

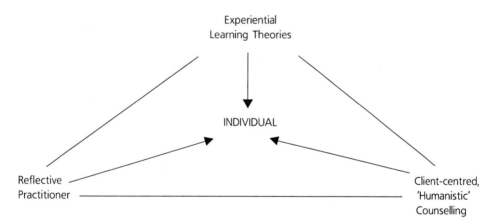

Figure 1 The Humanist paradigm

The role of discussion

Many of the ideas which underpin this book derive from this interlocking paradigm, but the aim of the book is not to 'teach' humanism or to 'train' client-centred counsellors. We believe in the power of group discussion in constructing knowledge and in reaching new understanding. We believe, following Vygotsky (Vygotsky 1978 and Chapter 3), that new understanding and knowledge is not solely an individual entity, but is a social entity, created through discussion. It is hoped that through doing the tasks in groups and discussing these tasks, users of this book will not only fully internalise and understand the ideas behind the theories, but will also go beyond them to create their own understanding and interpretation of these ideas.

From the explanations offered in Part 1 of the book, readers will be aware of the paradigm but need not feel constrained to remain within it or accept all that it postulates. For example, it is realised that the ideas involved in the 'humanist' approach are very sensitive culturally, and that not all advisors, teachers and trainees will necessarily share the same philosophical point of view. The ideas put forward in the book are therefore provided as frameworks for discussion both on a cultural and a personal level and are not intended as panaceas for action or ready-made solutions for all situations.

How to use the book

Organisation

This book is divided into two parts. Part 1 discusses general issues concerning learning to teach, teaching practice supervision, giving advice and feedback. The discussion is based on research in the area as well as the authors' experiences of working with mentors and supervisors in a number of countries.

This section of the book begins and ends with an examination of the context within which advisors work. Chapter 1 looks at the different contexts within which advice is given – the institutional framework – and the final chapter looks at the wider cultural framework within which advisors work. Chapters 2 and 3 examine the 'cognitive aspects' of learning about teaching – looking at what learning theories can teach us about the development of professional practice. The book then goes on to discuss in depth the 'psychodynamic aspects' of providing advice, by examining the way that feedback is delivered through the perspective offered by different theories of counselling.

In Part 2, a series of tasks are included which aim to raise awareness of the key issues identified in Part 1. We have used these tasks with different groups in training and development sessions throughout the world, in order to raise awareness amongst teachers and trainers of the issues involved in learning about teaching and in reflecting on the way that feedback can be provided to teachers.

Each chapter in the first section is followed by

- a summary which reviews key features
- a list of tasks in Part 2 which can be used to explore and reflect on the issues raised in the chapter
- advice for further reading

Contents of Part 1

Chapter 1 provides a discussion of the contexts in which advisors work. Different training situations (e.g. pre-service teaching practice or in-service advisory support) will have important effects on the way advice and support are given. Within these different contexts, the chapter looks at the critical issue of teacher assessment vs teacher support and development.

Chapter 2 then examines the nature of teaching and the way that the skill of teaching might best be learnt. From the focus on the 'context' and the advisor's role provided in Chapter 1, this discussion focuses on the subject itself (i.e. what is to be learnt) and the role of the teacher/trainee. This chapter involves the discussion of

- how skills are acquired
- the differing needs of teachers at different stages of development
- the Reflective Practitioner model of the teacher

Each of these will have a major impact on the way that the advisory process is carried out.

Chapter 3 then focuses on the structure of the teaching practice/advisory cycle and the way that the cycle can be used to enhance teacher learning. In particular, the chapter looks at the advisory cycle through the framework provided by two powerful models of learning:

- Kolb's Experiential Learning cycle
- Vygotsky's interactive model of learning

Chapters 1 to 3 locate advising within institutional, pedagogic and theoretical frameworks. Chapters 4 to 9 provide an overview of different counselling approaches as they relate to advising in ELT. This book proceeds from the belief that it is important for advisors and trainers to reflect upon the methods they use in giving advice and feedback to teachers. In order to do so they need a 'vocabulary' with which to describe what happens in feedback sessions. The vocabulary of interpersonal interactions can be provided from within theories of counselling. In Chapters 4 and 5, three different backgrounds to the advisory cycle are introduced. Chapter 4 begins by looking at different styles of supervision which have been used in ELT education and then, in this chapter and Chapter 5, two influential contributors to counselling practice are discussed with a view to providing a framework to reflect on the professional practice of giving feedback. These are:

1. Egan's Three-Stage Model of helping, which is used to examine the overall shape of the advisory encounter.
2. Heron's Six Category Intervention Analysis, which is used as a vehicle for investigating the detailed way in which advisors talk to teachers in the feedback session.

Using these models as a framework, the following four chapters consider the interpersonal skills involved in providing feedback. Chapters 6 and 7 explore the emotional aspects, with Chapter 6 examining the generic skills of creating an appropriate climate for helping and Chapter 7 examining the way that emotional aspects can be dealt with in a feedback session. Chapters 8 and 9 then go on to look at the specific moves that advisors can make, first of all to lead and direct teachers and then to facilitate teacher/trainees in arriving at independent reflection on their teaching.

Finally, the book examines a series of different factors which affect the way that feedback is provided. The way of delivering, and the interpretation of, different interpersonal messages are highly sensitive to a number of factors, of which culture is one. However, there are also linguistic and personality factors which play an important part in the choice of feedback and the particular style of advice. This final chapter in Part 1 explores the relationship between these factors and offers a model for an explanation of the way that they operate in an advisory situation.

Throughout Part 1 there are references to Tasks from Part 2 which are intended to illustrate and provide a platform for discussion of the issues raised within each chapter.

Contents of Part 2: the tasks

The tasks are designed to provide opportunities to examine the advisory process and increase the reader's repertoire of advice-giving skills. This is done through reflection on personal experience, through group discussion and through the analysis of data, including transcripts of advice-giving encounters. The tasks are designed to allow the reader to consider their own experience of issues involved in feedback, to provide opportunities for groups of teachers/ advisors to try out giving advice in different situations and – through discussion with colleagues – to pinpoint central issues which are important. Through this process readers are led to develop their own perspective on these issues and to develop their own repertoire of advice-giving skills. Each activity includes

- the task itself with photocopiable pages for use in group situations
- trainer notes with a suggested procedure for managing the task
- a commentary on the activity giving an indication of possible outcomes
- references to Part 1 of the book, detailing where the key issues to which it relates are discussed

The tasks are organised in sections which roughly follow the order of material in Part 1, but there are many instances where the implications of the role play or discussion will be dealt with in a number of different chapters in Part 1.

The role of the commentaries on the tasks

Commentaries on outcomes are provided after each activity. These are provided as a guide for the trainer using the book with groups to illustrate the central themes which could come out of the activity, but they are not provided as 'solutions' or 'model answers'. It is intended that the users of the tasks will devise their own solutions to the problems set, and will compare these solutions with the discussion of issues provided in Part 1 of the book. Thus, each task has a cross-reference to the sections of Part 1 which discuss issues which may arise from the task.

Ways of using the tasks

The tasks have been designed primarily to be used in groups to generate discussion and debate. However, it is also possible for an individual reader to complete tasks and keep a record of their reactions and thoughts, then compare these reactions either with colleagues or with the explanations and models provided in Part 1. Alternatively the reader might like to further examine an issue raised in Part 1 by looking at the relevant task(s) in Part 2.

Language note

Finally, a note on the terminology. Although the process of advice is relevant to both serving teachers and pre-service trainees, the term 'teacher' has been used throughout to signify the recipient of advice, rather than the term 'teacher/ trainee', or 'client' which is generally used in counselling. We have also employed the device of using 'they' as the generic singular as is used in sociology rather than the somewhat clumsy 's/he'. Within Part 2 of the book, we refer to those carrying out the tasks as participants, although as previously noted these tasks can be completed by individuals.

1 Contexts: when and why advisors advise

This book argues that the feedback discussion is the critical part of the process of providing advice and support to teachers. This discussion is undertaken by individuals, and the roles and positions they create in this feedback session will be of crucial importance to the success of the advisory process. In later chapters we shall explore the psychodynamic processes which take place in these sessions, but any relationship which is built during the session will be affected by the institutional and formal contexts within which the advisor is working. It is the aim of this chapter, therefore, to explore first the implications of these contexts for the advisor.

1.1 Pre-service and in-service contexts

There are many contexts in which feedback is given to teachers covering both pre-service and in-service teaching. Much pre-service advising operates within the context of teaching practice supervision. With in-service teachers, contexts range from the informal discussions which might occur between colleagues (often called 'critical friends'), through to the more formal visits of a head of department in a school or an area advisor, and to the official annual inspection of lessons by ministry officials. The observation of lessons on pre-service and in-service TEFL courses such as the Cambridge RSA or Trinity Certificate and Diploma programmes provides another context in which advisors work. Each of these contexts will have an effect on the conduct of the feedback session, inasmuch as each situation will provide its own set of participant preconceptions of the purpose of the session. This will define the roles of the advisor and the advisee within the session. The contexts which we shall examine are:

Pre-service   Teaching practice supervision
                    Mentoring
                    'Private sector' TEFL certification

In-service   'Private sector' TEFL Diplomas
                    Internal appraisal (Head of Department, Headteacher)
                    Inspection
                    Colleague to colleague ('Critical Friends')

The pre-service/in-service dimension will have an important influence on the areas that advisors will discuss with teachers, on the content and focus of the teacher learning process and on the degree of experience which the teacher brings to the discussion. These issues will be discussed in Chapter 2 (see particularly the discussion of teacher life cycles), but in this chapter we wish to concentrate on the wider social and institutional contexts within which advisors work.

1.2 The issues

There are three interrelated 'dimensions' which are common to all situations and which are likely to have a powerful effect on the feedback discussion. These we will characterise as the Interpersonal Climate, the Institutional Role, and the Purpose:

INTERPERSONAL CLIMATE	*Formal*	*Informal*
INSTITUTIONAL ROLE	*Technical*	*Professional/Personal*
PURPOSE	*Assessment*	*Developmental*

Figure 2 Three dimensions which affect feedback discussion

Before examining the different contexts in which advice is given, we shall briefly look at each of these dimensions.

1.2.1 Interpersonal climate: formal vs informal

The provision of effective advice depends to a large degree on the perceived status of the advisor by the advisee and the consequent interpersonal 'distance' between them. We shall argue that situations in which the advisor and the advisee trust each other and feel relaxed are more effective for giving advice. Although there are cultural differences which must be taken into account (in some cultures, extreme informality in a feedback situation may be inappropriate), the less formality that there is in the situation the more likely there is to be a degree of perceived 'equality' between the advisor and the advisee. In this situation, it will be easier for the advisor to provide supportive and non-threatening advice than in a more formal setting.

The above contexts in which advice is given obviously differ greatly in the degree of informality involved (the critical friend being potentially highly informal and inspection being potentially highly formal). This arises from the external social/work relationships between the participants. Although these factors will be difficult to change, an advisor who is aware of the potential constraints of the external circumstances can aim to counteract them by altering other, more immediate, factors such as the place of the feedback or the seating arrangement (see Chapter 6 for a discussion of the role that body language can play in providing advice).

1.2.2 Institutional role: technical vs personal

Later in this chapter we shall discuss the connotations associated with terms used to describe the advisor's role (e.g. inspector vs advisor, supervisor vs mentor). Here we merely point out that the very terms used to describe the role are descriptors of the function that advisors play within institutional frameworks. The teaching practice supervisor's role will usually be defined in documents produced by the college or university running the Teaching Practice. An advisor visiting a newly qualified teacher will have a specific role to play within the qualifications framework for that country. Both may have schedules of competencies based on standards (see Chapter 2) which will need to be completed as part of the visit. All of these documents provide a background to the feedback discussion and accumulate to form an institutional 'discourse' (Fairclough 1992) of inspection/advice. This discourse may have a technical agenda which is at variance with the professional/personal agenda which the advisor wishes to emphasise. The presence of such discourses cannot be ignored and, again, the advisor will need to be aware of this framework and, if necessary, take action to counteract their effects on the relationship in the feedback discussion.

1.2.3 Purpose: assessment vs development

If any one of our dimensions epitomises the dilemma faced by teachers and advisors, it is the tension between assessment and development. For teachers and for trainees, the issue of assessment is probably the most problematic in any feedback process. In any advisory encounter, even in the relatively non-threatening situation of advice being given by a colleague, there lurks the fear of being assessed and thus criticised. This is a central issue which must be confronted by anyone involved in providing advice (for an exploration of this issue, see Task 1.1). The emergence of the non-judgmental, humanistic counselling tradition in the West (see Chapters 4–6) is a response to just this issue and will provide one of the constant themes to which we shall return throughout the book.

However, if we look at the advisory contexts which we have outlined above, they nearly all involve assessment. No matter how supportive the teaching practice supervisor may be or how much the inspector sees their role as one of developing the in-service teacher, this intention may be completely misread by the trainee/teacher if the institutional outcome is to provide a report on the trainee/teacher for the purpose of certification or employment. Thus, the advisor will need to be keenly sensitive to this issue. They will need to be completely honest with the advisee about these two conflicting roles and, where possible, will need to separate them.

1.3 Pre-service contexts

1.3.1 Teaching practice supervision

This is perhaps the most common situation in which advice is given to pre-service trainees. Most initial teacher preparation throughout the world is carried out in post-school tertiary institutions, either teacher training colleges or universities.

Theory vs practice

In many contexts, it is colleges of education who train primary level teachers, while the training of secondary teachers is often exclusively the province of the universities, who may not appreciate the value of practical teaching at all. In some countries, the preparation of secondary teachers may contain no practical element. In these cases, future English teachers follow a general degree course which usually has a 'methodology' component but no teaching practice element. Good examples of this system can be seen in Poland, Russia and Tunisia. In Poland student teachers follow a five-year academic *Magister* programme and in Tunisia a four-year degree in Arts and Civilisation. In this type of situation, academics deliver plenary lectures on educational psychology, philosophy and sociology while 'real' teaching is left until later. This produces an 'educational intelligentsia' comprising those who teach methodology in university departments (the 'methodisti' of the Pedagogic Institutes in Russia are a good example) and who place a great deal of importance on theoretical knowledge but have little or no practical experience of teaching.

  This situation is now changing. In many countries in Central and Eastern Europe, the language teacher training departments were established to train teachers of Russian. With the increased demand for English in schools following the political and economic changes in Central and Eastern Europe, the need to train English language teachers has necessitated the establishment of new programmes to train teachers. For example, in Poland and the Czech Republic, there have been a number of colleges established offering 3-year Licentiate degrees which train language teachers for the middle schools. These colleges were founded and are supported in their efforts by the British Government through the PACE/PRINCE/FASTTRACK projects and have built in to their programmes the idea of teaching practice as a central part of the degree programme. However, these colleges are not totally independent as they are validated by established universities. This involvement of the university sector in colleges of higher education means that the ethos of the 'methodisti' or curriculum expert can continue to have an effect on the way that supervision is carried out. It can affect the view that supervisors have of their role and the view the trainee teachers have of the visiting supervisors. Although there have been moves in this region to move to a mentor-based supervision system – in some areas all supervision is carried out by the school-based mentor – under the traditional system, the supervisor is expected to provide answers to the trainee's problems based on knowledge gained from theoretical models based on 'scientific' research; yet it may be practical insights which the trainee most needs. In addition, supervisors working within this institutional culture often have little practical classroom experience and so may use theoretical explanations of teaching as a defence against this lack of experience. Thus, the situation is exacerbated by the theory/practice divide and the 'distance' between the advisor and the advisee is emphasised and amplified by the imbalance of theoretical knowledge possessed by the two.

Technical vs personal roles: assessment vs development

The potential conflict between the technical and professional/personal roles of the supervisor and between assessment and development is perhaps the clearest within the pre-service context. Teaching practice, although having a central pedagogic role in developing the novice teacher's teaching skills, also has an important gateway function for the profession. The time spent in the classroom not only plays an important part in the development of the teacher's basic teaching skills, but is also a time for the novice to demonstrate their level of competence in such skills. As such, this dual role poses a real dilemma for the supervisor. Is the role primarily one of attempting to develop the teacher's skills and understanding of teaching, or is it one of assessing their performance? The former role might well lead the supervisor into a more supportive and less authoritarian role whereas the role implied by the latter is more authoritarian, prescriptive and judgmental.

One solution to this dilemma is suggested by Stones (1984). He argues strongly that as few undergraduates are ever failed on teaching practice the teaching profession should essentially ignore the judgmental aspect and concentrate instead on the developmental side. Trainees, he argues, should be judged on *ipsative scales* (scales relating to their personal development) rather than on absolute measures of competence. Whilst this does offer an attractive solution to the dilemma posed by the dual roles, in political terms such a position is untenable. Quite reasonably, society will continue to demand that certification courses act as gateways to the profession and that the certification which they offer should indicate that teachers have the necessary skills and competencies to fulfil their roles. If practical teaching is to play a part in this certification process, then advisors acting as teaching practice supervisors will continue to be asked to provide judgments on suitability.

This tension is recognised in a number of curriculum models used at the pre-service level. The fact that on most undergraduate degree programmes in the UK teaching practice does not aggregate to the overall degree classification is an indicator of the difficulty of assessing teaching practice in the same way as other subjects. For further discussion of curriculum models and assessment/development, see Task 1.2.

1.3.2 Mentorship

An increasingly popular method of providing feedback on teaching at the pre-service level is that of mentorship. Starting in the British education system in 1992, it has spread widely and is increasingly being used in ELT contexts overseas, particularly in Eastern Europe (see Malderez & Bodóczky 1999, p. 3).

The mentor on pre-service teacher education programmes is a classroom teacher who accepts a novice into their classroom for a period of teaching practice. On the superficial organisational level, this person appears very similar to the teacher who, under the old system of teacher education, accepted a student from a teacher training college on a block teaching practice period, the 'co-operating teacher' as they are often called in overseas contexts. Many of these teachers did, in fact, provide extremely helpful advice and guidance to young trainees and performed many of the functions that are provided by the present mentors. However, previously this help and guidance was provided on an *ad-hoc* basis; those who received it profited, those who did not lost out. Ultimately, although the classroom teachers and the schools provided reports on the student teacher's period in the school, the responsibility of providing both developmental advice and assessment lay with the training institution. In the present system, mentors have a specific and defined responsibility for training and, ultimately, for assessment. Thus, the mentors not only have a professional/developmental role (as did co-operating teachers), but also an institutional role and an assessment function.

The roles of the mentor

In addition to having an institutional role in assessment, the mentor, in accepting a student for a long period, can also be asked to perform a wide range of roles. These include:

- **Technical/assessment roles**
  Coaching the teacher in classroom-based skills
  Informing the teacher of wider curriculum issues
  Helping in goal formation and clarification
  Evaluating classroom performance
- **Personal/developmental roles**
  Motivating the teacher
  Confidence boosting
  Counselling – listening to problems; helping to reduce feelings of anxiety
  Helping the teacher settle into the school
  Problem-solving

Many writers place a great deal of emphasis on these developmental and personal/professional roles and it is these functions which are perhaps seen as the most important by many mentors and trainees (Fish 1995, Smith and West-Burnham 1993).

However, as mentioned above, the mentor does play a technical institutional role in the gateway process by providing input to the assessment of the trainee's teaching practice performance. The difference is that, unlike the traditional supervisor, the mentor does not work alone. On British mentor programmes (probably the most developed models of mentoring) the overall grade of the trainee is decided in a three-way conference between the mentor, the trainee and the college tutor. Thus, the inherent tension between development and assessment is structurally removed to the teaching practice conference where the trainee, the mentor and an outside 'moderator' jointly negotiate the overall assessment profile for the trainee. This system has a number of attractions: In removing the burden of overall assessment from the mentor to the conference, it frees the mentor to be supportive and developmental in the day-to-day process of giving advice to the trainee; by involving the trainee in the decisions about their strengths and weaknesses, it allows for effective 'ownership' of any future action plan by the trainee; by involving a college supervisor in the final decision about the trainee it provides a check that standards are maintained between different teaching situations. This, then, is a structural approach to a resolution of the essential tension between assessment and development. The conflict is resolved through a combination of personnel (the involvement of the college supervisor) and process (the negotiation).

Formal vs informal: the mentor as guide

From an examination of the institutional roles and purpose of the mentor, we now turn to the interpersonal implications of the role. The term 'mentor', in itself, is a highly attractive one for native English speaker teacher educators. Although few would recognise its precise etymology, the connotations within the language are those of a warmth, experience and sympathetic guidance, and these connotations probably account for its success as a term.

Within the literature on mentorship, the following definitions have been offered:

> 'Mentoring is a process by which an older and more experienced person takes a younger person under his/her wing freely offering advice and
> encouragement.'   (Jeffrey and Ferguson 1992)
> 'The role of the mentor is to act as "wise counsellor", guide, adviser to younger or newer colleagues.'   (Smith and West-Burnham 1993)
> 'The mentor will be a senior colleague whose role is to support, facilitate and coach the new teachers.'   (Earley and Kinder 1994)

The above discourse is one of warmth and 'natural' teaching and learning. It clearly involves an asymmetrical knowledge relationship between the mentor and the mentee, but the relationship portrayed is largely informal, a relationship which is reinforced by the long timescale involved in such partnerships. The formality which can characterise the relationship between the formal teaching practice supervisor and the trainee is largely absent in the mentor/mentee situation. In addition, as discussed above, the tensions between development and assessment are to a degree ameliorated by the system of mentorship, allowing the mentor to concentrate more on the former. These are probably two powerful reasons why mentorship has become such a popular model for pre-service training both in Britain and, increasingly, in overseas contexts.

1.3.3 Private sector TEFL certification

This may seem to be an odd classification of training/advising situations. However, deriving from the lack of any government-recognised qualification for teaching EFL in Britain, entry to the profession for British teachers is largely in the hands of private examination bodies such as the University of Cambridge Local Examinations Syndicate (UCLES) and Trinity College. Unlike overseas teachers who generally pass through a tertiary level training programme at college or university, British teachers entering the profession do so through intensive post-graduate training programmes run largely by private institutions and validated by one or other of the examining bodies. This training situation provides a rather unique set of circumstances. At the Certificate (pre-service) level many courses are delivered as short, intensive programmes lasting less than 6 weeks. These types of courses are not only restricted to the UK. The intensive certificate programme is a very common method of inducting new teachers and has attracted some research interest (e.g. Richards, Ho and Giblin 1996). It is for these reasons that we feel justified in including it as one of the contexts within which advisors work. Specifically, we shall examine the implications of the intensive training programme.

The relationship between trainer and trainee

Given the intensive nature of these programmes, trainees and trainers often form extremely close ties. The relationship is usually highly informal, both in the methods of teaching (workshop style input sessions held in plenary) and in the manner of providing feedback to the trainees. The atmosphere is usually close to that found in private language schools – not surprisingly, since this is the location of many courses. In addition to the obvious influence that the location has on the social practices, there is also a tradition of 'teaching by example' on pre-service programmes, and thus the informal learning approaches of the training programmes mirror the pedagogy espoused for adult language teaching. The trainees will often be newly graduated students and in many circumstances the trainers and the trainees may not differ greatly in terms of age. All of these factors combine to produce a very different atmosphere from that found in other classroom supervision situations, such as in state schools.

Whilst this apparently 'democratic' and informal relationship may well form a facilitative backdrop for the acting out of more humanist approaches to counselling and learning, it is important to appreciate the peculiarities and uniqueness of the social setting. The learner/trainee may well not be familiar with such an egalitarian approach. Their experience of previous learning may well lead them to the belief that a greater social 'distance' and more formal system of feedback is more appropriate for learning. Thus, the advisor will need to convince the learner that this approach is, in fact, productive. As a corollary to this, the advisor who may have learnt feedback skills on such intensive programmes yet who is working in a state-school environment will need to be aware of the large differences that exist between the two contexts.

Technical vs personal roles: assessment vs development

The intensive nature of these programmes and the stress that they place upon trainees means that tutors are often involved in wider issues than the purely pedagogic. Even within the professional domain, the tension between supportive development and critical assessment is highlighted and intensified by the nature of the courses. This is particularly true of the weaker trainees whose confidence is low and who need to be supported carefully to develop as teachers. Such trainees can take up large amounts of tutor time and attention so that trainers working on such programmes often complain of the exceptional stresses imposed by the necessity to undertake a wide variety of personal and technical roles. Earlier courses of this type used external examiners to provide the final assessment of the teacher. Increasingly, the regulatory examination bodies are using external moderation of the *course*, rather than the teachers, as their means of guaranteeing standards and quality. These wider curriculum changes, in which the external assessment of the candidates has been replaced by external assessment of the providers, only add to the difficulties of acting as both a guide to professional growth and an assessor of sufficient competence for certification as a teacher.

Although these tensions are not unique to this situation (see the description of the mentor roles above), in the intensive training context, there is not the time offered by the mentor context for many of the problems to be resolved. In providing feedback, the advisor in this situation will need to be aware of which 'agenda' is being addressed; is it social, personal, technical? Is the advice provided for professional development, or is it to indicate a level of assessment? (for further discussion of agendas as viewed by Heron, see Chapter 5).

1.4 In-service contexts

1.4.1 Private sector TEFL Diploma courses

There are many similarities between these courses and the pre-service certificate courses discussed above. This is particularly true in terms of the micro organisation culture within which they both work. Most are located within schools and colleges which deliver mainly language classes, and are associated with a 'hands-on', highly practical approach to learning about teaching, in stark contrast to the often heavily theoretical approaches of the traditional tertiary sector previously described. Associated with this philosophy, there is often a highly informal interpersonal climate, in the same way as we noted with pre-service certification courses. Many of the courses at this level are delivered on a part-time basis, although not exclusively so, and this allows for a more relaxed and less frenetic relationship to develop between the advisor and the teacher/trainee.

However, there is a major difference between the two types of course; the level of experience brought to the feedback session by the teacher/trainee. On pre-service courses there is a highly asymmetrical relationship between the tutor and the trainee; the trainee is by definition a novice, and the tutor is to a large extent the 'expert'. This relationship will be recognised, at least tacitly, by both parties; although the tutor may well take a more 'reflective approach' to the teaching (see Chapter 2 for a discussion of the reflective practitioner), both parties will acknowledge the greater experience of the tutor. With Diploma courses, the differential between the advisor and the teacher will be considerably reduced. Given the fact that the age gap may also be reduced (a factor involved in many in-service situations), advisors will need to appeal to other bases than established, traditional social status values (e.g. age, experience, tutorial position) on which to 'validate' their claims to be able to offer advice (for a further discussion of validity claims, especially in cross-cultural contexts, see Chapter 10).

In this situation the tutors on such courses tend to ascribe to a reflective approach to learning about teaching. They place a lot of importance on teacher self-reflection and self-evaluation, and feedback sessions are often highly trainee-centred using a 'democratic' form of counselling (see Chapter 4 for a discussion). However, as with the changes mentioned above in the pre-service context, curriculum changes have shifted the burden of assessment from an external examiner to the tutorial team. The implications of these changes are that there is apparently a mismatch between the espoused philosophies of self-evaluation and 'democratic' counselling, reinforced by the highly informal atmosphere in which it all takes place, and the institutional function of assessment. Unless this is understood by the trainer/advisor and dealt with honestly, the 'messages' sent by the advisor may well be interpreted in quite a different manner by the teacher receiving them. Thus, advisors need to be aware of these factors when providing feedback on such courses.

1.4.2 Internal appraisal and staff development

In addition to the use of advice in teacher training, managers will also be involved in providing advice to teachers for the purposes of staff development or appraisal. Thus, Heads of Departments, headteachers and Directors of Studies will be asked to watch teachers and to provide feedback on the way that lessons are conducted. This can happen for a number of reasons:

- to provide support for a newly qualified teacher (NQT)
- to monitor the way that teachers are performing as part of routine staff appraisal
- to help a teacher who is perceived to be having problems
- to assess staff development needs of such a teacher

In many ways, this context overlaps to some degree with the next context, that of inspection. What differentiates it, however, is the close working relationship between the advisor (the manager) and the advisee (the teacher) and the power relationship between them.

The level of formality

In providing feedback to teachers in a managerial context such as this, there are a number of factors which will affect the level of formality involved:

- the hierarchical structure of the school
- the organisational culture of the school
- the leadership style of the manager

Most schools and colleges have a relatively 'flat' organisational structure and 'managers' are often not very remote from the teachers they manage. Indeed, the term 'manage' in education still sits rather uncomfortably with many involved in the process, possibly indicating a degree of disquiet within the profession about hierarchical structure. Heads of Department and Directors of Studies generally work with their teachers as 'teams', i.e. they operate as a group to provide lessons and often teach alongside the colleagues that they supervise. Thus, there tends to be an atmosphere of shared responsibility for getting a task done (i.e. teaching) in which there is generally not a great distance between the manager and the worker. This closeness is reinforced by the size of most educational institutions. Although secondary schools and colleges are large organisations, they are often broken down into departments and sub-departments which are rarely larger than 20 people. Similarly, private language schools also operate as small units even if they are members of large chains. Thus, hierarchies in such organisations tend to be small and relationships close. These factors should provide the opportunity for a relatively informal approach to the feedback process. However, this will depend on the institutional purpose of the feedback.

The institutional role and purpose

If we examine the range of reasons for an internal appraisal given above, its function will often have an important effect on the way that it is carried out. Clearly the degree of formality and the atmosphere when approaching the induction of an NQT will be quite different from that of supporting teachers who are having problems in their classrooms. It is also likely that the purposes and even procedures to be followed in these situations will be prescribed by the organisation. Thus the purposes of staff appraisal, the possible outcomes and even the way of approaching the observation of lessons may well be laid down in official documents. It is important that both sides are quite clear about the procedures to be used and also the likely outcomes of the appraisal.

Appraisal and staff development systems, then, carry with them a number of established institutional procedures and these procedures will have scripts which will carry messages about the interpersonal and institutional roles and functions the advisor will be taking up. The advisor needs to be aware of these messages and will be working within them but need not be totally dominated by them. In this context the advisor is the manager of staff and thus has power over the microculture of the department or school. Although not responsible for the overall organisational structure, the individual manager can affect the organisational culture within the department and can operate staff appraisal to maximise the supportive and developmental potential for teachers.

1.4.3 Inspection

The functions of inspection systems

Inspection systems can be broadly divided into

- those which primarily inspect schools as institutions
- those which primarily inspect teachers, i.e. their principal function is to report on the quality of the teaching rather than the overall quality of the school

Thus, from an institutional viewpoint, inspection/advisory systems have two functions; one is to monitor the provision of educational services and the other is to provide support and advice to the teacher in the classroom. In Britain this was historically provided by different bodies at different levels in the education system, the Local Education Authority (LEA) and central government inspectors (HMI). The HMI provided a monitoring role, whilst the LEA provided help and support for teachers through a system of advisors.

In other parts of the world, the two functions are not so clearly separated and one person often carries out both functions. Thus, in the Middle East for example, a subject inspector will be 'in charge' of a number of schools with a certain number of teachers. In such systems, the inspector is expected to see each teacher a specified number of times in the year and to produce a report on that teacher at the end of the year. This system seems rather 'Orwellian' viewed from the perspective of a British system which has traditionally given a great deal of autonomy to the classroom teacher in terms of curriculum, materials and methods. However, in practice, the system is less a system of constantly auditing performance than one of the provision of advice and support. It is important that an inspector working within such a system is clear about the role that is being adopted when debriefing teachers. In the best situations, the inspector can build up a close and supportive relationship with the teachers and can be a powerful tool for teacher development.

1.4.4 Critical friends

Action Research has been one of the most important in-service teacher development techniques of the last twenty years. It essentially involves teachers in researching their own classroom practice in a rigorous and systematic manner (for a description of Action Research in language teaching see Wallace 1998). A 'critical friend' is a colleague who is chosen to work with a teacher on such an Action Research project and, in particular, a colleague who is invited to observe lessons and provide feedback. The concept has also been used in peer-driven teacher appraisal systems (Hancock and Settle 1990). It has also been used successfully on undergraduate teacher preparation programmes in the UK, on overseas initial training programmes in Romania (Mace 1996), and as part of pre-service teaching practice in Egypt (CDELT 1992).

Advantages and disadvantages of peer observations

The use of peers for providing feedback to teachers has a number of attractions.

On the management level it has the advantage of low costs. The provision of skilled supervisors for anything like the amount of observations necessary for effective development is prohibitively expensive.

On the pedagogic level it also has advantages:

- The use of a friend to observe, on the face of it, should remove many of the tensions involved in the assessment/development debate. The critical friend clearly has no formal assessment role and thus should be able to offer advice untainted with at least the formal necessity to judge.
- The very act of observing and offering advice should benefit not only the one being observed but also the one observing. Being able to discuss lessons with your peers in a non-judgmental and open forum is seen as an essential step along the road to being an autonomous and reflective practitioner.

However, this idealised view of the situation may be nothing like the situation in reality. Although there are no formal requirements for assessing, any observation of a lesson is going to involve, by its very nature, judgments about what has been seen. This is perhaps the central conundrum of all teacher observation and feedback. Unless the feedback is to become so bland as to be of no use in moving a teacher on, the observer will need to make judgments about what went on in the lesson. These need to be expressed to the one being observed, and any criticism will at least have the capacity, if not the actuality, of causing pain. The use of peers and critical friends is supposed to reduce the incidence of such pain. What it does, supposedly, is remove the possibility that the comments made are in any sense due to the observer making them from a position of personal feelings, particularly those of hostility. A friend's comments are unlikely to be ascribed to antithetical personal feelings. However, the degree to which they are 'objective' is less clear. In fact, the comments are likely to be coloured positively by the personal friendship. Unless critical friends are aware of this problem, it is unlikely that the situation will produce the suggested gains.

There are great strengths in the concept of the critical friend. However, the phrase itself is in one sense only a slogan. In its juxtaposition of the two central tensions involved in observation and feedback – criticism and personal feelings – into one phrase, it highlights the central problem. In the sense that phrases can be used to focus attention on problems and indicate ways to overcome them, then it can be useful. However, careful preparation of a critical friend situation needs to be undertaken if it is to be successful. This preparation should involve the participants in some understanding of the ways to advise and the effects that different types of advice can have.

1.5 What's in a word? The terminology of advice

We have examined a number of different contexts in which advice can be provided to teachers and have suggested that the social practices involved in these different contexts will have an important effect on the way that advice is provided to teachers. Throughout we have used a number of different labels to describe the advisor – inspector, supervisor, mentor, critical friend and so on. Each term has its place within the discourses of supervision. As yet we have not examined the differences between these terms and the nuances they convey.

In a paper given at IATEFL in 1987, Roger Bowers suggested that we should examine the language used in teaching and examine the implications for the different metaphors we use. He gave the example of the implication of the term 'headteacher' as against 'manager' or 'director'. We have argued above that the latter two terms have yet to become accepted within British education, although the present emphasis by the British government on management rather than classroom issues has undoubtedly had an important impact on education practices. Similarly, the change of emphasis from a largely Local Authority-led advisory system to a centrally organised school inspectorate has had a major effect on teachers and their professional lives. This latter change is also accompanied by a shift in terminology – from advisor to inspector. It is for linguistic philosophers to debate the causal issues involved in such linguistic changes – do changes in social practices lead to changes in discourse or do discourses influence social practices? However, it is generally agreed that the two are closely connected, and without taking sides on the issue of primacy, it is useful to examine the terms used for describing the advisor's role.

1.5.1 Interpersonal relations

One of the first attempts to unpack the concepts underlying the metaphors used in teacher education was Stones' reflections on the meanings underlying the term 'supervision' (Stones 1984: vii). He mused on the types of 'sight' which could be involved in the term – super-vision, eyesight, insight, foresight – yet, surprisingly for a book avowedly following a counselling approach to supervision, he did not discuss the interpersonal social relationships involved in the term. Supervision overlaps with the discourses of industry and has strong hierarchical implications. The analogy to be drawn from the use of the term is that of the line manager checking the competence and performance of workers. Thus, the use of this term carries with it clear hierarchical implications.

'Mentor' and 'mentoring' carry a completely different set of associations in English. The term 'mentor' is still asymmetrical in terms of its power relationship with the mentee, but this relationship is much more 'organic' and 'natural' and less technical and institutional. The authority implicit in the term derives from a more 'traditional' personal respect rather than the institutional and hierarchical authority implicit in the term 'supervisor'. It is also noticeable that in the new discourse of supervision associated with mentorship, the tutor from the college now provides a 'link' between the mentor and the institution, rather than an all-knowing super 'vision' function.

1.5.2 *Institutional vs professional*

This book uses the term 'advisor' as a generic description of a trainer, teacher, tutor involved in the process of giving advice. However, as we have seen, the term appears within the contexts of advice in contrast to the term 'inspector'. This use of the two terms within English seems to us to encapsulate the central tension which we have identified between the institutional, technical and professional-developmental functions of providing advice on teaching. This contrast is reflected in many other languages. Arabic also has two words to describe the inspector: *muffatish*, which means 'official' and is very similar to the concept of inspector, and *muwajah*, which means 'leader/guide' and is closer to the idea of 'advisor'. The *methodisti* of the former Soviet states contrast with the in-service 'advisors', the latter often being experienced teachers quite removed from the intellectual intelligentsia of the colleges and universities. In a similar vein, the *animateurs* of Madagascar and Togo contain the concept of facilitating local teachers' groups and the idea of grass roots help for the teacher. *Animateurs* exist alongside the *conseilleurs pedagogiques*, the teacher advisors, who perform a more official function in many ex-French African territories, although not as formal as *l'inspecteur* who has a very formal institutional role in the education department.

The function of each of these personnel, their job descriptions and their position within the educational hierarchy will be the most important determiner of exactly what the term means in the culture. There are many examples of mismatch between the job and the title, the latter being 'political' rather than descriptive, but such 'political' labelling should not be ignored. By choosing to identify a position with a particular label, systems are indicating their beliefs about the position; such beliefs and validity claims are as important a part of the way systems operate as the physical realities of the situations. In an overt attempt to harness the power of discourse to implement changes, the Minister of Education in Oman issued a decree in 1982 that all inspectors (*muffatish*) were to be called advisors/guides (*muwajah*). The system changed little, but on arrival in a school, the children could be heard to call out a warning that the *muffatish* had arrived, whilst the headteacher (in Arabic the 'director') greeted him as *muwajah*. Although the changes to social practices took much longer to have a real effect, the use of the terms indicated the direction that the Ministry wanted the inspection service to follow.

1.5.3 The terms used in this book

As we have indicated, this book will generally use the term advisor in a generic capacity. However, there will be other terms which are used when we come to consider different approaches to learning and giving advice. Thus in this chapter we have used the term 'critical friend', an oxymoron which encapsulates the tension between the personal and the judgmental, closely associated with the issues we have identified in the different contexts. Other terms will be used such as Schön's 'coach' (Schön 1984) when discussing his model of the reflective practitioner (see Chapter 2) and trainer/trainee within the context of training programmes. Each of these terms will carry with it a host of associations, concerning both the interpersonal relationships and the critical/judgmental purposes.

Furthermore, different discourses use yet other terms. Within the discourse of counselling, advisees are referred to as 'clients' and advisors as 'practitioners'. As a major part of the book will be using ideas and concepts from counselling theory we shall, at times, also borrow from this discourse.

1.5.4 Terms in translation

Finally, in a book concerned with advising language teachers in international contexts, it is impossible not to add a footnote to this discussion concerning the translation of the different terms into other languages. The term 'mentor' is a good example of the problems which can be encountered. There is no Arabic equivalent of the term and thus it is impossible to translate. The potential, then, for any change in social practices by using the mentor metaphor, is lost. Also, in some Slavonic languages (e.g. Czech) the term is a 'false friend', implying the giving of advice in a dictatorial fashion. Thus, although this book will use terms in English and discuss them in their English connotations, advisors working with non-native speakers will need to be aware that the terms may have completely different connotations when translated.

1.6 Conclusion

In this chapter we have looked at a variety of contexts in which advice can be given. We have suggested that these contexts will play an important part in the way that the advisor approaches the business of giving advice. Within the contexts, there are two major issues:

1. pre-service vs in-service training, which relates to the teacher's level of development
2. the institutional vs the professional role of the advisor

This chapter has examined issues contained in the latter and in terms of the three dimensions which we used to examine the contexts, there is generally a cline operating across the different contexts which we have described, with certain contexts having a high degree of assessment and others a lower degree of assessment.

FORMAL
HIGH INSTITUTIONAL
HIGH ASSESSMENT
LOW PROFESSIONAL
LOW DEVELOPMENT

INFORMAL
HIGH PROFESSIONAL
HIGH DEVELOPMENT
LOW INSTITUTIONAL
LOW ASSESSMENT

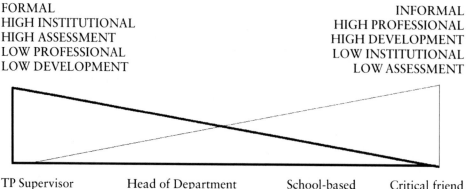

| TP Supervisor | Head of Department | School-based | Critical friend |
| Inspector | (Internal appraiser) | mentor | |

Figure 3 The degree of assessment in different advice contexts

In the next chapter, we shall examine the way that knowledge about teaching is gained; this will involve a discussion of the different needs of teachers at different times in their career, most notably the pre-service and in-service stages.

Summary

The following issues have been raised in this chapter:

- The different contexts in which advice is given: pre-service and in-service
- The effects of context on giving advice; formality, institutional role and purpose
- Teaching practice supervision, mentoring, appraisal and inspection
- Different contexts and the degree of assessment expected from the advisor
- The institutional setting and how the advisor is viewed
- The different terms used for describing advisory roles and their implications

Tasks

The following tasks can be used to introduce/explore issues raised in this chapter:

1.1 What does it feel like to be inspected? Inspection in various contexts
    Purposes of assessment
1.2 How do different systems deal with the issues of different roles and functions of advising?
    Separation of assessment and development roles
1.3 An examination of the strengths and weaknesses of inspection/advisory situations
1.4 What problems have researchers found on British teaching practice programmes?

Common difficulties within advisory systems
Ways of solving difficulties
1.5 The value of peer observation and 'critical friends'

Advice for further reading

Stones, E. (1984) *Supervision in Teacher Education*, London: Routledge.
   This is a very sensible, easily readable book dealing with a host of issues connected with supervision including what is meant by the term, the roles of the supervisor and the dichotomy between assessment and development. Although written some time ago, the issues it discusses are still very much of relevance today.
Edge, J. (1992) *Co-operative Development: Professional Self-development through Co-operation with Colleagues*, Harlow: Longman.
   A very practical book containing discussion on the use of critical friends as well as a range of activities for teachers to engage collaboratively.
Montgomery, D. (1999) *Positive Teacher Appraisal Through Classroom Observation*, London: David Fulton.
   This book describes how advisors and other professionals can set up and engage in classroom observation. It also looks at the use of focused appraisal sessions and how to deliver feedback interviews within this context.
Malderez, A. and Bodóczky, C. (1999) *Mentor Courses: A resource book for trainer-trainers*, Cambridge: Cambridge University Press.
   A definition of a mentor and the required roles are dealt with in the early parts of this book. The later section contains a range of activities for use with mentors on trainer training courses.

2 Learning to teach

Much of the literature on advising and mentoring concentrates on the skills and qualities required by advisors to fulfil their role competently (Parsloe 1992) with little attention paid to the recipients of that advice. To us, this is rather like looking at the teacher without considering the learner. Later we will look at the practical aspects of what the advisor needs to do, but in this chapter and the next, we examine how a teacher learns to teach. If the role of the advisor is to help the teacher become an effective practitioner, then we should look at the processes by which teachers reach this level of classroom competence. We need to examine what is involved in learning to teach – to look at what teachers should be able to do and what they need to know. This chapter looks at the 'types' of knowledge involved in teaching, including the difference between theory and practice, and the different approaches which have been used in teaching teachers how to teach.

2.1 Theory vs practice in teacher education

Teaching is a profession, and one of the most important aspects of professional training is that knowledge needs to be integrated with practice. This balance between theory and practice is critical in any professional training programme, and ELT is no different. As we have acknowledged earlier, teacher support and training involves a wide range of activities, not just that of providing feedback and discussion about teaching. Although this is the central interest of this book, we must examine the issue of the theoretical knowledge(s) involved in teaching in order to see how advisory discussion with teachers fits in with the wider context of teacher education. As advisory discussions with teachers take place in the school, the advisor is working at the 'interface' between theory and practice. It is the aim of this chapter to examine:

- the types of knowledge that teachers need
- the theoretical learning perspectives which apply to skill learning
- the approaches which have been adopted for the practical training of teachers

and to examine, within each of these areas, the implications for the advisor.

The challenge for those concerned with teacher education is how to integrate the theoretical knowledge about language and learning with the actual process of utilising such knowledge in the classroom to encourage effective learning. The issues which underpin this discussion of theory and practice can be expressed as the following central dilemmas:

◆ To what extent is it possible or advisable to describe teaching in purely theoretical terms, or should teaching be seen instead as an essentially practical process?
◆ Should the training of teachers concentrate on specific classroom behaviours and routines, which can best be learned through observation of others and practice, or should these surface routines be integrated with the theoretical perspective provided by discussions of methodology?

These questions will be addressed in this chapter as we examine the different approaches which have been used for training teachers (see Task 2.1).

2.2 The knowledge involved in teaching

2.2.1 Shulman's categories of knowledge necessary for teaching

Much has been written about the types of knowledge involved in teaching. Shulman (1987) lists seven types of knowledge base which are important for the teacher, regardless of their subject specialism. It is worth examining these types of knowledge with regard to English language teaching and looking at the role of the advisor in helping the teacher to assimilate these effectively.

Content knowledge

This refers to the teacher's knowledge of the subject – in this case the English language. It encompasses the teacher's own proficiency in the language (Spratt 1994) and the degree of knowledge the teacher has about the formal aspects of English such as syntax, phonology etc. Areas such as culture may also be included in content knowledge (Cullen 1994, Murdoch 1994) (see Task 2.2; 2).

It may often fall to the advisor to provide guidance in this area – both information on linguistic aspects and training in language proficiency. Given the fact that many advisors in ELT will be dealing with non-native speakers of the language and the advisor, although not always a native speaker, will usually be at least more formally qualified in the language, the issue of giving advice about content knowledge will be one which is dealt with in the feedback session. Indeed in some contexts, comments about teachers' language form the major part of the advice given to teachers in feedback sessions. (El Naggar 1986). Furthermore, as Cullen (1994) points out in the context of Tanzania, language improvement and the need to feel secure in one's own language competence may be the overriding personal goal for many teachers. The interpersonal implications of giving advice in such situations are discussed in Chapter 8 (see Informative interventions), but it is important to remember that the teacher may expect the advisor to give direct advice on the language itself and on aspects of that teacher's proficiency in the language.

General pedagogic knowledge

This refers to general issues such as classroom management and control which are common to a range of subject disciplines. It is interesting that in ELT, such issues are usually contained within the mainstream methodology component of courses rather than treated as separate 'generic issues' (but see Underwood 1987, Wright 1987).

This is an area which is clearly related to the practical activity of teaching; as such it is closely connected with classroom practice and will be one of the major areas on which the advisor will focus.

Curriculum knowledge

This refers to knowledge about the particular materials used by the teacher. These are frequently given a lot of emphasis on ELT training programmes, particularly within national educational systems where changes of curricula require reorientation of large numbers of teachers (Sheldon 1989, Nunan 1990, Johnson 1996).

As such, advisors may find that giving information about this area is one of their primary responsibilities, particularly when new coursebooks require a change in teacher thinking.

Pedagogical–content knowledge

This refers to the way that the target language may best be presented and learnt: the 'methodology' of language teaching. Within ELT, this tends to dominate training programmes. Theories of how languages are learnt and how these relate to approaches, methods and techniques used in language programmes form the core of most approaches to language teacher training throughout the world. Much of the recommended reading for teachers in training at both pre- and in-service levels falls within this area (see Freeman 1994). Such an emphasis is understandable since the issue of how the subject is taught is clearly of central interest to teaching, but it is also perhaps an indication of the strong link between the practical aspects of ELT and the more theoretical area of Applied Linguistics.

An analysis of feedback sheets written by inspectors in Oman suggests that this is the major area of commentary by advisors (Khalfan 1987).

Knowledge of learners and their characteristics

This area has begun to receive a lot of attention in recent years with the research into different learning styles and strategies of learning (Ellis and Sinclair 1989, Oxford *et al.* 1992, Skehan 1989). However the degree to which these have been implemented in mainstream teaching is arguable.

Nevertheless, if we agree that the purpose of teaching is to promote learning, it is the duty of the advisor to highlight the centrality of the learners and to make teachers aware of how their behaviour in the classroom will affect how individuals learn.

Knowledge of educational contexts

This refers to how the sociocultural and institutional context will affect learning and teaching. What is acceptable or appropriate in one educational system will not necessarily be so in another (Holliday 1994).

This may be an important area when advising teachers working in educational contexts other than their own (e.g. expatriate teachers in the Middle East, or native speaker teachers preparing to work in different contexts overseas).

Knowledge of educational ends, purposes and values and the philosophical and historical issues

Although the study of the sociology, philosophy and history of education often form a major element of general initial teacher training programmes run within tertiary institutions, such a knowledge is not usually seen as important on language teacher preparation programmes and is usually confined to a historical survey of methods in ELT (Richards and Rodgers 1986).

It is rare for the advisor to comment on this area (although see above about cross-cultural situations), but it is important to be aware of these issues in the specific context within which the advice is being offered.

2.3 Theoretical perspectives on the learning of skills

As we have indicated, learning about teaching involves not just the acquisition of theoretical knowledge, but the application of that knowledge to a practical context, the classroom. In order to implement the theories of learning, teachers need to acquire a set of classroom skills. This section will look at two views of skill learning; a cognitive psychological perspective and a perspective which draws insights from the development process undergone by teachers.

2.3.1 Learning skills – a psychological perspective

Psychologists have long been interested in the way that basic skills and routines are learnt through practice. Developing from the work of the behaviourist psychologists, which emphasised the value of practice followed by reward on the successful learning of skills and routines, Anderson produced a model of learning which provides a cognitive explanation for the effectiveness of practice as a method of learning. His ACT model of learning (Anderson 1983) places more emphasis on the way that the learner learns rather than on the way that outside factors, such as reward, influence learning.

2.3.2 Anderson's ACT model of skill learning

Anderson's model is based on the assumption that there are three types of memory involved in skill learning; the short term memory, the declarative memory and a memory which he calls the procedural memory.

The short-term memory

The short-term, or working, memory is the memory which we all use for controlling our minute-by-minute thoughts. Such a memory is crucial in language comprehension. It is like a 'notepad' on which we record things for a short time while we wait for new information to come in. It is also crucial in helping us to perform new tasks. It allows us to 'talk to ourselves' while we are trying to perform unfamiliar routines, such as trying to mend a car or use a new computer program. He argues that the explicit instructions which we use to perform new tasks are supplied from the declarative memory.

The declarative memory

This is the memory which stores 'rules' for doing things. In language learning terms it may contain the explicit rules for the construction of a particular tense, for example. It is the sort of memory which will benefit from the more academic, theoretical approach as well as a competency-based approach. For example, when learning how to organise pairs or groups in the classroom, a teacher can use ideas derived from theory – *'I mustn't put all the strong students in one group'* – or from a competency list – *'I must set this up efficiently and quietly'* – to guide them in the process of carrying out the task.

The procedural memory

However, as we have said, learning about teaching should not end at this point. Rules and knowledge need to be applied to the classroom. The experienced teacher does not need to stop and think about every action in the classroom, but has a fluent and intuitive knowledge about what to do. This intuitive, automatic knowledge of how to perform an action is supplied from the third of Anderson's memory types, the procedural memory. Actions which are controlled from this memory do not need to be consciously thought about. They are triggered directly from the preceding action, not from rules retrieved from the declarative memory.

He argues that skills and routines move from the declarative memory (where they are under conscious control) to the procedural memory (where actions are carried out unconsciously) through three different stages:

- cognitive
- associative
- autonomous

Routines move from one stage to another through practice. The more certain routines are practised the less we need to consciously control them and the more automatic they become.

Any of us who have learnt to drive a car with a manual gearbox will immediately understand the logic of such a process in the painful course of mastering the accelerator and the clutch; a complex series of actions which experienced drivers use totally automatically. This type of learning progression is found in many instances of skill-learning (see Task 2.1). However, it is one thing to recognise such processes in the complicated, yet still relatively simple world of the psychological laboratory (the source of much of Anderson's data) or the skills necessary for surviving in the modern world; it is quite another to suggest that the enormously complicated skills of teaching also conform to such laws. Let us then consider the extent to which this model of learning is useful for explaining the learning involved in teaching.

The cognitive stage and the novice teacher

In the first stage, the *cognitive stage*, the teacher needs to think about most of the actions which have to be taken in the lesson. The teacher needs to concentrate on the minute-by-minute progress of the lesson and has little or no chance to 'stand back' and consider what is happening in a longer time frame. This emphasises the need for novice teachers to plan even the simplest of routines quite explicitly and the importance of the detailed lesson plan to the process of learning to teach, and is the direct cause of the extreme pressures and chaotic impressions of the lessons reported by teachers during their early experiences in the classroom.

If we take an example of dealing with an error produced by a student, many novice teachers will not know how to react. They may ignore the error, not for a principled reason such as not wishing to demotivate the student, but for the simple reason that they are concentrating on carrying out their lesson plan and do not have time to consider any other factors. Even if they do notice the error, the teacher at this stage may well need to plan the actual language or signal used to respond to the student. How should they react to the student? Should they produce an explanation? Should they produce the correct language for the student to copy? Should they pull a face / make a gesture? Automatic routines of dealing with errors, derived from either the teacher's prior social experience, or from their own experience of learning, may not be appropriate in the new role. Thus, new routines will need to be learnt and, at this stage, will very much be under the conscious control of the teacher. In the turmoil of framing a response to deal with the immediate situation, the novice teacher will not have the time to consider the wider strategic issues involved in the correction of the error; either the psychodynamic/personal aspect or wider pedagogic/ linguistic ramifications.

The associative stage and the developing trainee

In the second phase of skill acquisition, the *associative phase*, the teacher begins to put together the different individual procedures into larger units. As certain types of declarative knowledge become involved in different situations, the novice teacher can gradually begin to automate certain procedures and use these procedures in a wider variety of situations, to make generalisations about required actions. This results in a lessening of the degree of verbalisation involved in problem-solving, so more of the behaviour can be described as intuitive or automatic. This allows the teacher to begin to think of more than just the immediate response. For example, to take further the example of the way that a teacher responds to an error, certain 'surface' routines of appropriate response will now have become automatic (such as adjusting language to the level of the learner, using different facial expressions and gestures) and the teacher can now concentrate on more 'strategic' aspects of the situation, perhaps employing a simple algorithm such as:

Is the error serious?

⇓

Is the error important?

⇓

Does it lead to a breakdown of communication?

⇓

Make a correction / Ignore the error

Figure 4 Dealing with student error: an example of a teacher in the associative stage of skill acquisition

The autonomous phase and the experienced teacher

Finally, in the *autonomous phase*, the learner is able to implement such skilled behaviour without any conscious control. This is the much-vaunted knowledge which is associated with the expert teacher. In this stage of development, there is no need to verbalise or consciously control a whole series of sub-skills which are necessary for teaching. The above algorithm will be reduced to the initial question only and will lead to the apparently intuitive teacher intervention, appropriate in terms of language and gesture, and in terms of the immediate teaching and learning strategy in the lesson. In the situation of handling feedback to a student, all the lower-level responses are entirely automatic, leaving the teacher free to concentrate on wider strategic issues such as reinforcement vs feedback and the particular nature of the individual concerned.

Although Anderson's model was derived from observation and experimentation with subjects undertaking limited, closed, problem-solving tasks such as mathematical problems, it does seem to match the experiences many of us have had as a teacher or have seen in our trainees. It explains the necessity for conscious control over actions when meeting new classroom routines or procedures and it accounts very well for the difficulties and stress faced by all novice teachers in the classroom when faced with new experiences. It also explains the importance of practice in the initial stages of learning how to teach. Practice is the essential mechanism for turning learnt rules into effective teaching; for converting theory into practice.

In addition, the model provides two central principles which are important for the consideration of the advisor's role in the process of teacher learning. It highlights the importance of conscious control over the early stages of skill learning, and thus underlines the possibility of talking about such skills. It also suggests that there is a development in skill learning from basic routines to more complex patterns, thus suggesting that for each teacher there is a zone of skill learning which is determined by their individual level of development. The first principle emphasises the advisor's role in helping the teacher to plan, prepare and execute new techniques, while the second emphasises the advisor's role in identifying the next stage of development for the individual teacher.

2.3.3 Skill learning and expert behaviours: the life-cycle approach

A parallel method of looking at the way that teaching is learnt is provided by studies of the life cycle of teachers. Rather than looking at the acquisition of particular skills or techniques in individual teachers, these studies have attempted to provide general descriptions of the types of behaviour exhibited by teachers at different stages of their development.

THE NOVICE	The novice teacher will concentrate on classroom survival by acquiring discrete instructional and managerial techniques and learning each element of a classroom task. The approach is recipe-based with the focus very much on short-term planning and discrete teaching techniques. Much of the learning at this stage takes place through imitation or following the advice of others, e.g. 'Don't smile before Christmas.'
ADVANCED BEGINNER	The classroom routines which were previously applied are now becoming increasingly automated. The teacher has acquired a certain degree of episodic knowledge and similarities across contexts are beginning to be realised. Rather than one-off reactions to difficulties, strategies for dealing with situations begin to emerge. The teacher is starting to shift attention away from his or her own performance towards the design of instruction and is starting to be able to question what he or she does in the classroom.
COMPETENT	The teacher now has strategies to cope with most common classroom events and will work to these strategies. At this stage teachers have the confidence to cope with more improvisational planning and are able to make conscious decisions about their own actions based on the context. Whereas at the previous two stages, the focus was still very much on the content of lessons, competent teachers are beginning to focus on the learner. They are able to set priorities and engage in longer term planning.

PROFICIENT	At this stage intuition and knowledge together are beginning to guide performance. Problem-solving takes account of the complexities of the situation and the focus is increasingly on the learner.
EXPERT	This stage is characterised by an intuitive grasp of situations. The teaching performance is now fluid and seemingly effortless. Planning is flexible. The expert is able to anticipate rather than merely react to classroom events, recognise global patterns and see how specific events are manifestations of these.

Figure 5 The typical life cycle of a teacher (for a task to discuss some of these issues, see Task 2.2; 3, 5)

While such a description is intuitively appealing (we can all remember what it feels like to be a novice), there have been criticisms of the life-cycle studies. A stage theory of teacher development implies that the earlier stages inevitably lead on to the later stages. However as Grossman (1992) points out it is by no means the case that once teachers have mastered techniques that work, they will move on to higher order concerns: 'As preservice teachers master the routines of teaching, many become satisfied with their teaching and are less likely to question prevailing norms of teaching and learning.' (1992 p.174)

What emerges from these studies is that different teachers will be ready to acquire different skills at different stages in their professional development. It may be then that the role of the advisor is to assist the teacher in moving through these stages. They will need to identify, develop and provide learning opportunities for the teacher – to question the applicability of existing routines, to widen the teacher's repertoire of strategies and techniques and to help the teacher move on to higher level concerns.

Thus, the teacher life-cycle studies and the psychological theories have a lot in common. Although the observations of teacher development are more detailed in their descriptions of the stages through which a teacher passes, the essential elements of the psychological model can be seen. Both are based on similar descriptions of cognitive development. Experts work intuitively, novices need to consciously control what they do. Experts recognise patterns and are able to work strategically, novices look at specifics and react to events as they happen. Experts can anticipate events, while novices can only react after the events have taken place. The two methods of examining the issue do differ, however, in providing an explanation of the phenomenon observed and a principled explanation as to how behaviour at one level of development can be transformed into behaviour at the next, how conscious control over actions can be transformed into automatic procedures. The Anderson cognitive model provides an explanation of the *process* of skill acquisition, albeit on a simple discrete task, whereas the teacher life-cycle studies provide merely a description of the skills, along with associated teacher thinking.

Both models suffer from being rather simplistic, perhaps dangerously so. The Anderson model suggests that the process from one stage to another is a smooth, simple process, and the life-cycle model might assume that the process of development is common to all and equally effortless for all. Whilst the models provide two useful metaphors for understanding the way teachers learn new skills and progress, they say little about *how* such learning takes place. In the next section we shall critically examine three major influential models of how professionals learn. These are:

- the apprenticeship models, which emphasise the practical acquisition of classroom behaviours through observation and replication of 'good' practice
- competency-led processes which emphasise the learning of different teaching skills and behaviours through a process of breaking them down into identifiable 'chunks'
- the reflective practitioner model which emphasises the role of reflection on teaching and the role played by a coach in this process

In each we shall examine the role that the advisor will play, and we conclude the section with a discussion of how advisors may use their roles to instigate teacher development through autonomous learning.

2.4 Approaches to training teachers

2.4.1 Apprenticeship schemes

One approach which emphasises the practical nature of teaching is the provision of opportunities for beginning teachers to learn from observation and from talking to those who are more experienced, in other words through apprenticeship. Such a model is referred to as the craft model (Wallace 1991) or in more pejorative terms 'sitting with Nellie' (Stones 1984). Such apprenticeship approaches emphasise the practical aspects of teaching. They provide practical workable tips for teachers yet the learning consists essentially of acquiring a set of observable classroom behaviours, rather than providing any insights into the deep structures of teaching and learning – the underlying principles which motivate teacher behaviour in the classroom. Such surface approaches to training are commonly found on a number of pre- and in-service training courses including short-term private sector certificate courses such as the Cambridge RSA CELTA (Certificate in English Language Teaching to Adults) programme, where trainees are expected to carry out a set number of observations of more experienced teachers. The emphasis is on trainees observing good practice rather than just watching their peers, the implication being that such observation will guide the new teacher towards the effective practice demonstrated by the more experienced professional. While such approaches would appear to have a high degree of face validity, as methods to be used with beginning teachers, they do suffer certain disadvantages.

Firstly, one of the characteristics of the mature professional is the seeming ease with which highly complex skills are carried out. The craft knowledge of such teachers is highly developed, apparently intuitive, and often not available for scrutiny even by the practitioners themselves (see Schön 1983). At the very best, even with carefully guided observation instruments, observation can only indicate the actual behaviours which are seen and does not uncover the hidden complexity of sub-skills and teacher thinking which underpins the behaviour. Observation of such teaching without the help of an experienced professional to focus the observation and, equally importantly, to unpack and explore the underlying reasoning for the actions being observed, may then lead the observer into believing that such behaviour is easily achieved.

Secondly, it is doubtful whether beginning teachers are even able to describe the complexity of classroom behaviours. In a study of 294 observation forms completed by Polish teacher trainees, Rybak-Dryniak (1995) found that not only were observers unable to identify the reasons for teacher behaviour but that they were in fact blind to many events in the classroom.

Furthermore, merely describing the behaviour of a good teacher will not necessarily help the novice. As with beginning readers, whose behaviour is very different from that of the fluent reader, the novice teacher's behaviour will be very different to that of the expert. A reader will use different strategies at different stages of learning to read. Beginning readers read aloud, most fluent readers read silently. However, it is difficult to imagine learning to read fluently without having first passed through the reading aloud stage. As Smith (1985) points out about reading, describing the processes used by the fluent reader does not necessarily give us information about how such behaviour is to be acquired. The same is true of the equally complex skill of teaching. It may be that teachers need to go through an initial novice stage which has its own defining characteristics. It may even be that expert behaviours are a distraction to the novice teacher. As with the teacher of reading, the advisor needs to keep the goal of the expert teacher in mind but needs to carefully structure the pathway so that the novice teacher will achieve that goal.

It follows from this discussion that simple apprenticeship schemes are not likely to be successful without the perspective of an experienced guide – the advisor – to interpret what is being experienced. As Stones (1984) points out, the essential goal of the analysis of teaching practice is to move beyond the surface structures of behaviour towards the 'deep structures' of teaching and learning. Thus, the role of the advisor is to relate this experience to some theoretical framework, to the 'deep structures of learning' (see Task 2.2; 4).

2.4.2 The role of competencies in learning about teaching

Another way of approaching what a teacher needs to learn is to make a list of the separate skills or competencies, in order to lay down a set of standards required by the successful teacher. Competencies are lists of exactly what a teacher at various levels should be able to do (the list of skill areas) plus descriptors of the type of behaviour required within these areas. Such an approach breaks down the process of teaching into a number of discrete skills which can each be monitored and learnt, and is based round questions such as: What constitutes the competent teacher? How can the teacher's performance best be described? What are the components of successful teaching? What skills are involved? How can these best be described?

One attempt to draw up such a list of skills within ELT is represented by the Cambridge RSA DELTA (Diploma in English Language Teaching to Adults) Categories for Comment. This checklist, possibly the most comprehensive ever produced in the field of ELT, contains 72 'teaching-related' categories and a further 10 'language-related' categories for comment. The following represents the sub-skill areas noted under the section 'Controlled and Semi-Controlled Practice Techniques':

6.1   Sufficient variety in techniques
6.2   Provision of meaningful practice
6.3   Appropriate balancing of teacher-learner, and learner-learner interaction
6.4   Appropriate balancing of class/group/pair/individual practice
6.5   Appropriate sequencing of controlled and less controlled activities

Although intended as a checklist for assessors, if we view these categories as important elements in successful teaching, there is clearly a very large number of aspects of teacher behaviour which need to be considered (see Task 2.3 for some examples).

The checklist acts as a reminder of all the elements to be taken into consideration and as such, provides a framework for the analysis and discussion of teaching, but it does not describe the level of competency required within each of the categories. While an experienced advisor can go into a classroom, make judgments about a teacher's ability and comment on areas that need improving, it can be useful for all those concerned to make explicit the underlying criteria on which assessment is based. It can be argued that without such lists the preparation and help that teachers receive will inevitably be a hit and miss affair, based on the hidden criteria of teacher educators, which may vary from one advisor to another or from one institution to another. Many educational systems have, therefore, drawn up lists of competencies to standardise expectations. The extract below is taken from British Teacher Training Agency (TTA) documentation describing what a newly qualified teacher in Britain should be able to do in the area of classroom management.

Those to be awarded Qualified Teacher Status, must [. . .] demonstrate that they

f)   ensure effective teaching of whole classes, and of groups and individuals within the whole-class setting so that teaching objectives are met and best use is made of available teaching time;
g)   monitor and intervene when teaching to ensure sound learning and discipline;
h)   establish and maintain a purposeful working atmosphere;
i)   set high expectations for pupils' behaviour, establishing and maintaining a good standard of discipline through well focused teaching and through positive and productive relationships;

TTA (1997: 7)

(see Task 2.3 for the design of more specific competency descriptors in ELT and Task 8.4 for competencies used for self-evaluation).

Such an itemisation of micro-skills is helpful particularly in terms of assessment and accountability, since in theory, all teacher educators will be focusing on the same areas and supervisors and others working from such lists will have the same expectations in terms of required standards. However, such competencies still need to be interpreted. For example, different educators may have different ideas about what constitutes 'a purposeful working atmosphere' (see TTA competencies above). In an effort to avoid variations in interpretation, there may be a tendency to break down competencies even further to make individual items more explicit and less prone to subjective interpretations.

Herein lies a major difficulty of using checklists in classrooms. In order to be effective in terms of specifying the goals for a series of lesson observations, they need to be detailed enough to capture the complexity of the teaching situation. However, such lists then become unwieldy and difficult to use. In addition, not all the categories (cf the techniques involved in controlled practice cited in the Cambridge RSA checklist above) will be appropriate in each lesson.

It is also clear that teachers will vary in the skills they need to acquire. There will not only be variation between different teachers, but there will also be different needs at different stages of their development. Thus there has been an interest in devising different descriptors for different 'levels' of teaching. The present British Teacher Training Agency competencies (TTA 1997) contain two 'levels' of competencies, but this approach tends to assume that all trainee teachers move through the competency levels at an even pace, a situation which evidently does not happen in practice (see Task 2.3 for an attempt to define levels in ELT).

To summarise, whilst competency lists and checklist-driven lesson observations have the advantages of making clear the micro-processes involved in teaching and the criteria expected from the teacher, they also have major drawbacks. The lists of skills need to be quite long to be able to capture the large number of skills involved in teaching. If we add to this the need to have differential descriptions of performance based on the teacher's stage of development, such approaches become difficult to manage. The crucial role of the advisor in this situation is to act as a guide to teachers to help them focus on relevant areas, as well as guide them towards the level of performance at which they should be aiming.

Therefore, a key role for the advisor is to assess the level of development and needs of the teacher and to produce an action plan of areas on which the teacher should work based on their learning needs and the requirements of the situation. Competency lists or standards can provide an important 'menu' for carrying out this function, for selecting the areas to be learnt.

2.4.3 The coach and the reflective practitioner

If you ask any group of teachers where they learnt most about teaching, the inevitable answer is something like 'on teaching practice' or 'in the classroom'.

There is usually a general consensus that teaching is best learnt 'on the job'. However, we need to consider what exactly is meant by 'on the job'. Where does such learning take place? Does it happen in the classroom (the mechanical reinforcement of skills by repetition), or does it take place during the whole process of teaching practice, which involves more than just the lesson in the classroom? Although the components of teaching practice may vary from one context to another, in most cases it follows a basic procedure which involves three principal stages: the planning of an activity or activities; the execution of the plan; and feedback on the plan.

This learning cycle can be seen as essentially a feedback control system. Such systems have provided powerful models for explaining behaviour in a number of areas of human thought (electrical, biological and social) during this century (Martin 1995). Central to this process is that comparing output from an action to the desired outcome provides feedback to inform new action. If the actual output and the desired output do not match, then adjustments can be made in the light of this feedback. In our situation, provision of feedback to the teacher leads to new ways of teaching based on this feedback. In this model then, learning does not happen directly during teaching, but it happens when the learner considers the teaching. This process of reflection has led to one of the most influential approaches to teacher learning of the last two decades, the Reflective Practitioner Model (Schön 1984, 1987).

Schön's analysis of professional practice is an attempt to describe the particular type of knowledge involved in professional occupations such as teaching and to describe the ways that such knowledge can be learnt. He believes that such knowledge is best developed in a learning 'practicum', the word he uses to describe the situation within which professional practice is developed. The practicum is a practice 'workshop' similar to the teaching practice situation. In terms of the learning processes involved, Schön develops three important concepts: reflection-in-action; reflection on action; the Coach.

Reflection in and on action

According to Schön, reflection-in-action is essentially different from reflection on action. Reflecting on action is thinking back over what has been done, whereas reflection-in-action is reflection in the midst of an action without interrupting it. He clearly considers the type of knowledge gained from this reflection to be powerful; his description of that knowledge is an eloquent expression of the intellectual processes involved in professional understanding. He defines knowledge-in-action as something 'which goes beyond statable rules – not only by devising new methods of reasoning, [. . .] but also by constructing and testing new categories of understanding, strategies of action, and ways of framing problems'. He describes it as 'a process we can deliver without being able to say what we are doing' (1987: 31). Thus Schön's concept of knowledge-in-action is very similar to the intuitive knowledge which we have discussed earlier and is closely analogous to 'procedural knowledge', in the Anderson model. Through a process of reflection-in-action the practitioners 'make new sense of uncertain, unique or conflicted situations of practice' based on the assumption 'that neither existing professional knowledge fits every case nor that every problem has a right answer.' (1987: 39)

If Schön is right and this reflection in action is important, then the ability to reflect while in the process of teaching is something which needs to be developed in teachers. We therefore need to examine the usefulness of this concept in the context of learning about teaching:

1. As we have argued above, teachers in the initial stages need to have conscious control over the skills they are learning, possibly even needing to verbalise routines until they become automatic and part of procedural memory. This conscious control over actions will inevitably take up processing space in the working memory of the teacher. Given the well-established fact that short-term memory has a limited capacity (Miller 1956), this leaves much less processing space for considering other things. As we said earlier, at this stage teachers find it difficult to consider longer term strategic issues, and it is likely that their capacity for reflection will be equally restricted. To put it simply, the teacher in the classroom does not have the processing capacity to both act appropriately and to reflect on what is happening.

2. If, as we argue, reflection-in-action is the same as intuitive knowledge, we need to ask what intuitive knowledge is available to the novice teacher. The automatic response from such a teacher may be based on their own past learning experience and possibly inappropriate in the circumstances. To take the example of dealing with a challenge from a learner in the classroom: the novice teacher might well produce an automatic response, for example, a sarcastic comment, which has the desired effect, in the short term, of making the student keep quiet. However, it can be argued that such an action is not the best way to approach situations in which teachers are challenged. The fact is the teacher produced an essentially 'coping' strategy. Mature reflection on this with an experienced advisor might elicit a more varied range of options the teacher could have used which would be more appropriate in the teaching context.

3. Schön emphasises the importance of the coach (advisor) in developing this knowledge-in-action and in assisting with the process of reflecting-in-action. How can this be done practically during the lesson? How can the advisor help the teacher develop such reflective skills? It is interesting to note that the types of example which Schön gives of the practicum in action are those of professions such as the architect. In such a situation, reflection-in-action is much more feasible as it is possible to work with such a person and ask them to think aloud as they work. Within the work environment of the architect, it is possible to interrupt the flow of creation to discuss what is happening on a moment-by-moment basis. In teaching such immediate joint evaluation is just not feasible, and the reflection on the process will need to take place on a more retrospective basis, i.e. at some time after the lesson in a feedback session.

Thus, while not denying the descriptive power of the knowledge- and reflection-in-action concepts, their actual application to teaching has difficulties. The way Schön describes the knowledge gained by professionals through practice is extremely eloquent and persuasive, and advisors need to be sensitive to the fact that teaching is not merely a set of routines to be mechanistically applied, but the situation does not allow for the advisor to sit behind the professional and develop this reflection while the action is taking place. In teaching, the advisor's role will be much more important in the feedback phase of the practice cycle, in guiding reflection-on-action. In this stage, according to Schön, their role will be to demonstrate, advise, question and criticise the performance of the student and enable the student to reflect.

The role of the coach

It is through the eyes and experience of the advisor that the teacher's experience in the classroom can lead to new learning. Schön argues, when discussing his concept of reflection-in-action, that this new construction of knowledge will be guided by the professional coach who will 'emphasise intermediate zones of practice' (identify the areas which the teacher needs to pay attention to / learn next – see Vygotsky and the ZPD, Chapter 3) and will draw out from the practitioner the concepts developed through 'reflective conversations with the materials and situation'. (1987: 39) Thus within Schön's practicum the coach plays an important role. The role of the coach or advisor is to structure the learning of the student by deciding which areas they should work on (emphasising intermediate zones of practice) and to guide the teacher into a critical dialogue concerning their current practice.

Thus, from the point of view of Schön's work, the coach is essential in providing the teacher with the framework to examine the teaching experience, and from that framework to provide explicit targets for the next experience. However, in addition to this process of individual target-setting within a teaching practice setting, we also need to consider the role of the advisor in setting the framework for independent teacher development.

2.4.4 *The reflective practitioner and teacher autonomy*

The ideal model of teachers as reflective practitioners, 'developing by reflecting on their professional experience and not simply [. . .] followers of instructions but professionals who are open to new ideas [. . . and who are . . .] flexible, capable of further independent study [and] able to resolve problems in a rational way' (Wallace 1991: 26) has lain at the heart of much of the thinking about teacher education in the West for a considerable time.

Such goals may well seem highly optimistic in many teaching situations around the world, where the resources are simply not available for a teacher to be provided with a long-term coach to guide them through the learning process. However, given these very restraints of time and personnel, teacher education or training can only be successful if it generates some degree of independent personalised professional growth which does not depend on the presence of an advisor or helper. It is quite simply not feasible to have constant access to an advisor at all times, yet we expect teachers to continue to develop throughout their professional careers. Thus, in providing support and help to teachers, it is necessary to consider how to provide the necessary structures which will allow teachers and trainees to develop autonomously. Such structures will involve helping the teachers and trainees to look critically at their own teaching (see Tasks 2.4 & 2.5). They will also involve helping the trainee teachers to learn to take responsibility and manage their own learning. The advisor's role might be to give them the strategies to identify their strengths and weaknesses and break down what it is they need to learn and to parcel it up into manageable chunks. Advisors will need to help teachers with the skills of prioritising, with short- and long-term planning and with techniques for monitoring their own progress.

A further role for the advisor within the reflective practitioner movement is to help teachers articulate and refine their views of the teaching process and their own learning. Alongside the focus on the practical skills of teaching and how they can be enhanced by reflection, there has been a growth in interest in values and beliefs held by teachers and the processes they use to make sense of teaching, that is, in teacher cognition (Calderhood 1987, Breen 1991, Burns 1996, Woods 1996). Teaching obviously includes both thought and action. The interest in the way that teachers conceptualise their teaching and the examination of teacher beliefs and values is perhaps inevitable, given the emphasis placed within the reflective practitioner movement on reflection and on the development of personal theoretical models of teaching. Here the role of the advisor will be to help the teacher in training to externalise such mental processes.

2.5 Conclusion

In this chapter we have examined teaching from the twin points of view of the type of knowledge necessary for learning about teaching and of some approaches which have been used to teach about teaching. A number of common conditions have emerged from this study. We have noted that there are important reasons for believing that there is a hierarchy in learning about teaching – both the psychological explanation of how skills are learnt and the study of teachers' life cycles agree on the types of behaviours exhibited at different stages. There is a general consensus that the intuitive knowledge of the expert is often difficult to access without the help of an expert guide. However, from these examinations of practice and learning theory, there are also powerful reasons emerging to believe that verbalisation and discussion of practice is an important element in learning about teaching. Each of these situations argues strongly for the important role of the advisor in the process.

We have also argued that teaching is more than a set of routines for acting in the classroom (although these do constitute part of the learning involved), and we have identified procedures which are involved in learning about teaching. In the next chapter we shall continue to examine learning about teaching from a cognitive standpoint by examining two powerful models of learning which provide theoretical support for the processes which we have begun to describe.

Summary

The following issues have been raised in this chapter:

- theory vs practice in teacher education
- the 'types' of knowledge involved in teaching
- Anderson's ACT model of skill learning
- the life-cycle perspective on learning about teaching
- apprenticeship schemes
- competency approaches to training
- coaching and the reflective practitioner approach
- reflective practice and independent teacher development

Tasks

The following tasks can be used to explore and reflect on the issues raised in the chapter:

2.1 What constitutes successful learning?
2.2 Beliefs about teaching
2.3 Developing teacher competency descriptions
2.4 How to help teachers to reflect in pre-service courses
2.5 Questions to aid critical questioning in the feedback session

Advice for further reading

On the role of theory and practice in teacher training:
Tomlinson, P. (1995) *Understanding Mentoring: reflective strategies for school-based teacher preparation*, Buckingham: Open University Press.
    This provides a very readable and persuasive overview of the way that effective advice can be provided and a useful discussion of the interplay between knowledge and practice in teacher education/training, and it discusses the relevance of learning theory as it applies to classroom practice.
Richards, J. (1998) *Beyond Training*, Cambridge: Cambridge University Press.
    This book contains a number of chapters touching on what constitutes skills and expertise in teaching. It examines types of teaching theories which influence the beliefs and practices of teachers and looks at teacher education from a more holistic viewpoint rather than seeing it at the level of 'training'.
On teacher thinking:
Burns, A. (1996) 'Starting all over again: From teaching adults to teaching beginners', in Freeman, D. & Richards, J. C. (eds.) *Teacher Learning in Language Teaching*, Cambridge: Cambridge University Press.
    This chapter provides an account of the way that teachers can reflect on their own classroom practice, develop their own concepts of teaching and apply them to provide professional development.
On the reflective practitioner and intuition:
Wallace, M. (1991) *Training Foreign Language Teachers: a reflective approach*, Cambridge: Cambridge University Press.

This book provides a helpful and very accessible overview of Schön's reflective approach as applied to foreign language teaching.

Atkinson, T and Claxton, G. (eds.) (2000) *The Intuitive Practitioner: on the value of not always knowing what one is doing*, Buckingham: Open University Press. This book contains a number of interesting articles which discuss how intuition can be used in teaching. Of particular interest is an article by Arleene Gilpin and Gerald Clibbon, 'Elaborated intuition and task-based English language teacher education' which discusses the way that intuition can be used in preparing English language teachers and discusses the difficulties of using intuition in teacher preparation.

On teacher life cycles:

Calderhead, J. (ed.) (1987*) Exploring Teachers' Thinking*, London: Cassell.

The chapter by David Berliner (pp. 21–59) discusses the differences between experienced and beginning teachers both in terms of classroom performance and in terms of teacher thinking.

Other chapters which may be of interest in this book are:

Carter and Doyle's discussion of teachers' difficulties in coping with the sometimes conflicting demands of classroom management and classroom instruction (pp. 147–160).

3 The role of dialogue in learning to teach

In the previous chapter we examined learning about teaching from the learner's viewpoint. We examined the role of theory and practice within the process, we looked at the type of knowledge and skills involved at different stages in the teacher's career and we began to discuss the role that the post-lesson feedback conference plays in the process of teacher learning. This concentrated on the need for the advisor to isolate and prioritise the skills needed by the teachers. In this chapter we want to examine the cycle of supervision in more detail and discuss the role of the advisor in this cycle. In particular, we will use two influential theoretical frameworks to examine the supervisory/advisory process: Kolb's Experiential Learning and the Social Constructivism of Neo-Vygotskian thinkers. Finally, we shall revisit the teaching practice cycle in more detail.

3.1 Kolb's Experiential Learning and the practice cycle

One of the most powerful models of learning which explains how people learn from experience is Kolb's Experiential Learning cycle (Kolb 1983). This theoretical model, which is particularly applicable to adult learning, involves four types of learning: Concrete Experience, Reflective Observation, Abstract Conceptualisation and Active Experimentation (see Figure 6, page 46). Although the framework can be seen as an essentially static taxonomy of learning styles (see Chapter 10), it is clear from Kolb's work that in addition to providing a description of learning styles, he is also arguing that such an experiential learning cycle is an effective method of learning. It is this aspect of his work which we intend to discuss here.

The experiential learning cycle places a great deal of importance on experience as an essential element in the process of effective learning. It seeks to explain the success that mature students often have in their approaches to learning, despite the fact that many of them lack formal academic qualifications. Kolb is essentially a humanist in that he places great emphasis on what the individual brings to the process of learning. Adult learners are particularly rich in the experiences they bring to learning. This is reflected by Carl Rogers, one of the most influential thinkers in the development of humanist approaches to counselling and learning.

> . . . there is only one truth about modern man and that is he lives in an environment that is constantly changing . . . The only man who is educated is the man who has learnt how to learn . . . The most socially useful learning in the modern world is the learning about the process of learning.   (Rogers 1969: 163)

Central to Rogers' thinking is the idea of the learner as an active and self-directed being, which forms an important underlying concept when we come to consider approaches to the feedback session. Such approaches have underpinned much of the recent thinking about adult learning (Gibbs 1981, Garry & Cowan 1986, Smith 1983) and form the basis of the rather ugly term 'andragogy' (adult learning) as distinct from learning approaches used in schools, 'pedagogy' (Knowles 1983).[1]

There are then, two powerful reasons for believing that Experiential Learning can provide a model for the way that teachers/trainees learn about teaching:

1. Teachers and trainees are adult learners and thus an approach which emphasises the strengths of adult learners is appropriate.
2. The subject matter we are concerned with has a large practical, experiential element which is critical to learning, and an approach valuing concrete experience is, again, highly appropriate.

The experiential learning cycle as devised by Kolb is, as indicated above, a four-stage process:

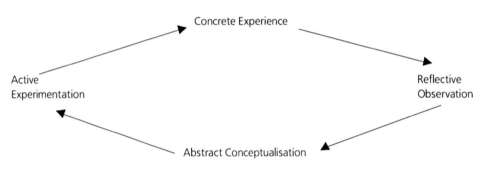

Figure 6 Kolb's Experiential Learning cycle

According to Kolb, effective learning takes place when concrete experiences are examined and reflected upon (Schön's reflection-on-action, Chapter 2). Based on this reflection it is important that the learner extracts principles and concepts which provide explanations for the experience. The principles so derived are then used to input another cycle of experience, reflection and conceptualisation through Active Experimentation; a conscious decision to test the principles and concepts in practice. Kolb argues that traditional academic subjects and tertiary institutions have placed a great deal of emphasis and value on the process of abstract conceptualisation and less on the value of concrete experience. What his model provides, however, is not just an explanation of the phenomenon of the

[1] Although we recognise the important distinction that Knowles makes between the two approaches (indeed much of the argument of this book will be underpinned by the concept of appropriate approaches to use with adults), we shall use the term 'pedagogic' in our discussion to refer to aspects which relate to learning and teaching theory and will not, unless specifically signalled, intend the term 'pedagogy' or 'pedagogics' to refer solely to approaches used with young learners.

'value of experience', but a principled approach which sees experience as an essential and critical element in the gaining of new knowledge. The model provides a description of the process by which theory is derived from practice and the way that this theory can then be tested in practice. It provides a more complex description of the operation of the teaching practice cycle discussed above. Crucially, it provides a role for the inclusion of theory into a model of learning. In addition, this model, drawing as it does on concrete experience as the primary initiative for the learning process, provides a useful framework for the discussion of the processes involved in the teaching practice cycle.

We can then relate the different types of learning involved in Experiential Learning to the teaching practice cycle as follows:

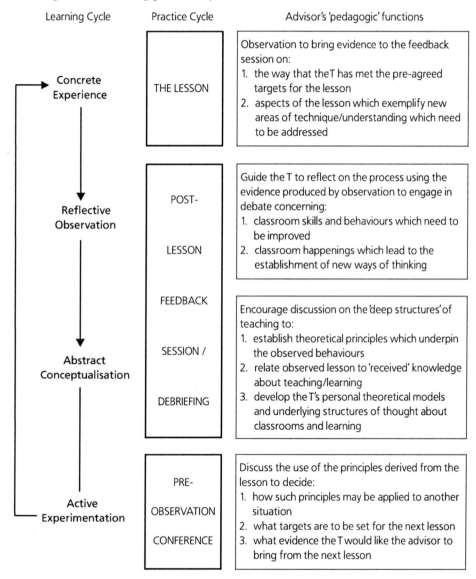

Learning Cycle	Practice Cycle	Advisor's 'pedagogic' functions
Concrete Experience	THE LESSON	Observation to bring evidence to the feedback session on: 1. the way that the T has met the pre-agreed targets for the lesson 2. aspects of the lesson which exemplify new areas of technique/understanding which need to be addressed
Reflective Observation	POST-LESSON	Guide the T to reflect on the process using the evidence produced by observation to engage in debate concerning: 1. classroom skills and behaviours which need to be improved 2. classroom happenings which lead to the establishment of new ways of thinking
Abstract Conceptualisation	FEEDBACK SESSION / DEBRIEFING	Encourage discussion on the 'deep structures' of teaching to: 1. establish theoretical principles which underpin the observed behaviours 2. relate observed lesson to 'received' knowledge about teaching/learning 3. develop the T's personal theoretical models and underlying structures of thought about classrooms and learning
Active Experimentation	PRE-OBSERVATION CONFERENCE	Discuss the use of the principles derived from the lesson to decide: 1. how such principles may be applied to another situation 2. what targets are to be set for the next lesson 3. what evidence the T would like the advisor to bring from the next lesson

Figure 7 The roles of the advisor in different stages of the TP cycle (see also Task 3.2)

In the above model, the role of the advisor is to provide guidance for the teacher, to critically analyse and draw out new principles from the teaching experience and then to use those principles in the next lesson through the drawing up of a plan of action. The function is less one of monitoring and training in techniques than of intellectual growth (for an exploration of advisor behaviour in different phases of the cycle, see Task 3.2).

It should also be noted that when viewed from the perspective of the experiential learning cycle, the pre-observation conference comes at the end of the learning cycle and looks forward to the new learning cycle. This perspective emphasises the fact that the purpose of the pre-observation conference is to look at what can be learned from experience and to use the lesson to put these conclusions into action. The advisor will thus be working from action plans drawn up from previous lessons, or from the teacher's own agenda of what they want to try out in the lesson. In the next chapter we shall look at the *psycho-dynamic* reasons for listening to the teacher's plans for the forthcoming lesson, but the experiential learning cycle provides the cognitive rationale for listening to the teacher's plans in order to help the teacher in drawing the appropriate lessons from experience.

Given the importance of concrete experience and reflective observation within the model, we need then to discuss the role of the advisor during the lesson and, in particular, the role of observation.

3.2 The lesson: observation for development

It was established in the previous chapter that novice and expert teachers differ not only in their ways of teaching but also in their perceptions of teaching, and thus observation instruments are particularly valuable as tools for teachers to be able to alter the way that they look at classes (see Task 3.4 for an exploration of the effect of observation instruments on perception of classes). Much has been written about observing language classrooms and it is not the intention of this book to repeat this work. Allwright (1988) gives a thorough introduction to the subject and there are plenty of examples of different observation instruments for teachers to use on their own classes or for teachers to use in peer observation situations (see Malamah-Thomas 1987, Wajnryb 1992). Such instruments are powerful developmental tools for teachers and for trainee advisors, allowing both to look at lessons systematically. Observation instruments can also be used very effectively in conjunction with feedback from advisors to allow teachers to follow through the advice given in action plans. For example, advice about the type of feedback given by a teacher to the students can be followed up by an instrument which specifically asks the teacher to record the type of feedback they provide to students (see Task 3.5). Finally, programmes of differentiated observation instruments can be used as an 'agenda' for observation of lessons in peer groups where there is little availability of advisory support for groups of trainees (CDELT 1992). Thus, advisors need to be aware of the use of such instruments for the development of teachers. Furthermore, such instruments are a valuable tool for the training of advisors in the process of lesson observation.

3.2.1 The lesson: the collection of data

In the model of learning which we have highlighted above, the function of the observation is to provide a description of what happens in the lesson – data of the actual experience to discuss, analyse and interpret during the feedback session. This can be done by the use of such devices as video recordings, and Turney *et al.* (1982) suggest that supervisors should use such evidence in the debriefing as a basis for discussion. However, in most contexts, there are neither the physical nor human resources to support the video-taping of lessons, the observation and editing of these tapes by the tutor prior to the debriefing and then their use as the material for the discussion as suggested by Turney *et al.* Thus, advisors will need to use other methods for collecting data about the lesson, and many use a system of making notes for later use in the feedback session (see Task 3.6 for an example of such notes).

The underlying justification for such a process of descriptive data collection is that learning proceeds best through a process of self-discovery. Thus Wallace (1991) contrasts the 'classic collaborative approach' with the 'classic prescriptive approach'. In the prescriptive approach, the function of observation would be to gather data about the way that a teacher was teaching: i.e. the data would be used to judge the effectiveness of a teacher. Using ideas from the clinical supervision approach (Sergiovanni 1977), Wallace sees the classic collaborative approach as emphasising the non-judgmental role of the supervisor. The supervisor 'understands' rather than 'judges' and the supervisor has no 'blueprint' of how a lesson ought to be taught. This humanist view of supervision emphasises 'looking with' rather than 'looking at'. The aim of the supervisor during observation is described by Turney as involving 'the supervisor in selecting ways of recording which will yield useful data and interpretation during the feedback sessions' and during the lesson to 'build up a clear record of what is observed' (Turney *et al.* 1982: 121). Thus, the emphasis is not on judgment but on providing a record of what happened in order for this data to be worked on by the advisor and teacher. This process of examination of the data will then lead to new insights being gained by the teacher in collaboration with the advisor. The supervisor's role is predominantly to 'help [the] teacher or trainee to develop autonomy, through practice in reflection and self-evaluation' (Wallace 1991: 110). Although this approach uses the concept of collaboration between the advisor and the teacher, it is important to note that this collaboration is seen as being a mechanism to support the teacher's personal growth and autonomy, i.e. the focus is centrally on the individual as a learner and the advisor as a facilitator.

3.2.2 The role of the advisor during observation

It is clearly possible for the advisor to observe from a number of perspectives during the lesson. Gebhard and Oprandy (1999) contrast the non-participant observer, who has no other role than to observe and take notes, with the participant observer, who may do other things during the lesson such as joining students during group work, monitoring pairwork, talking to students about their learning or even taking on a co-tutoring role. The nature of the data collected will obviously vary depending on the stance taken. Although observation will nearly always be a combination of the two approaches depending on the context and the teacher, it is important that the advisor negotiates their involvement in the lesson at the outset (see Task 3.3).

3.3 The feedback session: theory into practice or practice into theory?

We have discussed earlier the tensions between theory and practice which exist on teacher education programmes and Experiential Learning would seem to offer a solution to the dilemma.

Ramani (1987) argues that in-service teachers typically find theory to be somewhat remote from their actual teaching and Jarvis (1991) reports in a similar vein that in-service teachers on INSET courses require practical ideas to use in their classes rather than theory. Both authors thus highlight the theory/ practice dualism which arises from the difficulty of integrating theory into practice. A further example of this dualism is reported by Johnson (1996), who describes the turmoil experienced by pre-service teachers on initial teaching practicums where little 'theoretical' knowledge from the TESOL courses seemed to be of much use in their actual teaching practice situations. Johnson's suggested solution is to include more information about practical classroom management in the theoretical part of the programme. However, as Ramani points out, the very separation of theory from practice which derives from the division of knowledge into lectures on theory and practical teaching sessions on techniques is perhaps one of the central causes of the problems teachers encounter between theory and practice.

There are, then, two essential problems here. One is extrapolating the theory from the apparent chaos of classroom practice and the other is the failure of theoretical models to adequately contextualise their ideas into situations relevant to teachers. The first problem results from a lack of perception on the part of the teachers, the second results from the alienation of theory and practice. For successful resolution, both involve mediation: in the former, the data of experience needs to be made sense of through the application of rules and theories (a top-down approach) and in the other, theories need to be 'given flesh' through exemplification in actual experience (bottom-up). Following the model proposed by Kolb, the extraction of concepts from experience is a more effective method of working than the other way round. Such a method of working (i.e. from practice to theory) is also the essential model proposed by Schön in his professional practicum.

Thus, there would seem to be a general consensus that working on practical experience, working from practice back to theory, is the most effective way to approach learning about teaching. But whichever method is used (i.e. the top-down or bottom-up) there is clearly also a general consensus that it is essential for teachers to journey beyond the mere surface behaviours in lessons, and that the purpose of feedback and development is more than just providing 'tips for teachers', a danger if the feedback session concentrates solely on such surface features. Not only is there a myriad of things happening in the classroom in any one lesson (MacLeod and McIntyre 1977) which need interpreting, but apparently similar surface behaviours may stem from entirely different theoretical perspectives. Let us take the example of a simple I – R – E exchange (Initiation, Response, Evaluation: usually teacher initiates, students respond, teacher evaluates), an all-pervasive move in all classroom settings (Sinclair and Coulthard 1975). The purpose behind the use of such an exchange can vary from one of reinforcement and feedback to one of testing knowledge or to one of scaffolding new thoughts. On the superficial level, the exchanges are almost identical (and novice teachers need to be able to handle such routine patterns of interaction), but on the pedagogic level, such exchanges can be used in a variety of situations. The ability to match the uses of the technique to the general pedagogic purpose and the rationale behind the technique relates to theoretical models of learning, the 'deep structures' of teaching and learning. So, the advisor's role is to help the trainee/teacher 'see' the pattern and then to interpret the pattern in a principled way. It is in this extraction of patterns from practice and the mapping of theory on to practice where the advisor plays a crucial role in the development of the teacher.

3.4 Constructing new understandings: the Vygotskian perspective

Up to now we have considered the teacher or trainee as an individual learner. The models which we have considered focus on the individual as the central player in the learning process. The previous chapter looked at models of learning which examine the way that individuals acquire or gain knowledge and skills. Advisors here are seen as essentially aids to allowing the individual either to discover or learn new concepts. Even Schön, who talks about the collaboration between the professional and the coach, by his very terminology (coach, reflective practitioner) places the emphasis on the individual gaining insights into the way that professional practice operates. This concentration of attention on the individual learner from Piaget to Anderson is a central philosophical tenet of Western psychological thinking this century.

However, there is an alternative way of looking at the learning process which is proposed by the social constructivists and, most notably, Vygotsky (1978). They emphasise that knowledge is not something 'out there' to be learnt, but that knowledge is socially constructed through interaction and dialogue. There are a number of key concepts in the Vygotskian theory of learning, all of which are important to our understanding of the role of the advisor in the feedback session:

- Knowledge is constructed by dialogue, usually between a learner and a more expert individual.
- Knowledge/concepts exist first of all on an interpsychological plane (in social

interaction) and then on an intrapsychological plane (within the mind of the learner).

- Learning of new ideas, or 'appropriation', takes place when concepts move from the inter- to the intra-psychological plane.
- This process of appropriation is mediated by 'tools' – cultural symbols – the most important of which is language.
- For each individual there are concepts/skills which are 'on the edge' of their knowledge. They are said to be in the individual's 'Zone of Proximal Development (ZPD)'. These concepts/skills are activities which the individual can manage with help from another more expert individual, but cannot manage by themselves.
- The process of helping an individual through the ZPD and thus helping them to appropriate a new concept/idea has come to be called 'scaffolding' (Bruner 1990).

Let us consider some of these concepts in the light of the theories of learning which we have considered, and the way they may affect the role of the advisor.

3.4.1 Social interaction and the construction of knowledge

We have already seen that skill learning can be mediated by language in the Anderson model of learning, where skills pass from the declarative memory to the procedural memory (Chapter 2). Vygotsky's concept of learning through dialogue takes this one step further. New concepts and ideas are 'constructed' through interaction. The advisor helps the teacher to appropriate new ideas through a process of discussion, and through scaffolding in particular.

3.4.2 Scaffolding and the zone of proximal development

Vygotsky's concept of the Zone of Proximal Development is analogous to Schön's 'intermediate zones of practice' (see Chapter 2). Both thinkers refer to skills and ideas which are new to the learner/professional, yet ones which the learner/professional is ready to acquire. The concepts/skills which are in these zones are ones which the learner/professional cannot handle autonomously, but can handle with the help of a guide or, in this case, the advisor. Vygotskian thinkers emphasise that this is not 'telling' but constructing new knowledge through talk. The process needed to guide the learner to new awareness is 'scaffolding'; the provision of focused challenges and questions to allow (in our case) the teacher to internalise the new ideas. Through this process the teacher adopts and, more importantly, adapts the concepts thus constructing their own versions. In this way, appropriation is close to the concept of 'ownership', a key concept when we come to discuss counselling theories. The crucial role of the advisor is to identify the teacher's individual ZPD and to provide scaffolding for them to move forward and successfully internalise new ideas, concepts and skills (see Task 3.7).

3.4.3 Mediation through 'tools': theory as cultural signs and symbols

We have seen in the Experiential Learning cycle the importance of conceptualisation as a process of generalising from experience to enable the teacher to change their behaviour and undertake new experimentation. The social constructivists provide a much more proactive role for theory in learning. They see the concepts involved in theoretical models as 'tools' for mediating the learning process. In the case of ELT, for example, the constructs embedded in the terms used (e.g. from the macro methodological models such as 'communicative language teaching', through to micro techniques such as 'drilling') are tools which can help teachers to analyse, interpret and 'see' what is happening in their classes. Thus, a vital role of the advisor is to help teachers/trainees to learn to use the theoretical terminology provided in the methodological courses to understand what is happening in their classes. In this way, the advisor's role at the 'interface' between theory and practice can be further refined. The professional discourse (including the terminology) which has been provided by sessions on methodology will be used as 'tools' by the advisor to mediate learning and to help the teacher to understand the lesson and acquire new concepts.

3.5 The personal and the social; how they interact in practice

Vygotsky provides a framework for the understanding of both how knowledge is transmitted and how theory and practice interact in the process. To illustrate the interaction between these processes we shall use a model devised by Haste (1987). Her model involves three sets of 'factors' affecting learning; 'intra-individual', 'interpersonal' and 'socio-historical'. Intra-individual factors are those factors which stem from within the individual. They are the domain of the cognitive psychologists described in the previous chapter. They involve the way that the individual learns new skills through practice and they also involve the intuition of the teacher. The interpersonal domain is the domain of social interaction where meanings are negotiated through discussion with others. This discussion will ultimately involve the use of ideas and concepts from the third domain, the socio-historical. From within this domain will flow generally accepted cultural views of the world; in this case, the theoretical models of learning which form the basis of the educational and professional culture of the society in which the teacher works, or the one which is the model of the teaching programme. This can be represented diagrammatically:

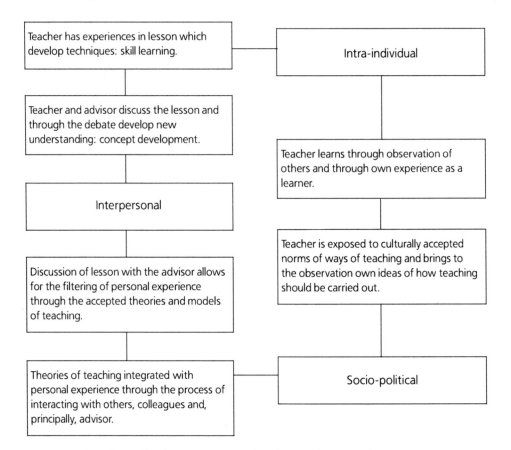

Figure 8 The relationship between personal and social factors in learning

3.6 Theory, consciousness and language

This Vygotskian perspective gives a clear role for theory in learning. Notice that both the cognitive and the Vygotskian explanations of learning place great importance on the role of consciousness. In cognitive theory it is the verbalisation of declarative knowledge which acts as a pathway to the automatisation of behaviour. From a Vygotskian perspective, language is one of the mediators of experience, operating alongside other cultural symbols. In this way, language not only operates to make routines explicit as it does in cognitive theory, but it is one of the systems of knowledge which carry within it embedded cultural values. This model provides an explanation for the way individuals learn accepted norms and values from society. Among these are the theories of teaching and learning which operate within the educational culture of the society. In the case of learning about teaching, these theories of teaching become the means by which the experience of the teacher is mediated and internalised. Through this process the accepted theories and teaching norms of the culture are integrated into the personal knowledge of the teacher. It thus provides a means by which the intuitive, intra-personal constructs of the teacher, derived from experience, are integrated with the professional theories of the professional subject culture.

Freeman (1996) describes just such a process acting on the way that four high-school foreign language teachers describe their teaching. Over the course of the programme, the intuitions and thoughts of the teacher, initially expressed in what Freeman describes as a 'local voice', became progressively reformulated in terms of the theoretical ideas provided by the programme, into the 'professional voice'. Thus the intuitions of the teacher become integrated with the established ideas of teaching. It is the articulation of thoughts about the lesson through discussion which provides the means by which teachers are able to understand and 'make sense of' the experience. Once this has happened, the ideas have become internalised. This internalisation will have transformed the way that teachers act in their lessons through the use of the language which was used to discuss the teaching, the special discourse of teaching and learning. This discourse is a sign system which embodies the concepts and ideas of the professional educational culture.

3.7 The inner dialogue and continuing professional development

The above argument stresses the importance of dialogue and interaction in the construction of knowledge and Vygotsky clearly believed that this construction of knowledge would take place between a learner and a 'teacher' (a person who had more knowledge of the subject than the learner). However, as we discussed in Chapter 2, learning about teaching needs to be an ongoing process and cannot be restricted to guided tutorial situations. Both pre- and in-service courses need to look beyond the restricted time frame of the course itself and thus advisors need to develop in the teacher the ability to continue to develop their teaching autonomously. The consideration of how learners can be encouraged to learn independently has formed a major theme in much of the recent thinking on teacher development, and encouraging self-directed learning and learner independence has become part of the orthodoxy of current paradigms on teaching and learning, especially with adult learners. With regard to the specific problem with which we are concerned, advising teachers, there is one perspective on continuing development arising from the Vygotskian perspective which deserves investigation: the Bakhtinian concept of the 'inner dialogue' as an explanation of how learning can take place without a 'teacher' to provide the interaction.

3.7.1 The inner dialogue

One of the central concepts in Vygotskian psychology is the mediation provided by cultural signs, and in particular language, in the internalisation of concepts. The other is the mediation provided by social interaction. However, it is clear that learning can take place without interaction between learners and teachers and, for the purposes of this discussion about promoting independent teacher development, we need to consider how such learning can take place within the Vygotskian perspective we have outlined.

To do this we need to consider the work of Bakhtin and Lotman (see Wertsch *et al.* 1993). Bakhtin's contribution to the debate concerning the mediation of learning involves the idea that there are different voices embodied in different social languages, language discourses of different groups in society. We have argued that the concepts and ideas of teaching are a specific discourse type deriving from the professional education culture of the society. We have also argued that part of the process of learning about teaching is to learn this social language or professional discourse, in order to both shape the perception of the teacher and enable the teacher to make sense of teaching. This happens through the interaction between their own experience and the concepts embedded in the professional discourse. Often such discourse, in the form of teaching theory, is provided through lecture input separated from the practical side of teaching. The problem with theoretical input which is provided in lecture format is that it is 'transmissive' in nature, its primary function is often seen as explaining ideas. This function is, in Lotman's terms, only one of the two essential elements of text as it is 'univocal' in nature. The other essential element of text is to generate new meanings, which is 'dialogic' in nature. This generation of new meanings involves the interaction between the individual and the message which is being transmitted. The interaction between the individual's knowledge (the individual's voice) and the social meanings encapsulated in the concepts about teaching (the social voice) provides the mechanism by which learning takes place.

Thus, with the extension of Vygotsky's ideas through the work of Bakhtin and Lotman, we have a principled explanation of a method by which learning can take place in a more autonomous manner. The essential element in the social constructivist view of such learning is the necessity of there to be an 'inner dialogue' between the listener/reader and the text. It provides an explanation for the effectiveness of 'Socratic dialogue', the most common technique used in teacher training (Britten, 1985). Socratic dialogue techniques, by which the trainer poses questions to / elicits suggestions from the trainees and then builds on their answers are effective because they allow the trainer to scaffold the thought processes of the trainees, but more than that, they provide training in the very techniques which are necessary for further autonomous learning. They provide a mechanism which can be used to structure the 'inner dialogue' necessary for independent development. Therefore, as explained in the previous chapter when we discussed autonomous development, one of the essential functions of the advisor during the feedback session is not so much to provide 'solutions' to the teacher's problems (although this is an important function), but to provide a framework for future development through the exercise of external dialogue which can provide a model for later internal, individualistic dialogue.

3.8 The teaching practice cycle: implementation problems

Having discussed the vital role that the advisor plays in the development of new concepts through the management of the experiential learning cycle and through the dialogic interplay with the teacher, it is now time to look at the overall TP cycle in more depth and to discuss the problems that may arise in many situations when trying to implement the model. Turney *et al.* (1982) divide supervision into 3 stages; the pre-observation conference, the lesson and the debriefing, and this model closely fits with the feedback control mechanism described earlier (Chapter 2):

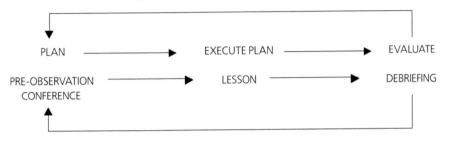

Figure 9 The three stages of TP supervision

This analogy is a rather mechanical and 'behaviourist' characterisation of the process of learning, in which the advisor is playing the role of providing the response to the teacher's actions in a rather simplistic stimulus – response – reinforcement model of learning. As we have seen, in a situation as complex as teaching, advisors are doing much more than commenting on performance; they are helping teachers to see things in new ways, developing new understandings.

In many contexts it may be impossible for logistic reasons for the advisor to provide each stage of the process in the order outlined above. For example, in many in-service teaching situations there may not be sufficient time between lessons to provide both a pre-observation conference and a debriefing session as separate events, so the post-lesson discussion will need to contain both a debriefing element and a planning element. In many contexts there may be little time to provide effective debriefing (for a discussion of some of the constraints faced by inspectors/trainers in developing countries, see Rees 1980). However, it is important that each *function* is fulfilled within the cycle. In some contexts it will be possible to provide an oral planning session in a pre-observation conference and an oral debriefing, but in other contexts it may be necessary to provide the planning function, for example, by other means than the face-to-face tutorial session envisaged by the original Turney model. Given the importance of these functions, we shall briefly discuss the problems associated with implementing the cycle and offer some suggestions about how the problems can be overcome (see Task 3.1).

3.8.1 Planning: the pre-observation conference

This can be a problematic stage to arrange effectively. As mentioned above, in many in-service situations where the teacher is rushing from lesson to lesson, this may be impossible to organise prior to teaching.

- If the advisor and the teacher are to work truly collaboratively on planning, then the planning conference needs to be arranged far enough in advance for the teacher to be able to act on any suggestions made by the advisor. Suggestions made to the teacher just before they teach a lesson can undermine a teacher's confidence.
- If such conferences are only possible immediately prior to the lesson, then the advisor should assume the role of 'listener and understander' (see Chapter 6) and should refrain from commenting on the plan other than to clarify individual points. This in itself is an important function of the pre-observation conference – to find out about the teacher's intentions as well as to establish a shared understanding of the purpose of the observation.
- However, if the essential function is that of planning, the teacher needs to have clear aims and goals which should derive from previous teaching. These goals and plans can be effectively discussed during the Action Planning stage of the Debriefing (see Chapter 8 for further discussion of Action Planning).
- It may be possible for trainees to submit written plans for the forthcoming lesson, for tutors to comment on (but see Task 3.3).

3.8.2 Execution: the lesson

Most would agree that it is important that the advisor has a chance to see the teacher actually teaching. However, even here there are problems which can arise.

- If it was not possible to arrange the pre-observation conference, the advisor may not be aware of the aims of the teacher. This may make it difficult to provide useful advice on the lesson (see Chapter 4, 'valuing the teacher's perspective' for a discussion of this issue).
- It may not be possible for advisors to see complete lessons. In this case the advisor will need to be aware that the view gained of the lesson was even more partial than usual.
- Peer observation can be used, especially in team teaching situations, and the resulting discussion between the observers and the teachers can be chaired by the advisor, who can extract important points from the discussion.
- Mechanical aids (videos, tape recordings) along with different devices for analysing the classroom (observation instruments, checklists etc.) can be used to provide the raw material for the debriefing. Such apparently 'objective' records may have advantages in that they provide non-judgmental evidence for the debriefing discussion. However, the complications of setting up such recording devices and the disruption they can cause to the lesson are factors which need to be considered.

3.8.3 Evaluation: debriefing

Again, this can be notoriously difficult to organise, especially with busy in-service teachers.

- If the debriefing is carried out in the corner of a busy staffroom (a not uncommon situation) then it can be very difficult for the advisor to listen effectively to the teacher and to avoid distractions.
- If the debriefing is carried out immediately after the lesson, the teacher may well be incapable of mature reflection, being too 'hyped up' by the lesson to be able to make any sensible evaluation of the experience or to take in what is being said by the advisor.
- One way of overcoming this is to provide written feedback to the teacher which can be reflected upon in less stressful surroundings (see Task 8.2 for samples of written feedback).
- Another method of providing feedback is to use prepared schedules of competencies which can be used for self-evaluation and evaluation by the advisor (for a description of the use of such schedules on an in-service programme in a developing country context, see Rees 1980).
- Another method is for the advisor to provide comments on written self-evaluations provided by the teachers/trainees. These can be written some time after the lesson and thus allow for more thoughtful evaluation from the teacher than that which can be provided immediately after teaching.

3.9 Conclusion

In this and the previous chapter we have examined the context of learning about teaching and considered various models of how knowledge is gained about teaching. We have examined the roles of an advisor within this pedagogic function. In terms of the different agendas which we outlined in Chapter 1, we have concentrated on the technical/professional and developmental functions of the advisor. We have characterised the advisor as someone whose primary function is to facilitate learning and development in teachers. Arising from this discussion, we have identified various roles for the advisor in the feedback sessions including guide, coach, tutor, expert (see Task 3.2). In the next chapter we begin to look inside the feedback session to identify the ways in which these roles can be implemented by considering different styles of supervision.

Summary

The following issues have been raised in this chapter:

- Experiential Learning and learning about teaching
- The role of observation in the teacher learning process
- The integration of theory and practice in the feedback session
- Vygotsky and learning through interaction and dialogue
- Continuing professional development and the inner dialogue

- The problems associated with implementing an effective teaching practice cycle

Tasks

The following tasks allow you to explore the issues raised in this chapter:

3.1 The adaptation of the Teaching Practice cycle to a local context
3.2 The roles of the advisor
3.3 The way to approach the observation of different teachers
3.4 Forms for providing data on lessons
3.5 Designing observation instruments for different purposes
3.6 Observation notes made by advisors
3.7 Providing scaffolding
8.2 Written feedback to teachers

Advice for further reading

On experiential learning:

Kolb, D. A. (1983) *Experiential Learning: Experience as the source of learning and development*, New Jersey: Prentice Hall.
    This really is a very important book on the area of experiential learning, in which, Kolb clearly outlines his theory of learning and provides a clearly argued rationale for the use of the experiential cycle in learning. Chapters deal with individuality in learning, learning and development in higher education as well as learning styles and the experiential learning cycle.

On Vygotsky:

Daniels, H. (ed.) (1993) *Charting the Agenda: Educational Activity after Vygotsky*, London: Routledge.
Wertsch, J. V. (ed.) (1985) *Culture, Communication and Cognition: Vygotskian Perspectives*, Cambridge: Cambridge University Press.
Vygotsky, L. S. (1978) *Mind in Society*, Cambridge, Mass: Harvard University Press.
    Vygotsky can be quite difficult to read in the original translation (Vygotsky 1978) partly due to the language and terminology he uses (he was writing in the 1920s). However, this book contains a series of articles which try to interpret his work and discusses issues from the perspective of a modern school.
    There are also a number of neo-Vygotskian thinkers who have used his ideas to look at classrooms, perhaps the most readable and accessible being Mercer (Mercer 1995) and interest is beginning to grow in applying his model to language learning (Lantolf and Appel 1994).
    Although not overtly Vygotskian in approach, Bailey has an interesting article on the role of dialogue in teacher education and on scaffolding in particular (Bailey in Freeman and Richards 1996).

On observation:

Wajnryb, R. (1992) *Classroom Observation Tasks*, Cambridge: Cambridge University Press.
    This book contains an excellent selection of different observation instruments and activities which can be used to investigate different aspects of language teaching. It also has a useful discussion of the reasons for observing teachers and the way that observation can be carried out.

4 Supervision and the three-stage model of helping

In the previous chapters we have examined the supervision process from a cognitive perspective. We have looked at learning theories to shed light on the most effective way to learn about teaching; the cognitive aspects of learning. In this examination we have established the importance of the feedback session in providing guidance and scaffolding for the teacher. We now intend to examine how this tutoring and learning is implemented in the feedback session by examining the interpersonal aspects of the dialogue between the advisor and the teacher; the psychodynamics of advising. This will involve a discussion of different models of counselling and their relevance to providing feedback, but before we start on this examination, we shall examine the different approaches or styles of supervision which have been discussed within ELT.

4.1 Styles of supervision: directive vs non-directive

One of the central tenets of humanistic counselling is that the process should be centred on the client. This derives from Carl Rogers' model of person-centred counselling (Rogers 1969). Freeman (1982) used this philosophical stance of person-centred counselling to suggest that there are three approaches to in-service teacher supervision; the Supervisory Approach, the Alternatives Approach and the Non-Directive approach, and that these are related to different stages of development and the type of questions which might be asked:

Stage	Question			Approaches
I	What do I teach?	T		Supervisory Approach: Observer as authority/arbiter
		R		
		A		
		I		
		N		
		I		
II	How do I teach what I teach?	N	D	Alternatives Approach: Observer as provider of alternative perspectives
		G	E	
			V	
			E	
			L	
			O	
			P	
III	Why do I teach what I teach?		M	Non-Directive Approach: Observer as understander
	Why do I teach the way I do?		E	
			N	
			T	

Figure 10 Three approaches to in-service teacher supervision (from Freeman, 1982: 27) (For an exploration of the issue of directive, alternatives and non-directive approaches, see Tasks 4.1 & 9.1)

This framework has informed much of the recent thinking about teacher supervision in ELT. Freeman further refined this basic concept of the training/ development continuum (Freeman 1982, 1990) and Gebhard (1984) extended the number of choices available to the advisor to six:

- Directive supervision, where the role of the supervisor is to direct and inform the teacher, model appropriate teaching behaviours and act as evaluator
- Alternative supervision, where the supervisor suggests a number of limited alternative actions to the teacher from which they are free to choose
- Collaborative supervision, where the teacher and supervisor work together to solve problems encountered in the classroom
- Non-directive supervision, where the supervisor acts as understander and allows the teacher to come up with their own solution to classroom dilemmas
- Creative supervision
- Self-help-explorative supervision   (Gebhard, 1984: 156–161)

While not dealing with supervisory styles as such, Edge (1992) has identified nine ways of interacting which are important for encouraging and nurturing collaborative development. He discusses the development of interpersonal skills which promote empathetic and supportive attitudes. Although these skills are intended for use between colleagues in the situation which we have described as that of 'critical friend', they are equally important to consider in any situation of providing advice where we want the teacher to develop independently. Edge's stages and skills are:

EXPLORATION: Attending (listening and understanding – see Chapter 6)
Reflecting (reflecting ideas to enable the teacher to get a clearer view of them)
Focusing (helping the teacher to focus on the personally important)

DISCOVERY: Thematising (linking things said by the teacher together or to a central theme)
Challenging (the coherence of the speaker's ideas)
Disclosing (talking about the advisor's own experiences for the teacher to use as comparison and contrast)

ACTION: Goal-setting (helping the teacher to decide what should be done next)
Trialling (actually talking through what the teacher will do)
Planning (making arrangements, administrative and otherwise to put the proposed behaviour into effect)

Figure 11 Edge's three stages of feedback and related generic skills

In this and subsequent chapters we shall examine the stages of the feedback session and the generic skills which are needed by the advisor at different points of the process, as well as examining the actual interventions which the advisor might choose to make, but it is worth noting at this point the similarities between the different views on supervisory styles.

All three writers emphasise the importance of exploring ideas with the teacher and of allowing the teacher to 'lead' the discussion of the lesson as soon as possible. They all agree that the end point of the process should be the teacher as the reflective practitioner, the autonomous professional, and that a non-directive and non-judgmental approach to advice is one which will achieve such a goal.

In Chapter 2 we also argued that the teacher should emerge as an autonomous professional at the end of a training or development programme, but we must not lose sight of the fact that this defines the goal of the programme and does not necessarily dictate the methods of achieving it. As we discussed in Chapter 2, a definition of the end point of a skills learning programme does not necessarily determine the steps taken to achieve this end. Self-directed learning and development are the goals, but there may well be stages on that road which need more directive approaches. The importance of the analysis produced by Freeman is a recognition of the fact that there is a continuum between training and development and that approaches may need to vary according to circumstances. At certain stages advisors will need to take the lead and prescribe; at other stages, and with other teachers, the teacher can be given more autonomy and freedom to lead.

However, fundamental to both Freeman's and Gebhard's ideas is the concept that supervisors/advisors have *choices* about how to intervene. Their models emphasise the importance of the teacher's stage of development on the style of supervision provided. This can be represented diagrammatically:

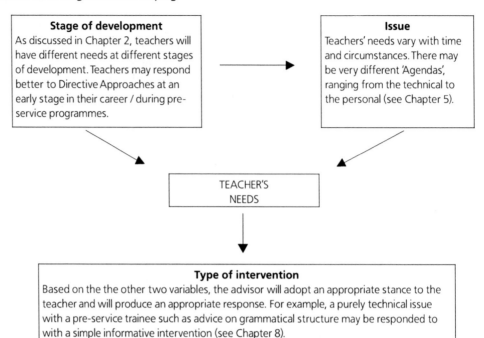

Figure 12 Criteria for choosing styles of supervision

It is thus clear that the advisor can adopt different styles of supervision with a teacher and that the style adopted will vary according to factors such as the age, personality and/or experience of that teacher. All are agreed that a successful learning process is one in which the teacher is empowered to make their own independent decisions about teaching and continue to grow as an independent professional. This growth will depend on the degree to which the teacher is able to reflect on performance and draw conclusions from this reflection. As discussed in Chapter 3, the dialogic process of the feedback session has the cognitive function of developing self-awareness in the teacher as a means of stimulating future independent development through the construction of new concepts about teaching. However, the process can also be viewed from another perspective, as a process of providing help to the teacher. It is this perspective which we shall examine next.

4.2 Providing help: the overall frameworks

In this chapter and the next we shall examine two frameworks drawn from counselling theories for looking at the methods by which the advisor can implement the broad objective of developing the reflective practitioner through the feedback dialogue. This chapter will provide a macro model of the helping and advising process as it relates to a teaching supervision cycle. It will examine the overall process of observing teachers and providing advice from a counselling/helping perspective. In the next chapter, we shall move on to consider how the advisor can 'intervene' in the advisory process and the effects of different interventions on the interaction.

The approaches described in these chapters have been developed within Western industrialised societies and are often described as 'democratic' models of counselling (Lee 1991). As Lago and Thompson (1997) point out, the wide range of counselling theories in use in the west at present rests on a common set of cultural beliefs and these will be discussed further in Chapter 10. These counselling theories are not offered as a prescriptive solution to the process of giving advice; rather they are provided as a point of departure for a discussion about the effective provision of advice. Various factors such as language, culture and personality play an important role and these issues will again be explored in Chapter 10. While reading these chapters the reader is directed to the accompanying tasks and to use them to evaluate the explanations offered from a personal point of view. It is important that the reader asks questions such as:

- Does this make sense to me as an individual/professional?
- Is the explanation offered one which is congruent with my cultural background / the cultural background of the teacher?
- Would the situation be changed if the teacher was of the opposite/same sex?
- Would I act differently with different teachers, taking into consideration factors such as age, experience and gender?

4.3 Counselling theories and the provision of advice

The role of the advisor is to 'focus on areas for improvement' (Chapter 2) and 'scaffold learning' through discussion (Chapter 3). The mechanism by which this is effectively carried out is a central issue in the training of advisors. Counselling theory has been developed by a profession which aims to provide help to people with problems and to effect changes of thinking and behaviour through discussion; such theories can provide a principled method for . examining what happens in effective feedback sessions. Although the basic belief in counselling is that individuals are capable of solving their own problems, the counselling process itself is where the client meets with a helper to talk over the problem, show it in a different light and come up with a plan of action. The Three-Stage Model of Helping (Egan 1994) adopted in this chapter and Heron's Six Category Intervention Analysis (Heron 1990) which forms the basis of the next chapter have both been chosen, not for theoretical reasons, but because they appear to provide models of giving advice and helping which make sense in the context of learning to teach (see Tasks 4.2 & 4.3 for an exploration of factors involved in giving effective advice). Both authors stress the fact that the skills they provide are useable over a wide continuum of situations, from professional psychotherapists through to informal helpers; 'since helping and problem solving are such common human experiences [that] training in both solving one's own problems and helping others solve theirs should be as common as training in reading writing and math' (Egan 1994: 4). It is this 'generic' approach to counselling theories which will be adopted by this book. We shall discuss counselling theories from the particular perspective of the teaching practice feedback session adopting an 'eclectic' approach to theory, borrowing where ideas seem important, editing and rejecting where ideas are not specifically related to our situation.

Although, as mentioned above, counselling theories rest on a series of cultural beliefs, the ultimate judgment of the efficacy of such theories must lie in their utility, not their underlying value systems.

4.4 Different approaches to counselling

Although there are many different approaches to counselling (481 different theories have been identified, Karasu *et al.* 1984 in Lago and Thompson 1997) we shall divide the approaches into four principal schools. The schools, their methods and their underlying assumptions are briefly summarised in the following table:[1]

School	Main Proponents	Methods Employed	Underlying Assumptions
Behavioural	Deriving from the ideas of Skinner (see Skinner 1993)	Training, control of behaviour through methods such as contingency management, positive reinforcement and shaping	Action is essentially driven by external events – we behave as we have learned to behave
Cognitive-behavioural	Ellis 1990, Beck 1976	Examination and change of beliefs as well as behaviour	Emphasis on both the beliefs and attitudes of the actor as well as their behaviour
Humanistic/person-centred	Rogers 1992	Prioritise the role of the client in solving their problems	The advisor and the client are trustworthy; the drive by the individual for self actualisation
Psychoanalytic	Deriving from the ideas of Freud (see Freud 1986)	Exploration of the unconscious and emotional sources of behaviour	Actions as caused by deep psychological processes of the individual

Figure 13 Four principal schools of counselling

---

[1] For a useful and approachable overview of different counselling theories see Nicolson and Ayers 1995, Lago and Thompson 1997, and for a more detailed discussion, see Cramer 1992.

Each of these approaches has different strengths, which may be related to the situations in which counselling or advice-giving takes place and to the ultimate goals of the counselling/advisory process. In the situation of providing advice to teachers and trainees, we are dealing with a particular type of advice, that of professional training. The goal of this advice is to provide a link between behaviour and theory, to enable the teacher to develop in terms of both classroom behaviour and cognitive understanding in the classroom. We need to adopt models of counselling which will address these issues and will produce effective advice within the confines of our limited goal. Thus, models which explore the deep psychological motivations for behaviour will not necessarily be effective within the field in which we are working.

4.5 Problem-solving and Egan's eclectic model of counselling

The model which we shall use is based on that provided by Egan (1994), often described as an 'eclectic' approach to counselling. Egan suggests that the effective helper aims to utilise good ideas from different approaches and integrates them into an effective model of helping. The essential elements of his model are:

Helping as a problem-solving process	The aim of the process is to allow the client to solve their problems
Helping as an educative process	The goal of the helping process is learning (unlearning, relearning and new learning)
Helping is a collaborative process	The process is a collaborative one between the helper and the client
Helping is a cognitive-behavioural process	The aim of the process is to help clients to change the way they act through a new understanding of what they are doing
Helping is a client-centred process	People are seen as active interpreters of the world. The aim of the process and the helper is to provide the client with the skills and knowledge to solve their problems

Figure 14 The essential elements of Egan's model

From these elements we can identify two central tenets:

- helping is a problem-solving process (deriving from the Cognitive–behavioural model)
- the client is the centre of the process (the Person-centred model)

These are put into practice through a three-stage model:

Stage 1	EXPLORATION ⇓	Looking at the teacher's current situation. Finding out what the teacher sees as problematic. Establishing the problems.
Stage 2	NEW UNDERSTANDING ⇓	Helping the teacher explore options and goals.
Stage 3	ACTION	Drawing up an action plan for achieving the goals.

Figure 15 Egan: a three-stage model

These stages are almost identical to those proposed by Edge (1992):

Egan	Edge
EXPLORATION ⇓	EXPLORATION ⇓
NEW UNDERSTANDING ⇓	DISCOVERY ⇓
ACTION	ACTION

Figure 16 Three-stage models: Egan and Edge compared

Both start from the exploration with the teacher of the experience of the lesson, then move on to the discovery of new insights and conclude with suggestions for action. We shall now examine each of the above elements and their central tenets in relation to the ideas we have developed about the way that teachers learn.

4.6 The principles of the three-stage model and providing advice to teachers

Helping as a problem-solving process

Egan's view of helping as a problem-solving process fits well with the goals which we have established for advising teachers; those of developing new understandings and new ways of teaching through the analysis of practice. Although Egan sees problems in a much wider social and psychological perspective than the teaching supervision process, the emphasis on the solving of problems is exactly the sort of mindset which is necessary for the reflective practitioner discussed in Chapter 2. The essence of the experiential learning cycle is that teachers should reflect on their practice, which involves identifying problems, understanding the sources of the problems, then drawing up a plan to solve the problems. It is important to note that 'problems' here is used in the widest sense of the word, i.e. areas of practice which are open to improvement or change. We do not wish to imply a deficit approach to teacher education.

Helping as an educative process; helping is a collaborative process

The view of the counselling process as being one in which learning takes place through collaboration fits well with the social construction of knowledge which we developed from the Vygotskian perspective of learning.

Helping is a cognitive–behavioural process

The cognitive–behavioural stance of Egan, where the goal of the helper is to effect a change on both the cognitive and the behavioural levels, reflects the importance of the integration of theory and practice in teacher training and development.

Helping is a client-centred process

Finally, by placing the emphasis on helping clients to develop the means by which to solve their own problems, the model provides a way for individuals to continue to develop independently as teachers.

4.7 Potential difficulties with the Egan model

Whilst Egan's model fits well with the theories of learning we have discussed, the adoption of the model is not without some difficulties. There are two issues which we would like to discuss; the person-centred approach and the place of psychotherapy within the helping process.

4.7.1 Providing advice is person-centred

This philosophical stance may be problematic for some advisors and in some contexts (cf in situations in which the advisor has a large assessment role – see Chapter 1). In its strong form as propounded by Rogers (1969), the counselling process starts from and is rooted in the person's experience and beliefs. The process tries to enable the person to establish a balance or congruence between their own view of themselves and other people's view of them as reflected by their position in society. The ultimate aim of the process is to develop a self-actualising person who is open to experience and has confidence in themselves and their own decision-making. Thus, the establishment of self-esteem is the principal goal of the person-centred approach. The two conditions on which this approach is based are that the client and the counsellor are both trustworthy and that the client has the potential to solve their problem themselves. Deriving from these conditions it is important that the counsellor gives the client unconditional positive regard and accepts the person non-judgmentally. These two concepts, the acceptance of the individual's view of reality as the starting point for exploration and the importance of a non-judgmental attitude towards the client have become central tenets in what have been characterised as 'democratic' counselling theories.

If taken literally and carried out to its logical conclusion, a person-centred approach would appear to argue for all learning and development to be instigated by the client. The role of the practitioner is merely as a facilitator of self-discovery leading to personal growth. The objections that many advisors have to such a model are that

- it is impractical
- it seriously reduces their role in the process

This approach is also often not appreciated by teachers, particularly in the early years of their career when they would prefer to be given solutions to their problems rather than work things out for themselves. In addition, advisors often complain that when teachers and trainees are offered the chance to evaluate or talk through the lesson, their accounts tend to be superficial and the issues raised are often trivial.

These objections are not to be dismissed lightly, especially the views of the teachers who, in the end, are the recipients of the advice. They are the clients and they should feel that the process is of value to them in their everyday lives, in this case, in teaching their classes.

One of the difficulties with an approach which focuses exclusively on the client is that it does not give sufficient weight to the role of others in the learning and development process. As with our discussion of western approaches to psychology in Chapter 3, the emphasis is centrally on the individual and on personal growth and the counsellor's role is to facilitate such growth. The great value of Egan's approach is its eclecticism. It accepts the importance of both the client and the helper to the process. In order for the process to work the client must want to change their behaviour and this involves the client 'owning' these changes by understanding what needs to be done and why it needs to be done. However, Egan also emphasises the need for a skilled helper as part of the process; he emphasises the collaborative nature of helping. Although not acknowledging the fact, Egan is arguing for the very dialectic which is incorporated in Vygotsky's approaches to learning discussed in the previous chapter. Vygotsky identifies the need for an 'expert' colleague to identify the learner's Zone of Proximal Development and to bridge that gap between actual development and potential development by providing scaffolding for the learner to progress. Egan's model provides a setting for the dialogue between the educator and the learner, the stage upon which new meanings and understandings can be constructed by meaningful interaction.

Thus, person-centred counselling does not diminish the role of the advisor, it merely changes it from that of the 'transmitter' of knowledge to the 'facilitator' of learning.

4.7.2 Psychotherapy or practical help?

The second possible objection to the use of counselling theories relates to the purposes for which they are used. Although Rogers later developed his ideas into wider fields such as education (Rogers 1983), the original purpose of the person-centred approach was psychotherapeutic. With such a personal/social goal, the exploration of the personal constructs of the individual and the discussion of their view of themselves and their world make perfect sense. Such factors are critical to helping people with social or psychological problems. What is, perhaps, not so clear is the utility of placing such critical importance on the teacher's view of events within the process of providing advice to teachers.

A clear case can be constructed for the importance of exploring the teacher's view of teaching in order to identify and solve issues which they feel are relevant to their situation rather than discuss issues identified by the advisor. It is also important to work with the teacher to develop new understandings about their role in the classroom rather than discuss general issues about teaching. But to make such an approach the sole basis on which to proceed is perhaps to place more emphasis on this aspect than the teaching practice situation demands. Advisors need to provide practical advice to teachers and the exploration of the teacher's and trainee's views of themselves is only part of the goal of giving advice. We need to review the person-centred approach in the light of the differences in context between the psychotherapeutic counsellor and the teacher advisor.

The teacher advisor differs from the psychotherapeutic counsellor in one crucial area: the degree of information which the former possesses of the situation. The psychotherapeutic counsellor does not have the 'fly on the wall' opportunity offered by the practice cycle. In the practice cycle, the advisor not only has access to the teacher's account of the lesson, but also has access, through observation, to the actual data on which such an account is based. The principal, if not the only, source of data on which the psychotherapeutic counsellor can work is the client's view of the situation. The counsellor does not have access to the situation or situations which are causing problems to the client. Thus, the client's story is the raw data on which the counsellor must work. Within the realm of psychotherapeutic counselling, it can be argued that this data is as important as the actual situations which gave rise to the problems in the first place. The counsellor is helping to develop in the client a way of dealing with social situations. An essential part of dealing with such situations involves dealing with the attitudes and beliefs which are held by the client which may have an important influence on, if not be the cause of, the problem the client is having. However, in the teaching practice situation, although the observer's view of a lesson will be coloured to a degree by the observer's beliefs, the teacher advisor has access to the raw data of the client's experience through observing the lesson. This added perspective on the 'problems' of the teacher must significantly change the tactics used by advisors in helping teachers.

The 'privileged' position of the teacher trainer and advisor in having access to the 'raw data of behaviour' thus changes the emphasis on using the teacher's account as the only evidence on which to work. The collaborative act of watching the lesson with the teacher is part of the process of 'listening' to the teacher's account and this extra information about the actual experience to be discussed alters the way that the advisor approaches the advisory session.

In the light of this discussion we shall, then, examine the teaching cycle from the perspective of a helping process, taking into account what we have just argued about the added dimension provided by the opportunity to observe the lesson with the teacher.

4.8 The practice cycle and the three-stage model of helping

We have established earlier that observation in teaching practice is an essential part of the process of Planning, Teaching and Feedback. We now want to look at how the functions of these different stages in the practice cycle relate to the three-stage model of helping as proposed by Egan.

We shall examine the way that this cycle integrates two central concepts of democratic counselling:

- valuing the client's perspective
- being non-judgmental in interpreting what is seen

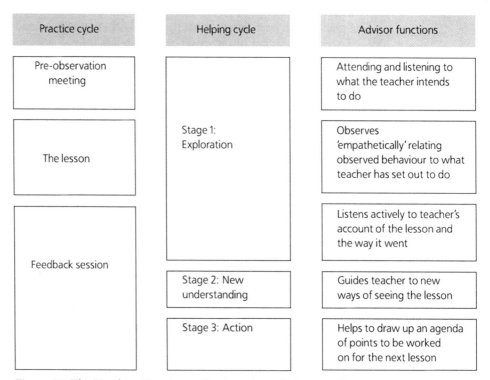

Figure 17 The Teaching Practice cycle viewed as a helping cycle

4.8.1 Valuing the teacher's perspective

The function of valuing the client's beliefs and constructs is provided for in the practice cycle by the fact that the advisor listens to the teacher before the lesson and decides with the teacher the things which the advisor will look for in the lesson. Then, during the lesson, the advisor observes 'empathetically', basing their observations on the issues identified by the teacher in the pre-observation meeting.

This perspective offers a solution to the often voiced criticism mentioned above that teachers are unable to provide significant insights into the lesson itself. It is often argued that it is too time-consuming to start with the often superficial accounts of the lesson provided by the teacher. This view, however, treats the feedback session as the only place in which the teacher is 'speaking' and the advisor is 'listening'. The analysis of the teaching cycle provided above provides a perspective which shows that the pre-lesson discussion *and* the observation are part of the listening process; they are both part of giving value to the teacher's view of teaching. The traditional counselling session begins with exploring the client's view of the problem. In the teaching practice cycle, this process has already been instigated before the beginning of the feedback session (the stage which is most overtly analogous to a counselling session). By discussing with the teacher before the lesson and by watching them teach the advisor will have gained a lot of understanding about the teacher and their situation. Such a view of the practice cycle emphasises the need to observe with empathy, the 'looking with' rather than the 'looking at' which we discussed in the last chapter (also see Tasks 3.6 and 8.2 for observation notes made on lessons).

4.8.2 Non-judgmental feedback and trust

Secondly, we need to further unpack the term 'non-judgmental' as applied to the teaching practice cycle. All observation, inasmuch as it involves interpretation, involves some level of judgment. If we examine the practice cycle in terms of a helping cycle, the term non-judgmental means that we value the teacher's views and ideas; that we use them as the starting point of the process of helping. We may well judge that certain things done by the teacher are wrong, misguided, and we may tell them so. These actions may well be based on what we judge to be inappropriate views of learning and teaching and perhaps even 'deeper' attitudes to students as people, such as racist beliefs, and we will seek to change these beliefs and attitudes. However, we will attempt to provide such feedback in a non-punitive manner; our comments on the lesson will be based on the behaviour and actions of the teacher and should not be based on our view of the teacher as a person. To be able to provide such feedback will not only need the consideration of the micro-skills of intervening (which we shall address in the following chapters) but they will also need to be based on an atmosphere of trust developed between the advisor and the teacher. A major component in the establishment of such a trusting relationship is the agreement of the terms on which the advisor will judge the lesson and the firm belief that the judgments made by the advisor are non-punitive and are motivated by empathy with and concern for the teacher's professional development (see Task 4.5 for a game to explore the feelings engendered by feedback on criteria which are not shared and Task 4.4 for an exploration of ways to create a positive relationship with a teacher).

Trust then becomes a generic prerequisite for the provision of effective help. It is central to the idea that the process is collaborative. Without such trust, collaboration between the advisor and the teacher cannot be undertaken. It is also of crucial importance in establishing the basis upon which the advisor can offer advice without being seen as critical of the teacher as a person. In Western democratic societies trust is generated by respect for the individual as a person. Within such societies the ultimate actor is the individual and the high point of the individual's motivation is the pursuit of self-esteem and self-actualisation (Maslow 1970). It follows from this philosophical standpoint that trust will be characterised by respect for the individual and for the individual's values and beliefs. It is, however, worth pointing out that both from within our own culture and certainly from other cultural perspectives, trust can be generated in different ways depending on the context and the individual (for a further discussion of this issue, see Chapter 10). Thus, when teachers have been asked to evaluate circumstances in which they have received effective advice (see Task 4.2), many have identified experience and wisdom as factors which they found important. In these cases, trust was based on the ability of the advisor to provide a good, workable solution. It was based on an unequal relationship (that of 'knower' and 'learner'), not on equality, but it was a relationship in which the receiver of advice trusted the advisor's ability to help.

As well as sensitivity to personal and cultural factors, the contexts in which the advice was being offered were important. Many of the contexts in which experience was considered important were concerned with seeking specific advice for a specific problem, a technical agenda. The advice we are offering in teaching is often regarded as technical in nature and thus trust is generated by respect for the experience of the advisor, rather than deriving solely from the advisor's attitude to the teacher. The factors which are seen as important vary when the problems are less technical and more personal (for an exploration of this aspect, see Task 4.3), and in these situations, the necessary prerequisites for advice to be effective are much more complex and problematic.

4.9 Conclusion

Egan's three-stage model of helping thus provides a macro model of the helping process which starts from the teacher's own view of the situation through a process of a pre-lesson discussion, an observation and a post-lesson debriefing session. As we have seen, the central elements of the process mirror the processes which are considered important from cognitive perspectives. Egan, however, begins to provide a psychodynamic explanation of this process as against the cognitive explanations which we discussed in the earlier chapters.

As part of this psychodynamic explanation, the aims of the helping process are:

- Establishing an *appropriate relationship* with the teacher
- Ensuring that the teacher uses their own *inner resources* and accepts *responsibility* for their own improvement
- Helping the teacher to formulate an *action plan*
- Helping the teacher to *transfer* newly acquired skills to new situations
  (adapted from Nicolson and Ayers 1995)

In Chapter 6, we shall examine the way that these aims can be achieved through the operation of generic micro-skills such as listening and creating empathy. Before that however, we shall examine another model of counselling, Heron's Six Category Intervention Analysis, which we believe offers a useful tool for the examination of the individual actions an advisor can take to create the specific conditions under which learning can take place.

Summary

The following issues have been raised in this chapter:

- Supervision styles: Directive, Non-Directive and Alternative
- Supervision styles and stage of teacher development
- Counselling theory and feedback
- Different approaches to counselling
- Egan's three-stage model of helping
- Egan's model and learning about teaching
- The person-centred counselling approach and teacher supervision
- The three-stage model of helping and the TP cycle

Tasks

The following tasks allow you to explore the issues raised in this chapter:

4.1 Supervision styles
4.2 Providing effective advice in general life situations
4.3 A role play to explore different contexts of giving advice
4.4 A pre-observation conference role play
4.5 A game to investigate the feelings involved in negative feedback
9.1 Examination of a lesson feedback transcript
3.6 Observation notes on lesson
8.2 Written feedback

Advice for further reading

On styles of supervision:
Richards, J.C. and Nunan, D., eds. (1990) *Second Language Teacher Education* Parts III & IV: Cambridge, Cambridge University Press.

These two sections in the influential book on teacher education contain articles about the teaching practicum and on supervision. The section on supervision contains articles by Gebhard on the choices available to advisors, a discussion of clinical supervision by Gaies and Bowers, and the paper intervening in practice teaching by Freeman gives a clear description of the directive, alternatives and non-directive options.

On activities to be used during discussions:

Edge, J. (1992) *Co-operative Development: Professional Self-development through Co-operation with Colleagues*, Harlow: Longman.

This contains a lot of activities which can be used to encourage reflection in teachers, and a simple overview of the different stages of helping, although not in the same form as Egan.

On approaches to counselling:

Nicolson, D. and Ayers, H. (1995) *Individual Counselling Theory and Practice: A Reference Guide*, London: David Fulton Publishers.

Designed as an introduction to counselling for those involved in counselling in schools, it provides an overview of the main counselling approaches and introduces the fundamental aspects of the counselling relationship.

Lago, C. & Thompson, J. (1997) *Race, Culture and Counselling*, Buckingham: Open University Press.

This is an excellent overview of different theories of counselling and the philosophies which underpin the approaches to counselling in the West. It also contains an interesting and useful discussion of culture which is relevant to the discussion of culture in Chapter 10.

5 Providing a framework: Six Category Intervention Analysis

In Chapter 4 we examined the overall 'game plan' for the feedback session. We indicated that the set of goals as identified for the different stages of the advice session will need to be implemented by the advisor through different interventions – verbal or non-verbal actions by the advisor. In this and the next four chapters we shall examine the different skills and interventions which are at the disposal of the advisor, paying attention to the intentions behind different interventions and their results in terms of the interpretations placed upon them by the teacher. We shall begin this examination by establishing a framework within which to locate these actions. In this chapter we shall outline elements of Heron's (1990) Six Category Intervention Analysis which we consider useful for understanding the way that advice can be effectively provided.

5.1 Six Category Intervention Analysis

The previous chapter, then, identified three 'stages' of providing advice, and Edge (1992) suggested different macro-skills which were appropriate for each stage of the process.

The problem with the 'stage' approach is that it is overly simplistic; there is no one-to-one relationship between the skill or the intervention type and the stage of the helping cycle. Attending and reflecting are skills which will be used all the time. Similarly, 'challenging' and 'disclosing' are interventions which could be used at any stage of the process. What is required is a framework for describing different interventions and then to look at their use in a complete cycle. For this we shall turn to a model provided by Heron.

Six Category Intervention Analysis is an overall framework for the description of interventions which can be made by any person involved in giving advice or feedback to others. Heron sees the system as being useful for a whole range of different professionals within the caring professions from school teachers providing counselling to students through to lawyers with their clients or psychotherapists providing psychological support to clients.

> The six-category system is a practical working hypothesis, not a dogma. It is in principle open to being checked and rechecked, amended and modified, by personal experiential inquiry, by testing it against the evidence provided by using it in action. There is nothing sacred about the number 'six', or about the whole way the system is put together. (Heron, 1990: 7)

Thus Heron, like Egan, sees the system which he describes as 'eclectic'. We shall use this framework in the way that he intended, relating the interventions to practical experience we have gained over the years in providing feedback to teachers and trainees. The following description is not intended to be exhaustive. It is a selection of ideas from his analysis which we feel are of particular relevance to providing advice in teaching. There are three main concepts which we feel are particularly useful as a way of examining interaction in the feedback session. They are:

- The six categories and their division into Authoritative and Facilitative approaches
- Different agenda types
- Degenerative interventions

5.2 The six categories

Heron divides the possible interventions which can be made in a counselling situation into two broad categories, Authoritative and Facilitative. Within each of these two broad categories, there are three further categorised interventions making a total of six in all. These are conventionally displayed as the intersections of two triangles:

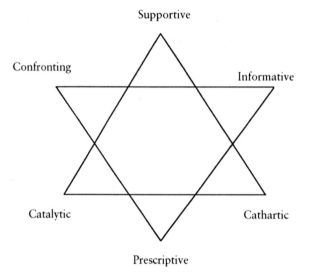

Figure 18 Heron's six categories of intervention

The categories are:

Authoritative
1. **Prescriptive.** Refers to interventions in which the advisor tries to directly tell the teacher what they should do, how to

Facilitative
4. **Cathartic.** This type of intervention seeks to allow a client to discharge their emotions and feelings, particularly

improve or modify the way they teach.

2. **Informative**. The advisor gives the teacher information or knowledge about the situation on which to base a new awareness and to facilitate personal growth.

3. **Confronting**. The advisor tries to raise the teacher's consciousness about certain aspects of teaching by sharing perceptions of the teacher's behaviour and challenging the teacher on areas which are seen as problematic and through this confrontation to improve their teaching skills.

painful feelings of grief, fear and anger.

5. **Catalytic**. This type of intervention from the advisor encourages self-discovery by the teacher by questioning on critical areas and by bringing knowledge and information to the surface.

6. **Supportive**. In a supportive intervention, the advisor affirms the worth of the teacher, primarily by praising and valuing what has been done.

In contrast to their general use in recent education discourse, Heron does not necessarily value one set of interventions over the other. The terms 'Authoritative' and 'Facilitative' have acquired associations within educational discourse over the last twenty years which make them difficult to use neutrally. 'Facilitative' is generally seen as a positive approach whilst 'Authoritative' is seen in a much more pejorative light. Within the system described by Heron however, the terms are used descriptively rather than prescriptively. They describe the degree of direction provided by the advisor in the process of discussion. Authoritative interventions are what Freeman would call Directive, and Facilitative are what he would call Non-directive. According to Heron, all of the categories are value free – they are all fundamentally supportive of the value of the individual and have as their implicit aim to increase the client's ability for self-direction.

5.3 Authoritative vs facilitative interventions

5.3.1 When are authoritative interventions appropriate?

We have suggested in Chapter 3 that one of the most important aspects of the advisory process is the generation of an atmosphere of trust and that this trust may be generated through a range of interpersonal/social roles. Thus, the teacher may trust the advisor because the advisor is more experienced, because the advisor is in a position of authority, because the advisor is a friend/equal etc. This trust is based on what Habermas (1984) calls different 'validity claims', an issue which we shall discuss in more detail in Chapter 10; here we intend only to look at the effect such different claims may have on the intervention style adopted by the advisor.

The following table illustrates the way in which the 'trust'/authority of the advisor is grounded in different social/personal roles and results in different ways of advising a teacher. At one end of the cline are interventions which are controlled by the advisor and which are based on trust generated by the advisor's position; at the other end are interventions which are teacher-directed and which rest on the trust which exists between the advisor as an equal adult, a colleague.

Advisor-directed	Commanding prescription	The advisor uses institutional authority (e.g. inspectorial position) to tell the teacher what to do. The reason for giving the direction and the reason for accepting the direction are those of authority.
↓	Benevolent prescription	The advisor suggests, persuades, proposes and advises and the arguments used are based on a wish to help the teacher. However, there is still no consultation with the teacher.
	Consultative prescription	The advisor not only proposes a course of action to the teacher, but also elicits their views on the proposal. However, it is clear that the advisor has the final say over the implementation of the proposed action.
↑	Negotiation	The advisor works with the teacher in a truly collaborative manner. Observations are shared and proposals discussed in a truly equal manner and the advisor and teacher work together to reach a fully joint solution.
Teacher-directed	Facilitation of self-direction	At this end of the cline, the advisor's main concern is to act as a catalyst for the teacher to arrive at their own solutions. The action suggested (e.g. some action research) is not only free for the teacher to accept or reject, but the intervention itself was intended to act as a stimulus for self-directed growth and evaluation.

(adapted from Heron, 1990: 32–33)

Figure 19 The effect of trust on advisor control in interventions

Thus, at one end of the gradient the advisor can simply tell the teacher what to do:

> 'You should discuss the situation with the class before you introduce them to the pictures'.

This might be appropriate in a situation where, for example, an advisor is helping to introduce a new coursebook in a country:

> 'The coursebook says that you should discuss the situation with the class before showing them the picture'.

In both examples the advisor is basing the advice offered and the manner of providing it on their institutional role within the system. The first is a *Directive Intervention* within Heron's category of *Prescription* and the second is an *Informative Intervention*.

At the other end of the gradient, a similar issue (the discussion of a situation before looking at the picture) might be approached like this:

'Do you think there might be a case for discussing the picture before showing it to the pupils?'

'I wonder if it might be worth trying to discuss the picture before showing it to the pupils. What do you think?'

In this case the advisor is negotiating with the teacher from a position of equality, as a collaborator. The advisor is providing the prompt for the teacher to evaluate the situation and a suggestion for a small piece of action research. *Action Research*[1] is an intervention within Heron's category of *Consultative Prescriptions*. If it is clear that the teacher is completely free to accept or reject the suggested action, then the intervention would become one which was *Catalytic* and thus Facilitative rather than Authoritative, and these we shall examine in Chapter 9.

Thus different intervention styles are appropriate in different contexts and will lead to different intervention types. (For an exploration of this issue, see particularly Task 5.1, although the issue will permeate discussion on many other tasks, especially 5.2, 5.3, 5.4, 8.1 and 9.1.)

5.4 Different agendas and types of intervention

Throughout the book we have suggested that the issue which the advisor wishes to raise is an important factor to be taken into account when deciding how to give advice. Along with Heron, we have used the term 'agenda' to cover this area.

Heron uses this term to identify the underlying issues which are being raised within an advisory session. He has a complex series of agendas, ranging from the purely technical (where 'client[s] lack basic skills in some specialist areas of professional competence') through to highly personal agendas such as emotional agendas (where 'client[s are] unawarely deficient in emotional competence') (Heron 1990: 49). Although not wishing to deny the importance of personal feelings in teaching and the complex relationship which exists between a person's beliefs, feelings and way of teaching (see Chapter 7), it is also clear that compared with psychodynamic counselling much advice in education, particularly when dealing with competency-based training systems, tends to relate to more technical agenda types than to the more emotional, intrapsychological agenda types.

Having said that, it is important when advising teachers to be able to differentiate issues which are merely technical or general from those which involve deeply held beliefs. For example, an advisor may wish to try to get a teacher to use a particular type of class activity such as pair or group work. On the surface this may seem to be a technical agenda. The teacher needs to acquire certain surface classroom management skills in order for the activity to work and the advisor may well decide that a directive intervention such as

---

[1] Action research here is used as one of Heron's intervention types (see Chapter 8), not as the general research approach widely used in education; although the type of suggestion is analogous to the research procedure, it is much simpler.

demonstrating the procedure with the teacher is an appropriate way to put the point across. However, the issue of classroom management may not be the reason why the teacher is not able to effectively use group work. There may well be (and probably are) many deeply held personal and cultural beliefs about what constitutes effective learning which are the underlying reasons for the teacher not using the technique. There may be underlying emotional reasons for not using the technique (e.g. lack of personal confidence and fear of failure). Such wider agendas will be better approached through other methods, perhaps by confronting the teacher with the issues rather than by directive interventions which can be used with technical agendas. This can be represented in the following diagram:

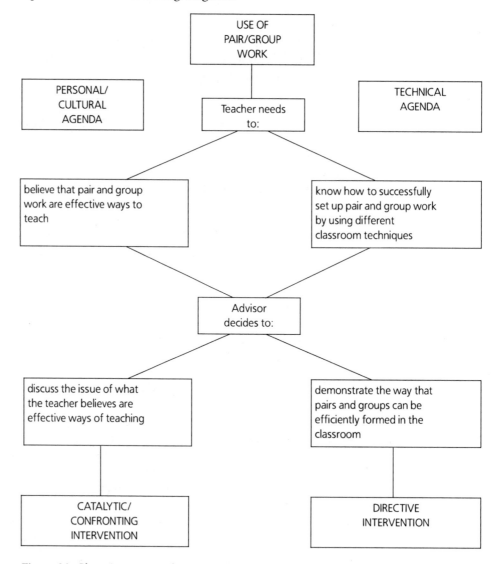

Figure 20 Choosing approaches to intervention based on agenda

Thus advice often needs to deal with both the technical aspects and the underlying belief systems.

Another agenda which is important in advising teachers concerns the relationship between advisors and teachers: interpersonal agendas. As we identified in Chapter 1, there will be different institutional roles and perceptions of the roles of the advisor. The advisor may view the session as a collaborative exercise whereas the teacher may well view it as an assessment. In such circumstances, the offer of a suggestion ('Why not put them into groups for this exercise?') will be 'heard' as a directive intervention although intended as a consultative intervention. Advisors need to be aware of the effect such agendas can have on the advisory process and bring these into the open if necessary (see Tasks 5.2, 5.3 & 5.4).

The third agenda type which advisors need to be aware of is that of the feelings and anxieties which are caused by the teaching situation or by the feedback session itself: emotional agendas. We mentioned above that lack of confidence may be a reason for not using a particular technique. Such an agenda may well be appropriately dealt with by using supportive interventions: valuing and praising the teacher's work. In Chapter 7 we shall discuss the effect that anxiety and defensive reactions can have on the feedback process. Again, as with the first two agenda types, advisors will need to

- be sensitive to the existence of such agendas
- be aware of the effect that these agendas are having on the advisory process
- make the teacher clear about the issue being discussed (raising awareness of the agenda)
- provide the appropriate interventions to make sure that the issue is resolved

5.5 Degenerative interventions

The third concept which we wish to adopt from Heron's model of interventions is that of the 'degenerative intervention'. In essence, a degenerative intervention is one in which the intention of the advisor is interpreted in quite a different manner by the teacher. We shall illustrate this idea by examining the way that an advisor approaches giving negative feedback to a teacher.

As the essence of providing help is to maintain an atmosphere of trust, the problem for the advisor is how to maintain a supportive and valuing atmosphere whilst raising uncomfortable and critical comments about the lesson. This will inevitably lead to raised levels of anxiety in both the teacher and the advisor. The effects of such raised anxiety on both the teacher and the advisor are summarised in the following diagram (adapted from Heron 1990: 46):

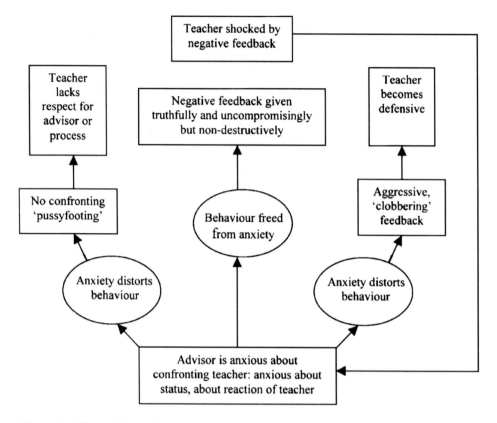

Figure 21 The problems facing the advisor and possible outcomes

The two degenerative scenarios illustrated in this diagram arise from a mismatch between the intentions of the advisor and the perception of the teachers. The advisor is seen as either 'pussyfooting' or 'clobbering'.

5.5.1 'Pussyfooting'

One path which the advisor could take is to shrink from giving negative feedback at all. The advisor's anxiety about upsetting the teacher leads to the advisor not confronting the teacher over important issues – to 'pussyfooting'. This anxiety arises from fear of the distressed reaction of the teacher to negative feedback which is perceived as punitive. Although such avoidance strategies are intended to enhance the supportive nature of the relationship between the advisor and the teacher, they may have the opposite effect. The teacher, although initially relieved by being 'let off the hook', may well finish up lacking respect for both the advisor and the process of feedback. In avoiding the important issues which arise from the lesson, little gets achieved in the feedback session. Such a scenario Heron classes as 'degenerative' in the sense that the intervention does not realise its intended aim; it does not raise the teacher's awareness of important aspects of teaching.

5.5.2 'Clobbering'

The other 'degenerative' scenario can also arise from the advisor's anxiety about the teacher's reaction to negative feedback. In this case the advisor reacts to the teacher by going on the attack. In response to the negative feedback many teachers will produce defensive reactions. Reactions from personal justification 'Well I tried it once but it didn't work with my class' through more overtly challenging statements such as 'You don't understand my class' to completely combative comments like 'What do you know about it anyway, you've only been here once' (often not openly verbalised) are all examples of defensive walls being set up by teachers in reaction to comments made on lessons. When faced with such reactions to suggestions, it is quite common for inexperienced advisors to react with overly aggressive interventions, by adopting an inappropriately authoritarian style. This is particularly true in a situation where the advisor is unsure of their status with regard to the teacher. The anxiety of the advisor leads to inappropriate levels of intervention and a situation entails in which both the advisor and the teacher are locked in battle; the teacher behind defensive walls and the advisor 'clobbering' with even more aggressive comments. The confrontation thus becomes 'degenerate' in Heron's terms. It becomes an intervention which does not perform its intended function. Instead of the confrontation leading to a raising of the teacher's awareness of an aspect of behaviour in a non-destructive manner, the intervention is 'heard' as punitive and hurtful, thus leading to a further cycle of defensive reactions from the teacher without the central issue being openly and calmly addressed.

Thus, the dilemma is that if the advisor confronts in a manner which is not seen as valuing the teacher, the teacher feels that they are being 'clobbered' whereas if the advisor does nothing, there is an air of 'pussyfooting'. The answer provided by Heron is the same as that provided by Egan in his analysis of providing help: the advisor should be honest and truthful in giving feedback, but this feedback should be free of any hint that it is in any way punitive. It is not the teacher who is being examined but the way that the lesson was taught. A 'problem' in the lesson is not a 'fault' in the teacher and this needs to be clearly signalled to the teacher.

5.6 Conclusion

In this chapter we have begun to look at the detail of the feedback session by providing a framework for the examination of the actual moves or interventions made by an advisor. We have also highlighted the importance of the agenda type to the process of giving advice and have suggested that the mismatch between advisor intentions and teacher perceptions, degenerative interventions, can be a major source of problems in the advisory session and can lead to raised levels of anxiety during the session. Throughout our discussion of the two counselling approaches we have emphasised the need for a positive and empathetic atmosphere of trust between the advisor and the teacher. Such an atmosphere of trust is essential for the giving of effective advice and there are a number of core counselling skills which are needed to create this atmosphere. In the next chapter we shall examine these core counselling skills and discuss in closer detail how advisors can deal with emotional agendas in the feedback session.

Summary

The following issues have been raised in this chapter:

- The Six Category Intervention Analysis framework
- Authoritative and facilitative interventions
- Different agenda types
- Degenerative interventions

Tasks

The following tasks will allow you to explore the issues raised in this chapter:

5.1 Feedback transcript examining authoritative and facilitative interventions
5.2 An activity to examine different interventions and the way that they are perceived
5.3 Examination of how different intentions are signalled by different language and contexts
5.4 Feedback transcript examining the difference that status can make in the way that advice is given and perceived
8.1 Feedback role play
9.1 Examination of a lesson feedback transcript

Advice for further reading

Heron, J. (1990). *Helping the Client: A Creative Practical Guide*, London: Sage Publications.
    This is perhaps the most accessible of Heron's books, in which he lays out his system and provides strong arguments for believing that the process of helping is a process of supporting and enabling the well-being of another person. In the book he argues strongly for a loving commitment from the helper to the client, and for some this may make the book difficult to take. However, although at times it is very involved, there is a lot of good common sense in the book and a lot of discussion about giving advice.

6 Ways of talking to teachers 1: creating the right atmosphere

Egan suggests that the skilled helper operates through the use of a number of core communication skills such as

- effective attending and listening
- active listening
- creating empathy
- probing

The first three of these communication skills will be considered in this chapter, as part of the essential skills needed by an advisor to create an atmosphere of trust. The fourth, probing, will be considered in much greater detail in the subsequent chapters as we begin to consider the way that advisors intervene to move teachers to new levels of understanding. This chapter, then, will deal with the emotional climate of the feedback session and will examine the generic skills involved in creating an empathetic and caring climate in the feedback session.

6.1 Effective attending and listening

The establishment of an appropriate relationship with the teacher is essential for the provision of effective advice. As we have argued, this relationship will be based on trust and should be collaborative in nature. The advice given should be perceived as useful by the teacher, it should be internalised by the teacher and it will need to be put into practice. In order to achieve these aims the advice must be 'owned' by the teacher. For the relationship to be fully collaborative, the advisor will need to listen to the concerns of the teacher and signal this to the teacher. Thus, listening skills will be approached from two perspectives; effective attending (relating to the way in which the advisor signals attention to the teacher) and active listening (relating to the mental processes and strategies being used by the advisor to listen not only to what is said but what is meant).

6.1.1 Effective attending

Effective attending is listening in a way that conveys to the teacher that they are being listened to.

It involves the use of body posture, gesture and other non-verbal parameters and includes such things as an attentive posture, eye contact, smiling, nodding etc. to signal concentration on the speaker. Egan uses the acronym S-O-L-E-R to characterise such effective attention-giving. This acronym stands for facing the teacher *Squarely*, having an *Open* posture, *Leaning* towards the teacher, maintaining appropriate *Eye contact* and being *Relaxed*. These suggested behaviours need to be treated with caution in that they describe what are considered to be effective non-verbal signals within a particular cultural setting and Egan is careful to describe such behaviours as those which work in a North American context. Not only is non-verbal communication (NVC) influenced by cultural differences but interpersonal distance, touch and body posture are also heavily influenced by other factors such as race, gender and status (for further discussions of NVC, see Graddol *et al.* 1987, Argyle 1988 and Pease 1997). Although the relationships between the different factors are complex, and there appear to exist wide personal differences in both postures used and their interpretation, it is important that advisors are aware of the different interpretations of non-verbal signals (see Task 6.1).

The processes involved in non-verbal communication are exactly the same as any other form of communication. Just as language forms can be interpreted differently in different contexts, so too can the messages conveyed by non-verbal communication be open to different interpretations. It is important that advisors are able both to signal their intentions and to read the signs showing how these intentions are being received by the teacher. The signals may be intentional or unintentional and it is important that advisors are aware of the likely interpretation both of their consciously controlled body language and of the effect of the signals which they may be giving unconsciously. Thus advisors need to be aware of the unintended effects that their body posture may be having on the feedback session and on the way that the teacher views them. This situation can be represented diagramatically:

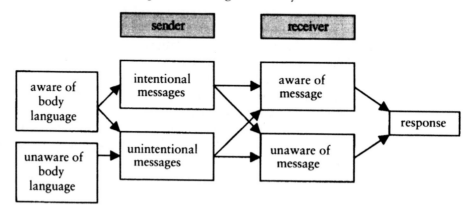

Figure 22 Possible effects of body posture on the feedback session (after Argyle 1988)

Thus, to use a phrase from Transactional Analysis (Berne 1964), it is easy for intentions to become 'crossed', or in Heron's model, 'degenerative'. Either the intended message is misinterpreted or an unintentional message is perceived from an unintentional action. One such example relates to body language during lesson observation. We have identified lesson observation as a part of effective attending (see Chapter 4). Thus advisors need to be aware of the necessity of signalling effective attention during the lesson. Exactly the opposite impression can be created, if, during the lesson, they concentrate too much on note-taking rather than signalling active engagement with what the teacher is trying to do and what is happening in the classroom. Accurate recording of the lesson may not be as important as signalling that the advisor is attending. The most important aim at this point is to establish a relationship with the teacher, to indicate a common interest in looking at the process of teaching with the teacher (for an exploration of the effect of taking notes while listening, see Task 6.2, Role Play 2).

6.2 Active listening

Listening has been described as a skill that is taught in inverse proportion to its use. Typically, an advisor will spend at least one half of each day in listening situations, yet they have frequently received little or no guidance in how to listen effectively. Active listening relates to the way that the advisor responds to both the verbal and the non-verbal behaviour of the teacher. It involves more than merely registering the surface meanings of what the teacher is saying. Egan puts it 'to be present psychologically, socially and emotionally' (1994: 111) and Heron describes it as 'Being here now, being there now' (Heron 1990: 96). Again, the phraseology here reflects one of the principal aims of Egan and Heron, that of providing psychotherapeutic help to a client, but the intention which underlies the phrase is clear; the advisor should communicate to the teacher that they are actively and closely interested in what the teacher is saying. Part of the problem of teachers not producing convincing or significant accounts of the teaching may be related to the often ritual nature of questions like 'Well, how did it go then?' asked in a manner which reduces the question to one of mere phatic communication, something akin to 'Well, how are you then?' The advisor's body language and tone of voice will provide a powerful signal to the teacher as to the way that the question should be 'read'; either as an 'ice-breaker' or as a seriously intended probing question. Neither of the readings is inherently 'correct'; either could be entirely appropriate in different phases of the feedback session. However, what is important is that the advisor should be in control of the manner in which the questions are delivered, should be aware of the likely effects of the different ways of delivering the questions and, crucially as far as active listening is concerned, should be able to provide and communicate the sort of active engagement with the teacher which is signalled by the term active listening (for an exploration of surface factors involved in listening, see Task 6.2, and for body posture, Task 6.1).

Thus, active listening is more than following what the teacher is saying. It can be signalled in various non-verbal and verbal ways, but it is more than a mere set of techniques. It is more the underlying intention and genuine warmth and support which is generated by the advisor than the implementation of a series of techniques.

Egan identifies four components of active listening:

- listening to the verbal language and understanding it
- listening to the body language, the non-verbal behaviour of the client and understanding what is being said
- listening to the whole person in relation to their social context
- tough-minded listening

Each of these components is important in advising teachers.

6.2.1 *Listening to the verbal account of the teacher*

Listening to the verbal account of the teacher involves the pre-lesson meeting, the lesson and the initial part of the feedback interview. It is important that advisors negotiate with teachers before the lesson starts in order to ascertain both the aims of the teacher in the lesson and, in training terms, the methodological goals which the teacher wants to work on. Thus, the observation should include the teacher's agenda in linguistic and developmental terms.

During the pre-observation conference

At this stage it is crucial that the advisor does not attempt to criticise what the teacher is attempting to do. The advisor should, at this point, listen with a view to understanding the teacher's aim, but should avoid challenging. The advisor may well disagree with the teacher's aims but even so should not attempt to try to 'rewrite' the lesson. Simple 'tips' may be offered if it is felt that they can be easily incorporated into the lesson (using an 'informative intervention', see Chapter 8) but it is important not to appear to 'judge' during the pre-observation meeting. This meeting should be dominated by the teacher's view of the intended lesson and the advisor should avoid judging, 'labelling' the teacher or dominating the discussion (see Task 6.2, Role Play 5). The agenda of issues raised by the teacher should be listened to, understood, and carried forward to the rest of the cycle, particularly the lesson observation phase. The different views of the advisor and the teacher will be considered as part of the process, but at a later stage in the practice cycle when such a challenging move will be more appropriate (for exploration of pre-lesson discussions, see Tasks 6.3 & 4.4).

During the lesson

At this stage the advisor should 'listen' (attend) to what the teacher is doing and try to understand the teacher's actions in the context of the intended aims, the developmental perspective of the teacher and the classroom situation. Again, it is particularly important here to avoid instant 'labelling' and judging actions as they happen. Within a lesson, teachers will do things which will apparently 'offend' the generally accepted view of how teaching and learning should proceed. For example, the teacher may not provide what the advisor considers to be effective pre-listening tasks for a listening passage. It is all too easy for the advisor in this situation to classify such behaviour as an 'inability to effectively introduce a listening passage'. Whilst such labels are important, and the process of learning about teaching involves the altering of the perceptions of teachers as well as their behaviour, at this point in the process of giving advice it is important that the advisor tries to understand the teacher's actions in the context of the lesson. There may be other equally important reasons for the teacher to launch directly into a listening exercise, and the advisor must remain sensitive to these factors, both within the classroom situation ('watching empathetically') and when listening to the teacher's account of the lesson ('listening empathetically'). During the lesson the advisor will identify areas which will need to be focused on in the discussion, often by indicating questions which might be asked of the teacher, but should avoid pre-judging the outcome (see Task 3.6 for discussion of what notes an advisor might make during observation).

During the feedback session

Finally, the advisor will need to actively listen to the teacher's account of how the lesson went. As we said earlier, often such accounts are rather superficial. This can be due to the fact that there is a great deal of anxiety on the part of the teacher immediately following the lesson and the advisor will need to be aware of such emotional factors which are being expressed. These emotional factors will not be expressed in words; they will be expressed through other paralinguistic features such as tone of voice, body posture and eye contact. Thus, active listening involves listening to and understanding the non-verbal behaviour of the teacher as well as the verbal behaviour (for an analysis of a feedback session, see Task 6.4; for an exploration of these factors through role play, see Task 8.1).

6.2.2 Understanding non-verbal signals

Listening to the teacher talking about the lesson, then, is an important step to understanding the situation from their point of view. But the surface meaning of what is said is only part of the message which the advisor needs to attend to. It has been said that 93% of what we hear is interpreted through non-verbal communication. The advisor needs to be able to decide on the significance to the teacher of what is being said. Teachers' accounts of their lessons and their reasons for doing things can be motivated by a host of different concerns. The teacher may well be telling the advisor what they believe the advisor wants to hear. The explanation may relate more to 'educational correctness' than to the real beliefs and cognitive structures of the teacher. An example might be that a teacher will criticise themselves for carrying out too much mechanical drilling, not because they believe that such drilling is wrong but because they believe that the advisor will think it is wrong. In fact, they feel that mechanical drilling is very useful, they use it a great deal and think it is effective, and do not understand why it has such a poor reputation in current approaches to teaching. It is vital that the advisor is able to understand and evaluate what is being said, not just on a surface semantic level, but on an unintentional, emotional one. Such underlying feelings can be signalled by body language and intonation as much as by the words actually used. There are a number of clues which can be used here: raising one's voice can be a sign of increased emotion; posture can indicate the degree of comfort and how willing the teacher is to listen to the message; turning away may signal indifference or discomfort, but such messages are easy to misread and the advisor will need to 'probe' the teacher to uncover these underlying feelings, to decide on the underlying agenda which needs to be addressed. (see 'confronting interventions', Chapter 8 and 'cathartic interventions', Chapter 7).

It is also important for the general establishment of an appropriate, caring relationship that the advisor listens to the emotional message being given by the teacher (e.g. 'Help, I'm in a mess' or 'I'm extremely worried about what you think of the lesson') and responds to that message. This may happen at the beginning of the session, but there will be changes in the teacher's feelings during the discussion. Thus advisors need to pay attention to such signals throughout the discussion to make judgments about how to move the discussion forward.

We should again reiterate that non-verbal communication is not universal. Non-verbal communication, and the interpretation of gestures, body posture and facial expressions in cross-cultural contexts needs careful consideration. There is evidence that the interpretation of many such factors, such as interpersonal distance and touch, are often culturally dependent. The classical work in this area was carried out by Hall (Hall 1959 and 1963, reported in Argyle 1988) on interpersonal distances which were used in different contexts in North America. He also found that comfortable interpersonal distances between Arabs were much less than those between Americans; the latter felt distinctly uncomfortable at interpersonal distances which were common amongst Arabs. Such studies of interpersonal distance have since been repeated and included studies of touching, gaze, orientation and voice (Watson 1970, reported in Argyle 1988), and studies such as this have indicated that societies may be classifiable into 'contact' and 'non-contact' societies. However, the relationships between these factors are complex and it is important to avoid adopting stereotypical attitudes; there also appear to exist wide personal differences within different cultural groups. Yet those who have experienced the apparent 'difficulty' faced by advisors from a European cultural background in reading the expressions of a Japanese teacher will testify to the importance of this area for those working in cross-cultural situations. In Japan the concept of 'face' and the inappropriacy of expressing negative feelings is much stronger than in European societies and thus it is much more difficult for the advisor to 'read' the feelings of the teacher in such situations.

6.2.3 Listening and understanding the teacher in context

Many innovations in ELT have failed because of the lack of congruence between the methods suggested and the needs of the local context (see Holliday 1995 for a further discussion of this issue). In a similar manner to the macropolitics of introducing new ideas into systems without due regard to the local situation, it is critical that the advisor actively 'listens' to the teacher in the local context. With the advantage of being able to actually observe the teacher in context in the lesson, the advisor is in an ideal position to put this part of listening into practice. However, it is important that the lesson is 'listened to' empathetically with the desire on the part of the advisor to find out what is happening rather than immediately labelling what is seen with reference to a pre-determined set of concepts of what is 'correct' teaching. The lesson should be viewed initially without preconceptions on the part of the advisor, who should have a genuine desire to understand the lesson from the viewpoint of the teacher and the context. Such an approach – starting from the actuality of the teacher in context and actively listening to that situation, including the teacher's own view of it – will certainly mean that the aims of the advisor with regard to new areas will necessarily be scaled down and be less ambitious. However, such a negotiation of the aims of and approaches to teaching between the advisor, the teacher and the context is exactly the negotiation of learning and the construction of new concepts proposed in the Vygotskian model of learning.

6.2.4 Tough-minded listening

Active listening needs to be genuine, and an understanding of this concept helps us to understand the concept of according the client 'unconditional positive regard' (Rogers 1969). This does not mean that we must agree with the teacher's view of what happened. As Egan points out, one of the components of active listening is 'tough-minded listening'. As proposed by Egan, this suggests that we must listen to the teacher's view of the lesson and we must accept that it is the teacher's view and understand that view. However, we must also recognise that this view can be distorted, that the teacher's view can be seriously at odds with reality. What the teacher believes/perceives is happening is seriously distorted. The process of active listening involves close psychological engagement with the teacher in order to explore their view of the events, in order to understand why they did what they did. We value their views as their views, but we don't necessarily accept that they are the only or the best explanations of the situation. Active listening, 'getting inside the skin' of the problem is an essential part of being able to diagnose and help the teacher develop, but it is important to produce the diagnosis in order to move the teacher on from their current level to new understandings. To do this, explanations will need to be probed, unpacked and analysed collaboratively; the process of scaffolding.

6.3 Creating empathy

All of the above micro-skills are related to basic, generic concepts such as creating an appropriate relationship between the teacher and the advisor; creating an atmosphere of trust. Underpinning this discussion is the notion that the advisor, in order to help the teacher, needs to understand the teacher and the teacher's motivations. The underlying concept is one of empathy, a central concept in democratic counselling. Empathy differs from sympathy in a similar way that 'looking with' differs from 'looking at'. Sympathy expresses the outsider's view of someone's actions; it involves a certain degree of understanding but one which is judged from a separate point of view. Empathy, by contrast, involves the ability to imagine oneself in another's place and understanding their feelings, thoughts and actions – looking at the situation from the teacher's angle and reserving judgment until the situation can be fully understood from their point of view. Empathy, then, is the essential goal for the process of advising. On the psychodynamic level it is an attempt to create a truly collaborative relationship; from a cognitive perspective, it provides a basis on which new understandings can be built.

Empathy can be enhanced by the use of different interpersonal skills such as effective attending and active listening. Limited self-disclosure (e.g. 'I had that problem when I was a teacher too') can also be a way of creating empathy. Within the verbal domain, empathy can be enhanced by the use of such moves as paraphrasing, reflecting, summarising and probing (these 'interventions' are discussed in further detail in Chapter 9). However, as we stated at the outset, whilst such skills can be practised and it is important for advisors to be sensitised to the effects of 'surface behaviours', empathy involves more than surface 'tricks'; it involves a deep commitment on the part of the advisor to want to understand teaching from the teacher's perspective (see 'being there, being here', Chapter 9). The danger of a communication skills training approach is that the training remains simply on the level of surface behaviours and does not address the inner concepts of helping. In order to be effective, advisors need to understand the intentions of the advice process, they need to explore and be comfortable with these inner concepts, including the philosophical approaches which underpin the ideas. Thus, it is not only aspects such as non-verbal communication which need to be explored in cross-cultural contexts. It is also the concept of empathy, a central theme underlying much of what has been said about effective helping, which we need to examine both in the light of individual and cultural positions on providing advice.

6.4 Supportive interventions

In all our reflections on our actions, rational thought and emotion are inextricably intertwined and advisors need to be aware of this when discussing lessons with teachers. In the realm of dealing with feelings, supportive interventions are central to all aspects of giving advice.

Supportive interventions

> affirm the worth of clients, of their qualities, attitudes of mind, actions, artefacts and creations. They do so in an unqualified manner. (Heron 1990: 116)

They are important for two reasons:

- as a basis for the establishment of the trusting relationship which we have identified as essential for any feedback situation (see Chapter 4)
- in the process of shaping and developing the teacher by emphasising the good work done (a developmental model) rather than being critical of performance (a deficit model)

They are essential for creating the atmosphere of trust and empathy which is central to the process of giving advice. Without this trust, as we have argued, there can be no successful relationship between the advisor and the teacher. The atmosphere created in the feedback session must be one in which the teacher feels free to talk and explore the situation with the advisor.

There are two aspects to support: one is being supportive and the other is providing supportive interventions. The general climate of providing support is closely related to the 'being here, being there' existential quality of signalling that you are close to the teacher and are providing your undivided attention to them and their concerns. The other is a series of interventions which can be made in order to affirm this. These interventions can be supportive in a number of different areas or agendas. They can be supportive of:

1.	the teachers as people	As we have said a number of times, the discussion of the lessons and any criticism of them should be just what this says. You still affirm the worth and value of the teacher as a person
2.	the positive qualities of the teacher as a person	Again, all teachers have qualities and these qualities need to be affirmed
3.	the beliefs, norms and values that the teachers hold	Although these may be up for discussion during the feedback session, they are still the views of the teacher and the advisor should acknowledge and respect them
4.	the actions of the teacher	The actual actions which the teacher has carried out in the lesson belong to them. The advisor must not appear to condemn them outright
5.	the products, projects and artefacts of the teacher	This will include the lesson plans, the materials and the lessons carried out by the teacher. Again, they need to be treated with respect

Figure 23 Supportive intervention (adapted from Heron 1991: 118)

6.4.1 Validation

On one level, the simplest way of being supportive is to show that the advisor values what the teacher has done by praising their work. Thus, advice to new advisors is often to 'start with the positive'. This very robust piece of advice is based on the idea that in order to provide constructive feedback it is important to 'get the teacher on your side' by saying nice things about the lesson, by making them 'feel good about themselves'. Such simple advice is clearly very sensible and it can be seen in many advice-giving situations (see Task 8.3 for providing written feedback and Tasks 5.4, 6.4, and 9.1 for spoken feedback).

However, such feedback as: 'I liked the way you introduced the dialogue but . . .' can easily become formulaic. The teacher 'reads' the validation of their work as a mere 'softening up' move prior to the sting in the tail. This is why Heron emphasises that providing effective advice is not merely a matter of following a formulaic series of steps or utterances, but must be felt and acted by the advisor. Providing support is more than using a form of words, it is a matter of living those words; it is 'intensely active but silent and unspoken . . .' (Heron 1991: 117).

6.4.2 Sharing and self-disclosure

We shall discuss the use of self-disclosure as a technique for helping the teacher to re-examine ways that they carry out certain actions in the classroom as one of the 'informative interventions' (Chapter 8). It is a powerful tool to lead into discussion of particular areas of difficulty a teacher may be having. Its power rests on the emotional signal ('I am not so different from you') that it sends to a teacher. It is a basic supportive intervention.

6.4.3 Apologising

It may seem odd to include such a basic human trait as this as a supportive intervention. However, it is important for the advisor firstly to be aware of any lack of respect or consideration which they may have signalled through their behaviour, and, secondly, to apologise for this. Given the in-built power relationships which exist in nearly all advisory situations, the humanity expressed by such an action is a very important signal to the teacher.

6.4.4 Expressing care by doing things and giving things

It is important to generate in the teacher the impression that the advisor really cares for the teacher and what they do. The way to do this is to really and genuinely care for them. Often inspectors and advisors are in a position to help the teacher by providing help, e.g. negotiating with the headteacher, lending them a book or getting information for them. All of these acts are supportive interventions and show that the advisor cares for the teacher.

6.5 Conclusion

In this chapter we have discussed the importance of the generic skills of attending, listening, creating empathy and supportive interventions in creating a positive emotional climate for helping. In Chapter 9 we shall return to them to examine their role in creating critical self-awareness (Heron's 'catalytic tool kit'), but in the next chapter we shall continue to look at the emotional aspects of advising and discuss how to deal with emotional agendas in feedback sessions.

Summary

The following issues have been raised in this chapter:

- Effective attending and listening
- Active listening
- Creating empathy
- Supportive interventions

Tasks

The following tasks allow you to explore the issues raised in this chapter:

6.1 Non-verbal communication
6.2 Role play situations for examining effective listening
6.3 Analysis of a pre-lesson conference
6.4 Analysis of a feedback session
4.4 A pre-observation conference role play
8.1 Feedback role play
2.5 Being a catalyst – how to probe teachers
5.4 Spoken feedback transcription and validation
8.3 Written feedback and validation
9.1 Spoken feedback transcription

Advice for further reading

Pease, A. (1997) *Body Language: How to read others' thoughts by their gestures*, 3rd edition, London: Sheldon Press.
    Although the approach taken may seem a little manipulative (you can use body language to make yourself likeable and get cooperation from people), it gives a fascinating insight into what common gestures and body posture may mean.
Argyle, M. (1988) *Bodily Communication (2nd Edition)*, London: Routledge.
    For further investigation of the issue of non-verbal communication, this is an interesting work which goes into some detail of the research into different aspects of non-verbal communication.

7 Ways of talking to teachers 2: dealing with feelings

In the previous chapter we examined the overall emotional climate of the feedback session and the way that an appropriate atmosphere can be established. In Heron's terms, the issues we talked about are part of the emotional and interpersonal agendas in giving feedback. In this chapter we intend to continue this discussion of emotional agendas by examining the negative impact that very common emotional reactions such as anxiety and defensiveness can have on the feedback session, as well as discussing the role of emotions in general in the analysis of teaching.

7.1 Anxiety and defensiveness

In Chapter 5 we discussed the part that anxiety can play in the way that teachers and advisors react to each other in the context of degenerative interventions. When interventions are 'misheard' or when advisors seek to point out new ways of doing things, the most common reaction of the teacher is to become defensive. Both of these issues lie within the area of emotional agendas and it is important that we discuss how to approach them and how to deal with such emotions, which are a barrier to carrying out effective feedback as we showed in Chapter 5 when we discussed degenerative interventions.

7.1.1 Recognising anxiety

Anxiety is perhaps the most 'public' of emotions in that it deals with people's fears about how others view them. It is particularly associated with the worry about 'making mistakes'. At a certain level, anxiety can be a positive force, focusing the mind and sharpening reactions to undertake a difficult task (facilitative anxiety). Thus, the 'nerves' many teachers feel before meeting with a new class play an essential part in preparing the teacher to produce good lessons. However, too much anxiety can be counter-productive, leading to the inability to act appropriately or be able to concentrate on the job in hand (debilitating anxiety). Anxiety, and its effect on performance, is portrayed in the following diagram:

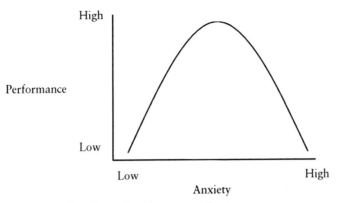

Figure 24 The effect of anxiety on performance

This figure demonstrates that if expectations are perceived as too demanding and anxiety is heightened, performance will be low. If, on the other hand, expectations are insufficiently challenging, performance will also be poor. For many individuals there is a stimulating level of stress which has a facilitating effect on performance. Anxiety levels also vary from person to person (trait anxiety) and there are teachers who will be more anxious than others.

Anxiety levels in the lesson phase of the practice cycle can become very high and can lead to a failure on the part of the teacher to produce an effective lesson. Advisors need to be sensitive to such factors, and the reading of these factors will be signalled by what the teacher says and their general body language in the pre-lesson discussion, during the lesson and afterwards.

The following are general factors which are seen to influence levels of anxiety (McIntyre and Gardner 1991) and we shall examine their relevance to our situation of providing advice to teachers. Depending on the context in which advice is being given, these factors can play an important role in heightening the anxiety felt by a teacher.

Factors affecting anxiety	Relevance to providing advice
Evaluation	The greater the perceived degree of evaluation, the greater the anxiety. As we discussed in Chapter 1, the institutional/professional tension in many contexts means that this factor is likely to be very important in providing advice.
Novelty	The less familiar the situation, the greater the anxiety. Although it may seem to teacher trainers (and to some teachers!) that teachers are always being observed, the number of times that an individual teacher or trainee is observed is actually quite low, and thus this is likely to be a factor in increasing anxiety levels. It is also worth bearing in mind that a teacher is likely to be more anxious teaching a class with which they are unfamiliar than with their regular class.

Ambiguity	The more ambiguous the situation, the more anxious people are likely to be. This is particularly true as regards the criteria on which someone is to be assessed. One of the strengths of an assessment checklist is that the criteria are 'transparent'. In this respect, the negotiation between the teacher and the advisor prior to the lesson should also reduce the ambiguity of the situation and thus reduce levels of anxiety.
Conspicuousness	The more conspicuous a person feels, the more likely they are to feel anxious. It might seem that teachers should not suffer from anxiety over this factor as teaching is a highly conspicuous activity. However, the presence of an advisor in the class is very different from the presence of students, and during an observed lesson, the teacher is likely to feel very conspicuous.
Prior history	The extent to which the situation in the past has created anxiety is also highly correlated with present anxiety. Thus, the previous experience of being observed, particularly if the experience contained a high degree of anxiety which was reinforced by negative feedback, is likely to increase levels of anxiety on subsequent occasions. It is interesting to note that in the Middle East, where classrooms are often visited unannounced by anyone from the headteacher through to the Minister of Education, the presence of observers per se does not seem to be such an important factor in creating anxiety.

Figure 25 Factors affecting levels of anxiety

Whilst the anxiety factors caused by the context are not usually under the control of the advisor, the advisor needs to be aware that contextual factors may increase anxiety. For example, one of the purposes of the visit may be to assess the teacher. Thus, the evaluation factor is likely to have an important influence on the feelings of the teacher. (Task 1.1 provides a useful exploration of some of these aspects.) The advisor will need to take steps to reduce feelings of anxiety through, for example, the use of an appropriate physical setting for the feedback session. Anxiety can be reduced by choosing a calm environment, by avoiding dominant seating arrangements, by maintaining appropriate interpersonal distance, and by adopting appropriate body posture and eye contact (for an exploration of the effects of seating and posture, see Task 6.1).

7.1.2 Recognising defensive reactions

Defensive reactions are common in all situations where advice is given. By defensive reactions we mean behaviour whose real purpose is not to seriously discuss the proposed changes, but to resist change due to feelings such as loss of face. Through such a reaction teachers are indicating that they view the suggestion of change as a threat to their personal or professional being. The likelihood of teachers producing defensive reactions can depend on factors such as:

- the degree of change required (the greater the amount of change envisaged, the more likely it is for a teacher to produce a defensive reaction)
- the experience of the teacher (the more experienced the teacher, the more

'face' may be involved; the less experienced the teacher, the more they are likely to feel threatened)

Defensive reactions will have a 'general' significance – deriving from factors outside the feedback session – and a 'local' significance – deriving from the way the feedback session is being conducted.

General significance: a particular teacher will tend to produce defensive reactions due to individual factors such as experience or personality

Local significance: a specific reaction to the manner in which a piece of advice is given in the feedback session. This may involve 'degenerative interventions' (see Chapter 5)

Thus, as well as being sensitive to the personal/social characteristics of the teacher, the advisor will need to be able to see if a specific meaning has been misinterpreted. Let us take the example of the advisor offering a 'tip' to the teacher in the pre-observation meeting. The intended message is non-judgmental but the teacher might not interpret it in this manner. The advisor intends to provide information as a neutral suggestion but this might be 'read' by the teacher as a 'criticism' and a defensive stance adopted. This defensive stance might be manifested by a string of reasons why the suggestion could not be implemented. What is said by the teacher may be a genuine explanation of the reasons why the suggestion is difficult to implement, or it might be an emotional refusal to listen to what is being proposed. In such a situation, the advisor will need to probe deeper into the motivations of the teacher in order to understand what they are saying at a deeper level, to decide on the appropriate agenda. Only then can the advisor begin to provide effective help.

What is actually said, whether it is a genuine explanation of the difficulties faced by the teacher or a defensive reaction, may be similar. The advisor will need to be aware of the teacher's body language as well as the actual language used; they will need to use their judgment of what the teacher is saying to them ('empathetic divining', Chapter 9). For example defensive reactions may be signalled on a non-verbal level by posture (crossed arms are said to signal retreat into the person and thus are seen as defensive) and avoidance of eye contact (again, see Task 6.1 for an exploration of typical gestures and expressions and their implications). Thus the advisor needs to attend to the non-verbal signals as well as the verbal account of the teacher in order to make valid judgments about what the teacher is saying emotionally.

7.2 Dealing with anxiety and defensiveness

When an advisor or counsellor attempts to probe emotional issues which are causing distress to the client, Heron categorises the intervention type as 'cathartic'.

7.2.1 What are cathartic interventions?

We have all experienced the way that our emotions can be released in some way. In a social game such as 'Crossed/uncrossed' (see Task 4.5) our inability to see the correct answer and our sense of frustration provides the 'fun' element. It is usually released through laughter, nervous laughter for those who still have not worked out the system, genuinely relieved laughter at others still struggling with the problem by those who have. Some people find situations like these rather unpleasant and threatening: not everyone finds them 'fun'. Not everyone sees the humour in the situation, and different cultures will have different ways of dealing with these emotions. However, the essential point is that for many people their underlying feelings and frustrations are released through laughter. Laughter is one of the cathartic reactions, albeit a social reaction in the example we have just looked at. We all know the relief that laughter can bring in such difficult situations, and the release of our emotions is the aim of cathartic interventions.

7.2.2 When are cathartic interventions appropriate?

There are situations in which catharsis occurs spontaneously. Thus, every advisor will have to deal at one time or another with a teacher who is just unable to cope with the situation or the pressure. Tears and sobbing during the feedback session or immediately after lessons are not uncommon and the advisor will need to empathise with the teacher and provide support to help to rebuild the ego which has been severely dented by the experience. Thus, 'valuing what the teacher has done' (a supportive intervention, Chapter 6) is an important intervention that the advisor can make at this point.

Heron suggests that the following interventions are appropriate in this situation:

Validation

The advisor will need to provide support for the teacher, affirming their deep worth. As we have discussed, feelings like stress and anxiety are sometimes a reaction to external circumstances such as the institutional purpose of the supervisory visit. However, such external circumstances can cause the teachers to doubt themselves. Affirming their value as people despite these feelings is an important supportive intervention to help them come to terms with their emotions.

Giving permission

It is important to make it clear to the teacher that their expression of emotion is acceptable behaviour; that the advisor will not view such expression in a negative light. Such freedom to express emotions will depend very much on the overall supportive atmosphere created by the advisor.

Holding

One of the common reactions for anyone within Western societies faced with a person in distress is to reach out and make physical contact of some sort, the most common perhaps being the holding of hands, and such intuitive reactions are quite valid. However, proximity and physical touching are non-verbal communication acts which are very sensitive to cultural variation, both between national cultures and sub-cultures within national cultures (for example between advisors and teachers of different genders). Advisors need to be sensitive to the different interpretations of such non-verbal behaviour within the cultural contexts in which they are working and act accordingly.

Ending

It is important that, at the end of an episode in which the teacher has discharged such emotions, the advisor brings the teacher back to the present and 'normality'. This will happen when the teacher has fully discharged their feelings and has stopped producing overt signs of release such as sobbing. This return to normality can usually be done by referring to the present problem of teaching or by looking forward to future plans.

(For an exploration of ways to deal with such situations, see Task 9.3, Problem 7.)

7.2.3 When should an advisor probe the emotional state of the teacher?

As discussed above, anxiety and defensiveness are common reactions encountered during teaching practice and observation. Neither is unusual and a certain level of anxiety is a healthy and productive emotion. Similarly, defending what has been done is not only a natural reaction, but it is an essential component of the dialogue during which new meanings are constructed. This dialogue is an essential component of the advisor 'listening' to the teacher. However, both states can interfere with the conduct of the feedback session and with learning about teaching if they are felt too strongly. The following are some of the common effects arising from severe anxiety or stress and if the advisor detects that the teacher is behaving in one of these ways, then probing the underlying emotional agenda is appropriate.

'Shutdown'

Teachers are so caught up with their fear of teaching that they finish up doing nothing positive. This is the level of anxiety we have all felt when faced with a task which we feel is beyond us. It is common in pre-service trainees when faced with the apparently limitless number of things they need to think about during teaching. Unless such feelings are let out and talked about, little positive can happen.

'Fascination'

Teachers become obsessed by a particular problem and continue to go on and on about it. Sometimes what to the advisor might seem relatively trivial issues, such as a language mistake made during the lesson, may be the only thing which the teacher wants to talk about. They are unable to 'move on' beyond this stage until they have been able to discharge their feelings about the problem.

'Distraction'

Teachers' attention is diffused by their anxiety and they are unable to concentrate on the problem in hand. This lack of concentration will severely affect what can be done in the feedback session.

In addition to the above, advisors will also need to use their judgment about wider global and political agendas. Cathartic interventions are useful in dealing with deep-seated feelings which are considered entirely inappropriate for effective teaching. For example, teachers may have underlying attitudes to race or gender which need to be examined through the release of feelings about the subject. The probing and examination of such issues could result in the sort of cathartic release of emotion described above.

7.3 Being in touch with emotions

In addition to dealing with such extreme feelings, it is also necessary that teachers to examine their 'feelings' with regard to events which happen in the classroom. Many accounts of successful teaching given by students stress the importance of motivational and affective variables in the classroom. They stress the 'fun' they had or talk about the pleasant and encouraging personality of the teacher. Because such variables are 'felt' rather than 'thought', it is important that teachers and trainees are directed to examine their feelings about the class, both to stress the importance of creating a positive atmosphere and to affirm the value of their feelings as an analytical tool for examining what happens in classes.

Goleman (1996) argues powerfully that psychology has been overly concerned with explanations of actions in terms of cognitive processing and has not paid enough attention to the part played by the emotions in both perception and decision-making. Indeed, evidence from neuro-psychological investigations of brain malfunctions seems to indicate that even such 'objective' processes as routine recognition of people are deeply influenced by emotional centres of the brain (Goleman 1996). He considers five areas important in emotional intelligence:

Knowing one's emotions	Being self-aware, being aware of one's true feelings towards something.
Managing emotions	Being able to change one's feelings so that they don't dominate our thinking and actions.

Motivating oneself	Being able to use one's emotions to achieve a particular goal.
Recognising emotions in others	This is the ability to empathise with others. As we have seen it is a critical skill in advisors, but it is also an important skill for teachers.
Handling relationships	As both teachers and advisors it is important to be able to handle emotions in others and thus form relationships which will help others to learn.

We have seen the importance of self-awareness in all the aspects of advising which we have discussed and, although we have largely explained the reasons for being critically aware in cognitive terms, we have also consistently had to discuss emotional issues related to the areas we have discussed. It is important to realise that the decisions which are being made through critical and reflective practice are made by thinking sentient beings who feel as well as think. Indeed Goleman argues that no decisions can ever be effectively made without the use of emotions; all judgments and evaluations must involve more than purely rational thought. He cites the case of a person who had his emotional brain surgically detached from his thinking brain and was completely incapable of making valid decisions, despite the fact that his intellectual capabilities were unimpaired. Thus, teachers and advisors need to use feelings as well as reason to analyse and reflect on their experience.

7.4 Conclusion

This chapter and the previous one have dealt with different aspects of emotions which will have a bearing on the advice session. In this chapter we have discussed two of the more common emotions which cause problems in feedback sessions. These two have been isolated because they can cause difficulties in the feedback session and so it is crucial that advisors recognise them and discuss them with the teacher. However, we have also examined the role that emotions play in any assessment or critical reflection of teaching. In the next chapter we wish to examine the way that advisors can help to develop teachers by looking at the more authoritative interventions which can be used to lead teachers to new understandings.

Summary

The following issues have been raised in this chapter:

- Anxiety and defensiveness
- Dealing with anxiety and defensiveness
- Being in touch with emotions

Tasks

There are no tasks which are specific to this chapter, but the issue of dealing with feelings will permeate discussions of many of the role play activities in this book. However, the following tasks specifically allow you to think about issues related to feelings:

1.1   An exercise to examine the anxiety involved in being observed
6.1   The way that feelings are expressed in body posture
4.5   A game which highlights reactions which people have in stressful situations
9.2   A situation to stimulate discussion of the ways to deal with distress

Advice for further reading

Goleman, D. (1996) *Emotional Intelligence: Why it can matter more than IQ*, London: Bloomsbury.
A very influential book on the role that emotions play in life. It does not deal with teaching and advising as such, but it discusses the way that inappropriate emotional reactions to events can cause severe problems. It is built around the discussion of a number of 'extreme' situations in which lack of understanding of the emotions has led to problems and suggests ways in which emotional intelligence can be 'trained' through becoming more aware of the contribution of emotions to action.

8 Ways of talking to teachers 3: directing and leading

In Chapter 6 we saw how there exists a gradient of intervention types from those where the advisor leads the teacher through to those in which the teacher is given the freedom to direct the feedback session (see Chapter 6, authoritative vs facilitative). We have also talked about the role of the advisor in probing and in taking an active role in scaffolding the teacher to discover new understandings. In this chapter we shall examine the range of interventions which are available to the advisor to take the lead in the feedback session. We shall also examine the way that the new understandings created by the feedback session can be incorporated into effective action through the formulation of action plans.

8.1 Prescriptive interventions

Heron identifies a number of different interventions which he classifies as 'prescriptive'. It is useful to examine those which are of particular relevance to ELT.

8.1.1 Directive interventions

The term 'directive intervention' is used by Heron in a more restricted sense than the more generalised 'Directive Approach' used by Freeman and Gebhard. In these types of intervention the advisor advises, proposes, recommends and suggests the teacher carries out certain things in the classroom. Through taking such a route the advisor thus takes the most hierarchical position as regards the teacher. Such a stance may well be highly effective for certain surface teaching behaviours in a lesson, such as the way to lay things out on the board, take the register, etc. The effectiveness of such an intervention will thus be determined by the agenda (i.e. they are highly suitable for technical agendas), the level of the prescription (i.e. some actions may be serious/dangerous) and also by the perceived role of the advisor (i.e. they may be more suitable in a supervisory, pre-service role).

Directive interventions are also likely to be affected by an interaction between language form and underlying intention. Linguistic forms for giving advice in English tend to be less directive and more tentative than they are in other languages. Thus, a typical form of giving advice such as 'Why don't you use the blackboard for marking the exercise?' uses the surface form of consultation, yet the illocutionary force can vary, depending on the pragmatic context, from true consultation through to a direct instruction. When the advisor and the teacher are working through the medium of English as a second language (as is the situation in many parts of the Middle East, for example), or have differential commands of the language being employed (where native speakers of English may be advising non-native English speakers), the underlying linguistic and pragmatic codes involved may well result in crossed communication at the level of intended and perceived intentions (degenerative interventions). Thus, it is important to explore the effect of different linguistic forms, especially in situations in which English is being employed as a second language (for an exploration of this, see Tasks 5.2 & 5.3).

8.1.2 Consultative prescriptions

Consultative prescriptions are those in which the advisor proposes a line of action to the teacher. In this situation the teacher is offered a possible way forward and then asked to comment on the action proposed, which thus allows the teacher to decide independently on whether to take the solution offered. This is similar to the supervision style which Freeman categorises as the Alternatives Approach. However, either explicitly or implicitly through the context of the situation, the advisor reserves the right to make the final decision concerning the course of action. This is what distinguishes the consultative prescription from the facilitative catalytic intervention in which the advisor and teacher work as equal collaborators in deciding on a plan of action.

In education, perhaps the most common example of consultative prescription is that of action research. As an intervention, the term is used in its widest sense – that of asking the teacher to try out a course of action which is different and in some way to analyse the outcomes from the new way of working.

In Chapter 3 we discussed the use of observation instruments to help raise teachers' awareness of a particular area. For example, the advisor may have seen that a teacher was only using a restricted range of prompts and the students were producing a restricted range of responses. The advisor could suggest that a teacher record a lesson and listen to the different responses produced for different types of teacher prompt (e.g. the responses to direct WH questions as against elicitations which begin with 'Tell me about . . .'). The intention of such an investigation would be to get the teacher to reduce the number of WH questions and increase the number of prompts designed to produce longer responses. The advisor could have tried to reach the same end

a) by making a direct suggestion: 'You should try to reduce the number of times you use WH questions' (a commanding prescription)
b) by making a benevolent prescription: 'I think you would get longer responses from the students if you used phrases like "Tell me about x . . ." rather than asking WH questions'

c) through consultation and an action research proposition: 'You could always record the lesson and listen to the different responses produced by the students to the different prompts. What do you think?'

By using a consultative intervention the advisor, in Heron's terms, is still being prescriptive; the advisor is telling the teacher to carry out a particular course of action, but the end point of consultation is personal growth on the part of the teacher. The actual form of the prescription is one of offering a hypothetical course of action with which the teacher apparently has the right to disagree. The advisor elicits the views of the teacher on the course of action suggested, but finally, in a prescriptive intervention, it is the advisor who decides on the course of action to be carried out by the teacher.

8.1.3 Demonstration

This type of intervention can be very effective for certain highly technical agendas involving surface classroom skills such as writing on the board, using gestures to elicit from students etc. It is usually carried out in feedback sessions by actions which can be modelled in a role play situation between the advisor and the teacher. Wragg uses demonstration as one of the three methods of providing effective feedback to a teacher in an appraisal setting (Wragg 1990). The advisor must be aware of the dangers of relying solely on demonstrating the desired behaviour – those of leading to a dependency on the part of the teacher – and of offering the demonstration in a commanding manner (thus flirting with rejection due to negative reactions to authoritarian behaviour patterns). However, such interventions, if offered in a benevolent or consultative manner, can be highly effective ways of providing feedback.

8.2 Informative interventions

In everyday life, one of the most common reasons for seeking advice is to gain information on which to base decisions. We generally go to someone who we consider is in a position to provide such information in a reliable fashion. This is a situation involving a 'technical' agenda. Although the informative interventions cover many more agenda types than this narrow technical agenda, it is clear that the provision of relevant information is one of the central characteristics of providing successful advice. It is highly prescriptive, but it is also highly valued and, on certain agenda types, highly effective.

8.2.1 Providing advice on language

One of the most common areas on which advisors give advice is that of language, both language competence (with non-native speakers of English) and language knowledge (El Naggar 1986). Teachers often need considerable support in their knowledge about or use of the language. However, the provision of information is not a simple open and shut case, even on a purely technical agenda such as language. The use of an informative intervention needs to be sensitive to the relative experience of the advisor and the teacher in the topic under discussion, and to the cultural norms of the society in which the teacher operates.

It is interesting to compare the situation involved in providing advice on the two technical agendas with which advisors work – classroom techniques and language knowledge. In most advisory situations there will be some sort of knowledge imbalance between the advisor and the teacher in either one or both of these topics. There will almost certainly be a difference between the advisor and the teacher in terms of linguistic knowledge and ability. The advisor will usually possess a much higher proficiency in the language than the teacher. There will also normally be a large difference in experience and in the understanding of classroom methodology between the pre-service or novice teacher and the advisor. In both situations it would seem that the advisor is in the situation of being the 'wise' counsellor to whom the teacher can come for advice and from whom information will be gratefully received.

However, the situation is not so clear with regard to the serving teacher, especially the non-native English speaking teacher. This teacher may well have much less command of the language than the advisor (both the native and the non-native English speaking advisor), but may well have considerably more experience of teaching than either, and certainly much more experience of teaching in the specific context of the school and lesson. This teacher will probably feel much more threatened all round than the pre-service trainee, but if one considers the two topics, those of language and methodology, the teacher may well accept, even welcome, information about the former (provided it does not become destructive to their image of themselves as a teacher) much more readily than comments about the methodology. The non-native English speaking teacher is perhaps more likely to accept information on a purely content agenda such as language from someone who clearly possesses much greater command and knowledge of the language than they are about the procedure used with the class, of which the teacher is an expert. However, even information about language which is offered in an advisory capacity may well be interpreted in a negative manner as any deficiency in this area can undermine the professional image of the teacher as 'knower' which is central to many cultural concepts of the successful teacher (see Task 8.1 for a role play situation involving language knowledge).

Thus, the above discussion illustrates that the provision of information to help a teacher, an apparently 'neutral' intervention when compared to prescriptive interventions is, in fact, implicitly hierarchical and authoritative and can be interpreted as such by a teacher. However, the fact remains that informative interventions are extremely useful, lying as they do between prescriptive and confronting interventions. They are less hierarchical than prescriptive interventions, allowing the teacher more latitude to develop independently, and less risky than confronting interventions, with all the dangers of defensive retreats (see Chapter 7) which they contain. The following types of informative interventions are particularly useful.

8.2.2 Personal interpretation

The advisor interprets the actions of the teacher and gives their opinion of the way that the teacher acted. This interpretation should be signalled quite clearly and should be offered as what it is – a personal interpretation – and should be open for discussion. In this sense it differs from providing negative feedback where the advisor provides an unqualified judgment. Thus interventions such as 'It seemed to me that the class didn't like the reading activity' or 'From what I saw in the lesson, it would appear that you are not particularly happy with the way the class is handling the written tasks' in which the advisor 'owns' the feedback are more useful than those which are purely judgments: 'The class didn't like the reading task'. It is a particularly good method of eliciting further discussion on the part of the teacher.

8.2.3 Presenting relevant information

This can be a particularly effective way of dealing with the subject of language accuracy discussed above. Instead of being prescriptive: 'You should always use the present simple when talking about timetables' or risking confrontation with negative feedback: 'You made a mistake when you used the present continuous in that timetable exercise', information about the language can be given either directly: 'The usual way of expressing the future when talking about timetables is the present simple' or by offering a reference for the teacher to use to improve their knowledge about the grammatical point. By offering such a reference the advisor is encouraging personal and educational growth in the teacher by providing information which will help them to develop independently.

8.2.4 Feedback

As discussed in Chapter 3, in the ideal supervision cycle the role of the observer is to provide information to the post-lesson feedback session as data on which to work. The providing of information about the lesson in an informative, non-evaluative manner is one of the essential procedures used by advisors. However, it must be emphasised that the manner in which this feedback is presented is crucial. If the teacher believes that the information has been selected to criticise the lesson, then the intervention may be seen as confronting and may produce a defensive reaction.

8.2.5 Self-disclosure

The advisor provides information about him or herself which helps the teacher to assess the situation. This is particularly useful in creating empathy with the teacher and in helping the teacher to deal with difficult issues or with things which are going wrong in the lesson. Such interventions would include 'I have always found it difficult to deal with vocabulary in elementary classes'. The admission by the advisor that they have had the same problem allows for a discussion of the topic and personalises the situation as does the personal interpretation intervention, but does so in a much less threatening manner. It enables the advisor to say directly to the teacher that they are the same, and is thus important in establishing a collaborative rather than a supervisory atmosphere.

(For practice in using of many of these interventions see Tasks 5.2, 5.3 & 8.1)

8.3 Confronting interventions

As discussed at the beginning of this chapter, the purpose of the feedback session is to scaffold new understandings, to move the teacher to a new level of awareness and through this to change the way that they see or think about the way that they are teaching. The provision of information, through the selection made by the advisor of the information to provide, begins the process by focusing on the problem areas. This is part of the process of giving feedback to the teacher. We have suggested that an important element of feedback is that it should be informative rather than judgmental. However, there will be times when it is necessary for the advisor to provide negative feedback. This feedback is a result of the 'tough-minded listening' which we discussed in Chapter 6. One of the principal reasons for such feedback is to provoke the teacher into the reassessment of actions, beliefs or attitudes of which they are unaware. The aim of the intervention is to make the teacher aware of these unconscious attitudes and to examine them. This is done by confronting the teacher with attitudes which are seen as problematic by the advisor.

The use of negative feedback and the decision to confront are extremely difficult areas for advisors. Advisors have nearly always served their apprenticeships as teachers. As teachers they will all have had a lot of experience in giving negative feedback to students; people with whom they have a particular role relationship in which they are in a dominant position. When dealing with teachers and trainees in the feedback session, the situation is different. Acceptable methods of providing feedback in a situation in which they have the high status of a teacher do not always apply in the context of the advisor, especially in in-service contexts. Furthermore, they will find that feedback which is not necessarily intended as confronting or even as negative may well provoke highly defensive reactions in the teacher leading to a highly charged, negative, confrontational situation. This is not the situation envisaged by Heron:

> A confronting intervention unequivocally tells an uncomfortable thought, but does so with love, in order that the one concerned may see it and fully acknowledge it . . . Its manner is deeply affirming of the worth of the client, however uncompromising is the spotlight that is thrown on his or her negative attitudes or behaviour (Heron 1990: 43).

8.4 **Providing negative feedback in a non-punitive atmosphere**

This is an extremely difficult area and there is no 'single' recipe for doing it. The general skills which we discussed in Chapter 6 of creating empathy with the teacher and valuing what the teacher is doing are centrally important in creating the right climate for negative feedback to be provided without becoming degenerative. However, the specific interventions which will lead to constructive, critical analysis of lessons and the establishment of new awareness will vary from situation to situation. The advisor will need to be clear about their intention all the time throughout the session, and be sensitive to the possible reactions from the teacher which indicate that the session is becoming 'degenerative'. Having said this, there are some issues concerning confrontation which are essential to discuss.

8.4.1 Raising consciousness of the agenda

In order for the intervention to be seen in a positive, non-destructive light it is important to make clear to the teacher the area of unaware behaviour which has been identified. Thus, it is important to:

1. **Identify the agenda.** Is the advisor talking about a technical matter of classroom procedure or a deeper level of understanding? Does the behaviour (e.g. correcting the students all the time) derive from basic assumptions about the teaching/learning process (such as the attitude to correction) which the advisor considers are dysfunctional for effective teaching or is it due to other factors (e.g. the particular class, topic or 'type' of lesson)? Is the behaviour due to routinised patterns of teaching? Do these errors derive from even more deeply held personal views of interpersonal relationships (e.g. the belief that teachers should be strict disciplinarians with their classes to gain respect)?
2. **Explain how the teacher is failing to meet the criteria set by the profession and discuss why this needs to be addressed and why it is relevant to raise the issue.** Discussing the 'ground rules' for raising the difficult issues and pointing out exactly what the teacher is doing wrong will help to dispel the idea that the confrontation is a punitive intervention at the teacher *personally.*
3. **Give the teacher plenty of space to react to what has been raised.** When confronted with negative feedback, possibly touching on well-established teaching routines or deeply held beliefs about teaching, the teacher's first reaction is likely to be very defensive. It is important that the advisor listens empathetically to these reactions and takes them seriously, yet is aware of just what they are – defensive reactions. Thus, the underlying agenda is not what the teacher says explicitly (e.g. 'I find the students like to be corrected all the time') but an underlying refusal to cooperate (e.g. 'This is the way I've always done it and I don't see any reason to change because you say so'). The advisor will need to deal firmly with such reactions and respectfully move the teacher back to the issue which is under examination.

4. Follow through. It is important that the advisor works with the teacher to examine the area of unaware behaviour and to work out a strategy, both for dealing with the unaware behaviour and for implementing new behaviour or attitudes in their teaching. Thus, the importance of an action plan.

8.4.2 Negative feedback

The provision of negative feedback overlaps with the informative intervention of 'personal interpretation' discussed above. It is important for the advisor to realise that what is being stated is exactly this; it is a personal interpretation of the event. The advisor should not shrink from owning the interpretation and of being clear to the teacher that this assessment of their behaviour or, more likely, this assessment of the underlying motivations for the observed behaviour, is that of the advisor. The interpretations should be offered in this light and should relate specifically to the behaviour or attitudes of the teacher. They are not an assessment of the teacher as a *person*, but as a teacher. Thus the negative feedback is localised and is in no sense punitive.

8.4.3 Educative feedback

The advisor offers an interpretation of behaviour in the lesson which has given the advisor the impression that the teacher lacks training or awareness of particular skills or areas of knowledge. An example would be the appropriate methods to introduce a listening exercise. If this is accepted by the teacher, then the advisor can go on to examine the particular area of skill or knowledge which the teacher needs to be aware of, such as the value of focused listening and the handling of receptive vs productive skills in a lesson. Clearly, the impression may well be initially challenged by the teacher, or there may be challenges to the ideas involved in the processes underlying teaching listening and receptive skills. At this point, educative feedback may well then become negative feedback. However, the role of the advisor is to focus the discussion on the general principles – on the positive developmental aspect – rather than let the judgmental aspect divert the process.

8.4.4 Direct questions

As an alternative to stating a personal interpretation of what the advisor considers unaware behaviours, the advisor asks direct questions concerning the issue which needs to be raised. This technique is particularly useful to identify the underlying causes of surface teaching problems. To continue with the example above of providing feedback on a listening exercise, it is very difficult from the point of view of the observer to ascertain the *reasons* underlying particular sequences in the classroom. Was the lack of pre-listening tasks caused by not knowing about the importance of such tasks, by not understanding the importance of such tasks, or by a fundamental disagreement with the theory of focused listening and its application in the classroom? By asking direct questions about the processes and the teacher's feelings about the exercise, and being sensitive to defensive reactions on the part of the teacher, the advisor can begin to arrive at the central issues involved (e.g. questions such as 'Why did you start the lesson with the passage?', 'Did you consider using pre-questions?', 'What is your feeling about pre-teaching lexis?' are ways of probing the teacher about the area which they want to discuss). This process provides the opportunity for the advisor firstly to understand the lesson from the teacher's standpoint (active attending and listening) and then to confront the teacher with what are perceived to be the underlying problems in the lesson (probing). If these questions are genuinely 'open' questions – there is more than one acceptable answer and the teacher is free to choose which to take – then the intervention becomes 'catalytic' (see Chapter 9).

8.4.5 Holding up a mirror

Finally, a very useful technique is to mirror to the teacher the behaviours which you want to concentrate on. In the absence of video and/or tape recording this can often be carried out effectively by role playing a section of the lesson with the teacher. The advisor thus takes the position of the teacher and the teacher takes the position of the student(s). Such a technique is very useful in raising awareness of classroom interaction patterns such as routinised elicitation or questioning sequences which no longer have any useful purpose in the lesson. However, care must be taken not to ridicule or mock the teacher by using this technique. The confrontational effect should be gained from the role-reversal of placing the teacher in the place of the student, not from any judgmental characterisation of the teacher's behaviour on the part of the advisor.

(See Task 8.1 for an exploration of many of these issues.)

8.5 Providing action plans

As discussed above, the end point of any feedback session should be the transfer of what has been discovered to future action. When teachers consider what makes advice successful (see Task 4.2), the defining element of successful advice was that it solved a problem, it helped, it was effective in terms of outcome. In contrast, unsuccessful advice was universally characterised as advice which was not used, and it is worth considering the factors which cause advice to be unsuccessful.

One reason for failure is when the advice offered is imposed by the advisor and the advisee fails to own the solutions which are offered. It is to avoid such a reaction that the helping model (see Chapter 4) places such emphasis on the skills of attending, listening and creating empathy. However, the offering of advice very often also breaks down in the final stage of the process; the failure to consider its implementation. If the suggestions offered are not clearly thought through and the implications of the advice are not transferred to future actions then the advice is not likely to be successful. This stage in the process of giving advice is quite critical in providing help to teachers. If we look at the Experiential Learning Cycle discussed in Chapter 3, the output from reflection on practice needs to feed into new experience through Active Experimentation. This sets up a learning agenda for the future development of teachers.

The importance of formulating action plans which are implementable is a process which has received a great deal of attention in a number of fields, notably in management. All emphasise the importance of being specific about plans, being realistic in what can be achieved, and monitoring to make sure that the plans are actually realised. Thus, according to the acronym SMART, plans should be:

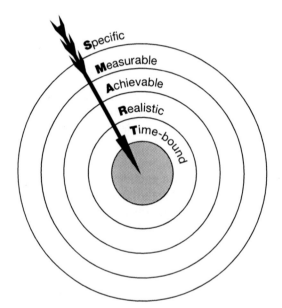

Figure 26 SMART: an acroynm for effective action plans

Specific

It is necessary at the conclusion of the advice situation to be quite specific about what the teacher is going to do. The advice needs to be concrete and expressed in terms which the teacher can put into practice. Thus, a general piece of advice to 'be more careful in selecting specific aims' is not likely to be as successful as a more specific piece of advice 'to consider structural, phonological, lexical and skills aims for each lesson'.

However, the advice may also be of an action-research type, such as to suggest an examination of the way that the teacher talks to the pupils. This type of advice also needs to be specific and a specific contract undertaken such as the undertaking to record a number of lessons and transcribe certain sections, or to invite a critical friend into a number of lessons.

Measurable

The collection and recording of evidence of achievement are central to the action planning process. Thus, the above planning aims are measurable in that they can be put into lesson plans and the lesson plans will provide evidence that the action has been carried out. Similarly, action research aims can be measured by the production of lesson transcripts and completed observation instruments (see Task 3.5).

Achievable

The goal must be within reach of the teacher at the present stage of that teacher's development. Typically, in the initial stages of learning to teach, the novice teacher will perceive weaknesses in many areas, not all of which can be worked on at the same time. The role of the advisor here will be to help the teacher establish priorities and negotiate targets.

Realistic

The goals set by the process must be realistic. They must be related to aspects of teaching which the teacher can actually control. Thus, the changes which are negotiated must be capable of implementation. We cannot change the colour of our skin or the way we look and, to some extent, we cannot change our personality. Very often we cannot make any changes to the physical circumstances in which we work or our family situation. Thus, it is important that the goals should take these factors into consideration. Time-consuming action research projects, for example, are not realistic given the real-life situations of many teachers in the world, where second jobs and family commitments mean that time that can be spent outside teaching is extremely limited.

Time-bound

While action plans can be either short term such as planning to implement a new teaching strategy over the next week, or longer term, such as planning one's own professional development path over the next year, the negotiation of targets will need to include timescales for their achievement.

Therefore, it is important that at the end of the feedback session both sides should be clear about the issues which have been raised and the steps which will be taken to work on these issues.

8.6 Written feedback

One way in which action plans can be effectively carried out is to record them in writing. Written feedback is a feature of nearly all training and advisory situations. Most in-service advice systems use some form of written feedback to teachers through the use of observation checklists, competency profiles or the even more universal 'blank page' with notes. Very often the teacher and the advisor each keep a copy of this feedback sheet through the use of carbon copies. Whilst all the comments we have made in this book about the provision of supportive and empathetic advice also apply to written feedback, the very medium of written feedback means that the interactional features of empathetic listening and supportive interaction are impossible to operate. Thus written feedback is much less likely to document the collaborative exploration of problems and solutions; it is more likely to record the outcomes of such exploration.

Although the medium of writing is not ideal for interactive problem-solving, it is better than speaking for the recording of negotiated action plans which emerge from the feedback discussion. It is vital that:

a) written feedback should contain the outcomes of the observation and the feedback discussion expressed in terms of action which is going to be taken
b) this statement of aims should be negotiated and agreed between the advisor and the teacher

Whatever else the feedback sheet contains, it must contain the record of these very important conclusions of the feedback session. Whilst oral interaction and discussion are important scaffolding tools to develop new understandings, to be effective such new understandings need to be implemented in practice through carefully agreed future actions. These need to be remembered and carried away from the feedback session. Thus written feedback acts as an aide-memoire to the teacher for development and, equally, as an agenda for the advisor and the teacher in any future advisory situations (for an examination of written feedback, see Tasks 8.2 & 8.3).

Action planning can also play an important role in pre-service training. In such training, the typical action planning process involves the student teacher in

- reviewing their strengths and weaknesses (recognising that even before the practicum has begun individual teachers will bring a number of skills and experiences to teaching)
- setting targets for development, usually in negotiation with another teacher
- reviewing progress towards the goal

As such the process recognises that learning is a partnership and that relationships are the key to learning. At the same time, the process itself enhances many of the teacher's skills such as planning, reviewing, negotiating, communicating. It encourages teachers to take some responsibility for, and therefore have some control over, their professional development (for an example of such a process, see Task 8.4).

8.7 Conclusion

In this chapter we have looked at the interventions which are available to the advisor in trying to direct the teacher. There are many ways that this can be done and the degree of control exercised by the advisor is variable. The interventions cover the areas identified by Freeman (1982) as 'Directive' and 'Alternatives' methods of supervision, but by examining the moves in greater depth we can begin to see the complexity and delicacy of choice of intervention available. However, the ultimate goal of a feedback cycle, as we have suggested, is to allow the teacher to take control of the analysis and to become self-directed both in the feedback session and in their professional development. In the next chapter we shall examine interventions in the feedback session which encourage such self-direction and independence.

Summary

The following issues have been raised in this chapter:

- Prescriptive interventions
- Informative interventions
- Confronting interventions
- Providing negative feedback
- Providing action plans
- Written feedback

Tasks

The following tasks will allow you to explore the issues raised in this chapter:

8.1 A role play on providing feedback
8.2 An examination of notes made during a lesson
8.3 A series of written reports given by inspectors
8.4 A self-evaluation form for target setting
5.2 An activity to explore the differences between what is said and what is heard
5.3 Exploration of the way that different intentions can be signalled

Advice for further reading

Gebhard, J. 'Exploring with a supervisor' in Gebhard, J. and Oprandy, R. (1999) *Language Teaching Awareness: a guide to exploring beliefs and practices*, 99–121 New York: Cambridge University Press.
In this section, as well as looking at general issues regarding exploring teaching with a supervisor, Gebhard gives very practical suggestions for ways in which the teacher can take more ownership of the process.

9 Ways of talking to teachers 4: towards critical self-awareness

In the previous chapter we examined the way that the advisor could intervene in various ways to move the teacher forward to new understandings. We believe that this scaffolding of understanding is necessary for effective advice. However, as in the earlier chapters where we considered that the goal of training should be to develop an independent, autonomous and professional teacher, the ultimate goal of the feedback session should be to develop in the teacher the skill of self-critical reflection. This means that the teacher needs to take control of their own learning and development within the session itself. In the end the agenda should be set by the teacher and the solutions arrived at should be owned by them. Heron characterises the type of interventions which create this type of situation as 'catalytic interventions' and we shall continue to adopt his terminology, although recognising that it describes more of an ethos than a specific set of interventions in their own right. We shall also examine a number of techniques for creating such an ethos which he describes as a 'catalytic tool kit' and we shall look closely at the role that different question types can play in opening up areas for discussion. Finally the chapter will close the examination of the counselling aspects of the feedback session begun in Chapter 4 by looking at the use of the different interventions within the overall structure of the advisory cycle.

9.1 Catalytic interventions

Throughout this book we have emphasised the importance of the experiential learning cycle to the development of new ideas in teaching. We have also suggested that the ultimate goal in the advisory process is to create in the teacher the ability to be self-evaluative and autonomous. Heron's view of effective helping shares the same goal. Working from experience the client is prompted to 'uncover' incidents which are important, 'reflect' on these incidents and to discover new meanings for these incidents, and then 'prepare' to put the learning from experience and reflection back into new experience. We have already indicated all of these stages as essential for effective learning. The aim of the advisor in the feedback session is to enable the teacher to reflect on their teaching experience and to critically reassess their understandings and teaching in the light of this reflection. In the last chapter we saw how the advisor can lead the teacher to consider their teaching by the use of various interventions such as directing them, providing information and confronting them with perceived problems. All of these strategies are designed to facilitate self-direction in teachers. Thus the advisor, by analysing and probing, is acting as a catalyst for the teacher to develop the skill of critical thinking. The interventions discussed so far can be expressed as part of a gradient, from prescription through to facilitation of self-direction:

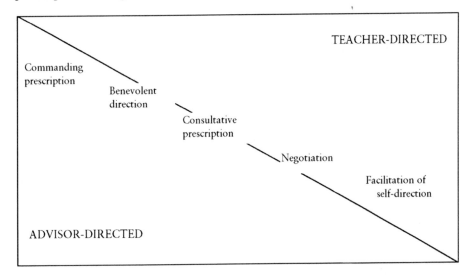

Figure 27 Catalytic intervention: towards self-direction (adapted from Heron 1990: 113)

Thus, catalytic interventions are the end point of a process. They are more of a methodological assumption which underlies all feedback encounters. They are those which expressly lead to the teacher arriving at their own solution to their own problem and they are closely associated with the process of developing critical thinking.

9.1.1 Developing critical thinking

The starting point for all approaches to critical thinking is to start from the concrete and to work towards the abstract (Brookfield 1987). Thus, the development of critical questioning – questioning designed to uncover the teacher's underlying assumptions and attitudes to teaching – starts from the raw data of experience. Critical questions start by asking the teacher to give their account of the lesson – to review the experience – and are typically signalled introduced by phrases such as:

'Tell me about the lesson'
'Just talk me through the lesson'

Starting from this, the advisor will provide prompts which enable the teacher to critically reflect on the lesson. These critical questions are important in uncovering the meaning of what has happened. Brookfield (1987) offers the following advice to those involved in promoting critical thinking:

> Critical questioners must be able to frame insightful questions that are readily understood by subjects. They must be able to explore what are often highly personal matters in a sensitive way. They must be able to ask what might usually be considered highly intimidating questions in a non-threatening manner. (Brookfield 1987: 93)

They are the 'scaffolding' to lead the teacher through their ZPD. He offers the following suggestions:

> **Be specific.** Questions should be related to particular actions, language or students. Thus, questions such as 'What did you think of the way the student in the corner dealt with your question about the house?' are a better starting point than 'What are your views on accuracy and fluency when answering comprehension questions?' although this may be the underlying issue which the advisor wants to discuss.
> **Work from the particular to the general.** Allied to the point above, he suggests that it is better to work from an actual incident in the lesson or in the teacher's experience through to abstract concepts than the other way round. This again follows what we have discussed about experiential learning.

Working from the teacher's account of the lesson the advisor may:

- identify data which need to be thought about (critical incidents)
- probe the teacher's views of the incidents
- negotiate with the teacher their view of the incident
- prompt the teacher to arrive at a new understanding

9.1.2 What steps can help the advisor be catalytic?

Heron offers four basic strategies to such 'scaffolding': following, consulting, proposing or leading.

Following

During the discussion of the lesson and the critical incidents, the teacher has already begun to identify problem areas which need resolution. For example, the advisor wants the teacher to discuss the use of games in learning following a lesson in which a game was used. The teacher may already have identified difficulties with discipline and control and already talked about the positive and negative effects that imposing strict discipline may have on the class. In this case, the advisor can follow the teacher down the avenue which has already been opened: 'You mentioned the problems of losing control of the class during a game'. Once the topic has been identified the advisor can then guide the teacher through a thorough discussion of the issues involved, leading to a resolution which will be implemented in future lessons.

Consulting

The teacher may have finished their account of the lesson and be unsure of what to do next. During the account the advisor will have noted areas which would seem to need further exploration, such as the issue of class control. The advisor can then consult with the teacher about the areas which would be worth exploring further. These can be

- elicited directly from the teacher e.g. 'This was an interesting lesson as you say. Are there any areas you would particularly like to discuss further?'
- selected by the teacher from a menu of possible areas which could be explored e.g. 'The lesson threw up a number of interesting points. You mentioned the difficulty of keeping discipline, the issue of when to use games in the lesson and the difficulty of trying to keep score during the game. Would you like to discuss any of these further?'

Proposing

The advisor suggests an area which needs exploring and asks for the teacher's agreement to explore this area e.g. 'You mentioned the problems of losing control of the class during a game. Can we explore this some more?' Such an area may derive from the 'tough listening' discussed in Chapter 6. The advisor will probably ask the teacher if there are areas which they wish to explore, but in the absence of a response which fits with the advisor's perception of the lesson, then the advisor may well simply propose that an issue is discussed and ask for the teacher's consent. Such a scenario could result from a game used in the classroom which became a little out of control. In this case the advisor will need to be careful that the intervention is not interpreted as one of confronting.

Leading

A further escalation up the ladder of techniques available to the advisor is that of directly asking a question about some aspect of the teaching, forcing the teacher to deal with the issue which the advisor sees as important. An example of such a direct approach might be 'Tell me how you viewed the game at the end of the lesson.' Following an account of the game which really did not begin to address the problems of discipline, the advisor could focus on a specific incident, on one individual: 'Can you tell me why you started to argue with the girl in the corner about her behaviour in the game?' and from this account, encourage the teacher to critically examine the issue of games and discipline.

The choice of strategy used will be very much determined by the situation, the teacher and the professional culture within which the advisor is working, but it is important to make sure that there is critical reflection on the part of the teacher. It is important in the process of listening to the teacher's account and facilitating self-direction through listening that the process does not become the product. In the end, advice needs to be effective. From the process of review, new insights need to be gained and these need to be put into practice. Listening can become a self-indulgent rather than a self-discovery exercise. The role of the advisor is to listen to the teacher and understand the concerns, but it is also to probe and to scaffold new understandings.

(For an activity to examine aspects of following and leading, see Task 9.1 and for some examples of leading and following, see Task 2.5.)

9.1.3 The 'catalytic tool kit'

Heron offers the following 'catalytic tool kit for promoting self-direction'. Whilst these techniques are primarily aimed at inducing self-direction in the teacher, we agree with Heron that these techniques 'are absolutely fundamental for every practitioner of every kind' (Heron 1990: 171).

Being here now, being there now and giving free attention

The first three techniques for eliciting self-directed learning are very similar to the general techniques which we described as part of 'effective attending' in Chapter 6. They involve the advisor giving the teacher total, undivided attention, and 'being with' the teacher in the feedback situation. As we discussed in that chapter, however, the 'being here' and 'being there' are more than merely exemplars of non-verbal behaviour, they are the description of a state of mind of the advisor in which the actual, real situation of the feedback session becomes the reality. What happens during the session is the centre of the universe and the advisor should attend to this situation unencumbered by ideas and thoughts from the past. The moment of the session is all, as is the intention to reach out and understand the teacher ('be there now'). This is a quasi-mystical description (Heron actually uses the term 'mystical') of the importance of effective attending; a re-statement of the importance of empathy to the feedback situation.

However, there are techniques which help to signal this close attention to the individual.

Simple echoing

This involves the advisor repeating the last word or phrase spoken by the teacher without any questioning intonation. It is intended as, on one level, a simple affirmation that the advisor is listening (signalling active listening and attending) and, on a deeper level, as a signal for the teacher to continue to explain or describe what happened or their feelings about the event under discussion (a catalytic intention).

> T: I liked the way that the pupils reacted to the prompts in the dialogue.
> A: The way they reacted in the dialogue.

The advisor needs to make sure that the echoing does not carry either an interrogative meaning through using a rising intonation or a closure of the topic, with a steeply falling intonation. In these situations the intention of the intervention may become ambiguous. Even when attention is paid to these linguistic features of communication, the teacher may well still perceive the echo in quite a different manner depending on the particular circumstances of the lesson and feedback (i.e. the teacher's evaluation of the event under discussion), on the teacher's preconceptions of the roles within the feedback session, or on their understanding of the socio-pragmatic processes involved in the session – their understanding of the tutorial 'genre'.

Selective echoing

The advisor listens carefully and attentively to both what the teacher says and the way that it is said; the advisor repeats something which they think the teacher needs to explore more fully.

> T: The dialogue was a difficult one for the pupils to handle and I left it out last year. However, I decided to use it this time to see if they could handle it, but I included a lot more preparation beforehand.
>
> A: You say the dialogue was a difficult one.

This intervention is designed to allow the teacher to explore an aspect of the lesson in more depth. For example, in the above example the advisor might want to get the teacher to explore their concept of 'difficulty'. This is an opening for the teacher under the guidance of the advisor to examine new ideas and to move into new territory. This is an example of the way that 'following' can be instigated and is the first level in beginning to focus the teacher and to move the teacher on to new insights.

Questioning. Open and closed questions

The use of appropriate questioning techniques is clearly a very important tool for the advisor to move the teacher on to new territory. We have already referred to the importance of developing a critical questioning stance as part of the development of critical thinking. In terms of enabling teachers to become self-directed, we need to consider the degree to which a question leaves the response 'open' to the teacher/trainee to develop their own line of thought.

The degree to which a question such as 'What do you feel about the use of games in lessons?' is an invitation for the teacher to talk about their feelings regarding games (an open question) or is a test of their theoretical knowledge (a closed question) will depend on a number of factors. It will depend, again, on the circumstances (Was there a game in the lesson? Did the game go well/ badly?), it will depend on the relationship established between the advisor and the teacher (Is it one of collaboration or one of leading/following?), it may well depend on the emotional state of the teacher (Is there a high degree of anxiety or defensiveness?) and it will depend on the perceived view of the feedback session (Is the main ethos of the session one of 'correcting mistakes' – a deficit model – or is it one of building on success – the supportive model?). Questions can be used to either follow the teacher's line of thought or they can be used to lead the teacher into new areas. However, it is all too easy for the session to become 'inquisitorial' through the use of too many questions, even supposedly 'open' 'WH' questions on the part of the advisor and thus threatening rather than explorative (Heron calls this type of degeneration 'scraping the bowl') (see Task 6.3). The art of being a catalyst for reflection involves knowing when to use different forms of question, their timing and of knowing when to move on to a new topic, or even to offer some form of prescription.

Empathetic divining

In Chapter 6 we discussed the importance of empathy in the process of giving effective advice. In particular, we stressed the importance in active listening of paying attention to both the words of the teacher and the manner and context in which they were being said. Empathetic divining is when the advisor communicates to the teacher the emotional message that they have heard in the situation. For example, when discussing the use of games in lessons, the teacher might give a number of reasons why it is not possible to use games with the class. It may be that such explanations are founded on genuine lack of knowledge about using games effectively. In such a situation the advisor may use either an informative or prescriptive intervention as a means of helping the teacher to be able to manage games in the classroom. If the advisor considers that the teacher has a deeper aversion to using games then they may challenge the teacher by getting them to consider alternative modes of teaching. However, the advisor may 'read' a certain defensive reaction behind the excuses offered by the teacher. In such a situation the advisor may indicate their empathy with the teacher by offering a statement which shows that the advisor has 'read' this reluctance on the part of the teacher. Thus, the advisor might offer something such as 'It seems/sounds as if you are somewhat worried about using games in the lesson.' By using such a statement, the advisor is indicating that they are 'in tune' with what the teacher is saying emotionally by paraphrasing (repeating, summarising and interpreting) what is being said. Obviously, such an intervention is closely related to an interpretative intervention, but whereas the latter is offered as an interpretation to be discussed, empathetic divining is, in emotional terms, the equivalent of the echo. It says 'I am with you. I recognise your worries, so continue' rather than suggesting that these might be worries which need to be discussed and modified in some way. Advisors will need to be quite skilled in reading body language and interpreting what teachers and trainees are saying in order to accurately judge the unspoken feelings and to use this intervention effectively, rather than imposing their own views on the teacher (Heron's 'information and prescription in catalytic clothing').

Checking for understanding

Given the problems of accurately divining what the teacher is trying to say, both in terms of content and implied meaning, it is often necessary for the advisor to check that the interpretation which has been arrived at is correct. Thus, where it is felt necessary, the advisor can offer the interpretation to the teacher for the latter to agree or disagree with. Interventions such as 'Let me see, are you saying that the students don't really enjoy playing games?' are the mechanisms by which the interpretations are offered to the teacher for agreement. It should be noted that such interpretations should be interpretations of what the advisor thinks the teacher is saying and not the views of the advisor. They are offered in the sense of 'This is what I feel you are saying/feel about the situation. Am I right?' Once this is established, the teacher is then free to continue with their account and to offer, if necessary, further views on what has been said. The object is to allow the teacher to discover the meaning of what has happened. The advisor will prompt the teacher to move on to new understandings through the use of more proactive interventions once the teacher's own account has been completed.

Paraphrasing

This is another technique for signalling to the teacher that the advisor is listening carefully and for beginning to guide the teacher into focusing on issues which are considered important. It involves expressing something important that the teacher has said in the advisor's own words. Such expression shows that the advisor is listening carefully and also gives the teacher the chance to check the formulation of the advisor against their own.

Logical marshalling

Paraphrasing also allows the advisor to 'give shape' to the teacher's view, to provide the link between the theoretical models of teaching and learning and the teacher's own experience. It gives the advisor the chance to explicitly organise the totality of what the teacher is saying and to put it into the context of the theoretical models of learning and teaching. Such arguments will hopefully prompt the teacher to reconsider what they are saying and to provide a springboard for evolving new understandings about teaching.

(See Tasks 2.5, 5.1 and 9.1 for exploration of these issues.)

9.1.4 *What questions are truly catalytic?*

As questioning is such a vital part of the feedback process, it is important that we consider the effects that different types of question will have on the process. We mentioned earlier when discussing the use of direct questions that open questions would be catalytic, implying that closed questions would not, and here we wish to discuss the difference between the two types of question.

The question of linguistic form, the use of polar Yes/No questions as against the use of 'WH' questions are not as important as the underlying intentions.[1]

---

[1] The Yes/No question such as: 'Did you feel that the class was able to handle the question form by the end of the lesson?' would grammatically be considered as restricted with the answer being either yes or no. However, the WH question such as: 'What did the student say in reply to your question?' would be analysed as less restricted and thus open in that the answer demands a longer response and one that is not contained in the question itself.

Thus, the 'WH' question *What do you feel about using games in lessons?* is not necessarily any more 'open' or 'closed' than the same question phrased as *Do you like using games in lessons?* Both can be perceived as requests for elaboration (a catalytic intervention) or in a more authoritative light as either confronting or challenging. The important function of this type of intervention is that it should provide space for exploration by the teacher of the lesson and the questions should enhance this exploration.

When we come to consider such questions in the feedback session, the degree of openness is not solely related to linguistic form. The first Yes/No question could be a genuinely open question – the advisor genuinely wants to know the teacher's thoughts and feelings. However, the same question in different contexts could be taken to be quite different in underlying meaning.

Question	Context	Teacher's Interpretation	Question and Intervention Type
'Did you feel that the class was able to handle the question form by the end of the lesson?'	A good, quiet class where the students worked well on a series of written tasks involving questions.	'Do your students find it useful to write questions and have you found it to be a useful way of approaching learning?'	Open Catalytic
	A chaotic lesson in which nothing really got achieved and the students never really got the chance to practise the question.	'Are you satisfied with this lesson? I wasn't. You never really got the children to practise anything.'	Closed Confronting
	A lesson in which some of the students were able to use the questions but others were having some difficulty. There was not a great deal of practice provided for the class.	'Do you feel that you provided enough practice of the question during the lesson?'	Closed Confronting

Figure 28 Advisor questions: the effect of context on teacher interpretation (see Task 5.3 for an exploration of the importance of context)

Similarly, WH questions will vary in their interpretation depending on the context. WH questions asking teachers to give reasons for actions can be particularly ambiguous. A question such as 'Why did you drill the class in the target sentence?' can have a number of interpretations depending on:

● the way the class went
● the views of the advisor / coursebook / education system about drilling

- the views of the teacher about drilling
- the teacher's interpretation of the advisor / coursebook / education system about drilling

Questions asking for explanations are, at least superficially, among the most open questions, but they can be extremely threatening in a situation where the teacher feels that they are being 'assessed' in some way. This atmosphere of threat is considerably enhanced, especially if 'why' questions are asked with negative verbs e.g. 'Why didn't you drill the class in the target sentence?' The use of such questions, according to normal discourse rules, rests on an assumption that there is an agreed 'positive' way of operating. However, such questions can be asked in a genuinely catalytic manner depending on the intonation used, but more importantly, depending on the atmosphere in the feedback session itself. In a truly collaborative feedback session with an advisor who signals that the teacher is free to explain and explore the situation from their own point of view, the negative sentence could be interpreted quite differently.

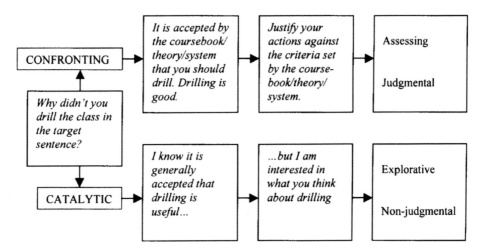

Figure 29 Advisor questions: the effect of atmosphere on teacher interpretation

In a genuinely catalytic intervention, the advisor should be using the question as an opening to a debate about drilling; they would then follow up the question with further probing questions to get the teacher to verbalise and discuss the issue of drilling and collaboratively come to a solution owned by the teacher and suitable to the local context (for an exploration of the effects of different question types and intentions, see Tasks 5.2 & 5.3. Also see Tasks 2.5 & 6.4 on the use of questions in feedback sessions).

9.2 Critical incidents as catalytic interventions

We have suggested earlier that the advisor can begin to focus the feedback interview by bringing data from short periods of the lesson to discuss with the teacher. These incidents will be examples of either bad or good practice which the advisor wants to explore with the teacher. If these incidents contain problem areas as identified by the advisor but not seen in the same light by the teacher, the intervention can be classed as either 'informative' or 'confronting'.

Such a process is a very valuable way of focusing the teacher's attention on areas and issues which need to be discovered. However, the process of selection of these incidents is in the hands of the advisor. To be truly catalytic, the incidents need to be selected by the teachers themselves.

Brookfield (1987) points out that the analysis of critical incidents has been used as a tool in social sciences and education for many years. Subjects are asked to write a detailed account of an incident in their lives or in their professional setting which held particular importance for them. They are asked to be quite specific about

- the location of the incident
- the people involved
- their own particular views of why the incident went the way it did
- their feelings about the incident

In this way it is possible both to identify issues which the subject thinks are important and, from their account, to uncover their underlying beliefs. By working on such accounts the initiative is handed to the subject, both for the area that is to be discussed and the issues which they see as important. (Task 1.1 is an adaptation of a critical incident methodology to examine what is important in being observed.)

This technique can be used for supporting teachers. It can be used as part of an action research project where teachers are asked to tape-record a lesson or lessons and then to transcribe a small section which seems to them to be particularly important, either illustrating something which went very well or something which went less well. They can then be asked to write about the incident, saying exactly how they felt and why they did what they did. They can also be asked to discuss alternative courses of action which they could have taken (see Nunan 1990 for a description of such an approach as part of an action research project).

However, the technique can also be used in a less formal manner in the feedback session, where the advisor asks the teacher to describe a part of the lesson which they felt was important to them and then use this as the basis for exploration of ideas about teaching – issues which are important to the teacher. In this way, the advisor is being catalytic – acting as facilitator of development by handing the initiative over to the teacher.

9.3 Sequencing the interventions

Over the last four chapters we have examined different interventions and discussed their effects and uses in the feedback session. We have mentioned earlier the generally-accepted wisdom of a 'good news followed by bad news' strategy, and when we looked at confronting interventions in Chapter 8 we suggested that the provision of negative feedback would, at times, need to be coupled with supportive interventions. Thus from the macro-strategic conduct of the feedback session exemplified by the three-stage model of helping (Chapter 4) to the micro considerations of the ongoing dialogue between the advisor and the teacher, we need to consider the appropriacy of different interventions in relation to each other. This is not to suggest that there is a single set sequence of steps to be taken, but we need to consider the aims of a feedback session and the way these aims can be implemented through different interventions.

Heron offers a number of different macro-models of helping, and perhaps the closest to our advisory situation is that of 'collaborative assessment'. If we combine his suggested interventions with the three-stage model of helping we developed in Chapter 4, we get the following uses of the intervention types:

STAGE 1. EXPLORATION

GOALS	INTERVENTIONS
• *Providing reinforcement* • *Highlighting strengths* • *Recognising difficulties*	Mixed informative, prescriptive and catalytic interventions negotiate a set of criteria for assessing performance: these criteria are mutually agreed, not imposed. The trainee makes a fully self-directed commitment to them.

STAGE 2. NEW UNDERSTANDING

GOALS	INTERVENTIONS
• *Examining data from lesson* • *Helping teacher to recognise problems* • *Identifying problems in the lesson* • *Inviting self-evaluation* • *Acknowledging problems*	Catalytic interventions elicit the trainee's self-assessment of his or her strengths and weaknesses of performance in the light of the criteria. Some confronting questions may be needed to help the teacher identify weaknesses. Informative interventions give the advisor's assessment of the teacher's strengths and weaknesses using the agreed criteria. During this, supportive interventions affirm strengths the teacher played down or ignored; confronting interventions identify the weaknesses glossed over or omitted.

STAGE 3. ACTION

GOALS	INTERVENTIONS
• *Determining priorities* • *Planning alternatives* • *Proposing focus for next lesson*	Catalytic and informative interventions negotiate an agreed final assessment. Catalytic interventions elicit from the teacher their plans for using the assessment, especially identified weaknesses, to direct future practice. Prescriptive interventions add the advisors' suggestions for the teacher's future practice. Supportive interventions validate the teacher's developing skills in self-assessment.

Figure 30 Collaborative assessment: a three-stage model (adapted from Heron 1991: 139/140)

(See the feedback transcripts in Tasks 5.1 & 8.1. The issue of sequencing is also something to be discussed as part of the role play in Task 9.2.)

9.4 Conclusion

In this chapter we have examined the way that different interventions can be used to develop critical thinking and new understanding in the teacher. Over the last four chapters we have described a feedback process from a counselling perspective which, as we indicated in Chapter 4, rests on strongly humanist principles. The aim of the session is to develop an independent and critically aware teacher and the means to do this involves collaboration with the teacher to analyse their behaviour and arrive at mutually agreed solutions to their problems. This philosophy, however, is closely associated with a predominantly humanist viewpoint of the world. In ELT we are dealing with teachers from widely different cultures, and, even within single cultures, there are many different individual differences and viewpoints. These differences may well cause problems when trying to implement the model of helping which we have described. In the last chapter we shall discuss the way that individual and cultural differences can affect the way that advising is carried out.

Summary

In this chapter the following issues have been raised:

- Catalytic interventions
- Developing critical thinking
- The 'catalytic tool kit'
- The effects of different question types
- Critical incidents
- Sequencing interventions

Tasks

The following tasks will allow you to explore the issues raised in this chapter:

9.1   Examination of a feedback transcript to look at ways of prompting awareness in teachers
9.2   A role play of a feedback session
9.3   A number of problem scenarios which allow discussion of a number of issues about advising
2.5, 5.1, 8.1 & 6.4 Feedback transcripts which in one way or another embody moves and interventions discussed in this chapter

Advice for further reading

Brookfield, S. D. (1995) *Becoming a Critically Reflective Teacher*, San Francisco: Jossey-Bass Wiley.
  Brookfield discusses ways in which teachers across disciplines can improve their teaching through critical reflection. He shows how we learn through the four key lenses of self, students, colleagues and theory, guiding readers through the process by which this is done.

10 Putting it all together: personal and cultural factors

10.1 Introduction

In Chapter 1 we examined the institutional contexts in which advisors work and saw the impact that such contexts can have on the teacher's perception of the feedback session. In the next two chapters we examined the cognitive aspects of learning about teaching: the light that learning theories can throw on the process of giving advice. Then we turned our attention to the processes of giving advice; we examined the feedback process from a psychodynamic viewpoint derived from theories of counselling.

Throughout this examination, reference has been made to various individual and cultural factors which will affect the feedback process. Chapter 1 examined the effect that the institutional setting will have on the advising process and highlighted the importance of assessment on the advisory atmosphere. In Chapter 2 we looked at the individual differences in content and approach which may be motivated by stages in a teacher's professional development and throughout the discussion of counselling skills we have made references to the necessity of paying attention to individual and cultural differences. For example, in Chapter 6 we discussed the culturally different interpretations of non-verbal signals and the way that such signals can be misinterpreted.

The importance of 'trust' is an issue which we have identified as central in establishing an effective relationship between advisors and teachers. The basis on which trust is established between advisors and teachers is something which will be influenced by both individual differences and wider cultural influences. It is these two factors which will form the basis for this concluding chapter.

Individual differences will be looked at from two perspectives:

- Learning styles
- Personality types

and the wider cultural influences will be examined within the following frameworks:

- Language and socio-pragmatics
- Cultural expectations

10.2 Individual differences and feedback styles

10.2.1 Learning styles

There is growing interest within educational research in the relationship between learning styles, cognitive styles and personality factors. There are a number of instruments in use to diagnose personality types (The Myers-Briggs Type Indicator, Myers and McCaulley 1985), learning styles (Honey and Mumford 1986, Kolb 1984, and Oxford 1991) and cognitive styles (Riding 1991) and interest is growing in the relationship between personality types, learning styles and cognitive styles. The connections between learning styles and personality types are based on tests which place individual learning styles on different dimensions such as convergent/divergent, accommodative/ assimilative scales (Honey and Mumford 1986) or wholistic/analytic verbaliser/ image scales (Riding 1991). Miller (1991) argues that these learner types derive to a large extent from Jung's typology (1923) of a basic attitude scale (extroversion–introversion) and two functional scales (sensation–intuition and thinking–feeling).

Researchers	Dimensions
Jung 1923	extroversion–introversion sensation–intuition thinking–feeling
Honey and Mumford 1986	convergent/divergent accommodative/assimilative
Riding 1991	wholistic/analytic verbaliser/image

Figure 31 Personality and learner types

Thus, he argues, there is a relationship on a theoretical and experiential level between different learning styles and personality types.

Within ELT, there have been a number of statistically-based studies which have tried to establish links between cognitive factors such as field dependence/ field independence and language learning with mixed success (for a critical review, see Griffiths and Sheen 1992), and there is now interest in relating learning style research to different cultural factors (for a review of cultural factors in language learning, see Oxford et al. 1992). Oxford identifies the following style dimensions which are relevant to all learning situations and to EFL/ESL in particular. These dimensions provide a useful taxonomy for us to examine the possible influence such styles may have on providing feedback.

Style dimension	Relevance to the feedback situation
global–analytic	Does the teacher see the lesson as a whole or do they prefer to break the lesson into separate elements? If the former is the case, then the teacher will respond better to overall discussions and impressions rather than analysing each separate element in detail.
field dependent–field independent	Does the teacher respond to the 'foreground' (i.e. details) more than the general context of these details? For example, is the teacher sensitive to individual events in the classroom rather than seeing these events as wider patterns? This factor is often related to the global–analytic and the extrovert–introvert dimensions.
feeling–thinking	If the teacher is a person who relates more closely to the emotional 'colour' of the situation, then an approach which explores the emotional aspects of teaching will be more effective than one which analyses things in a cognitive manner. This type of person will also be more sensitive to the 'human warmth' elements of the feedback situation.
impulsive–reflective	Teachers who prefer impulsive styles of learning may well be more ready to accept new ideas or suggestions enthusiastically, although they may make more mistakes. With such a person it may easier to motivate them to try out new ideas whereas with a more reflective teacher, it may be necessary to explore the implications of what happened in more depth before providing suggestions.
intuitive–concrete	Again, related to the global–analytic and the feeling–thinking dimensions, an intuitive teacher is likely to respond more to the colour and overall shape of teaching and can be encouraged to make hypotheses and theoretical models of teaching which rely on feelings rather than logical reasoning
judging–perceiving	Is the teacher someone who sees things in 'black and white' and will arrive at and respond to judgments, jumping to conclusions quickly?
extroverted–introverted	As discussed above, this dimension is seen by many as being a global dimension within which the detailed dimensions can be subsumed. Extrovert teachers are more likely to respond well in the feedback situation and enjoy the human warmth aspects of the discussion. They may well be less sensitive to criticism than the introvert, who is more likely to want to explore their own personal feelings with regard to teaching. It may be more difficult to 'draw out' the introvert, although the extrovert may well lack the skills to be properly analytic about their own feelings with regard to teaching.

Figure 32 Possible influences of learning styles on the teacher's response to feedback

The above table represents the different learning styles with which an advisor might be confronted; it does not necessarily indicate what effect these areas may have either for the giver of advice or the recipient. The emerging research does not make clear the degree to which learning styles can, or perhaps should, be altered. Alternatively, the degree to which teaching (and in this case, advising) styles should be altered to accommodate different learning styles is not indicated. If the latter is the case, then the advisor needs to be sensitive to the preferred learning style of the teacher and produce interventions which are congruent with it. If the former is the case, then one of the aims of the feedback session should be to raise the teacher's awareness of their own less 'effective' learning styles and to make them aware of different and more 'effective' ones.

Miller (1991) suggests that:

> Far from being simple habits which can be changed at will, some believe learning styles to be complex adjustments to life and remain held in place, as it were, by the demands of psychodynamics . . . Over time, we develop characteristic styles of selective inattention (defences) which, in turn, form the basis of personality types. (Miller 1991: 231)

Following this argument, it may not only be relatively difficult to change an individual's learning style, but it may also be highly disturbing for that individual to change. Their individual learning style may rest on personality styles which have been built up through reactions to events in their life. In most cases this personality style, being a combination of various tendencies such as introspection and extroversion, thinking and feeling, sensations and intuition, produces a balanced and well-adjusted person. Thus the individual's unique style has been developed to suit each individual. Unless this has led to a severely maladjusted personality, this style is perhaps the best for that individual. Given that the feedback session is not the place for an advisor to deal with severely maladjusted behaviours of teachers (these are best referred to professional help), it is questionable whether the advisor has the right to alter an individual's learning style. It seems sensible for the advisor to offer alternative methods of learning to the teacher, especially if the advisor is convinced that adherence to a particular style of learning is dysfunctional for that teacher's development. Thus a consultative rather than a confrontational/ prescriptive approach is probably more appropriate. This would then be a suitable 'agenda' which the advisor may wish to raise with the teacher, especially if the advisor feels that the teacher is unaware of the problems caused by adopting their approach to learning.

However, we have argued that the process involved in teaching practice is one which leans heavily on experiential learning for its success. Experiential learning may well be a method of learning which is unfamiliar to the teacher due to different cultural expectations of learning. Consequently, they may have little faith in this approach. In order for the teacher to make progress they will need to be convinced of the importance of learning through doing and reflection. Thus, this issue will need to be explored in the feedback process. As with other factors having an effect on the feedback process, it is important that the advisor

a) identifies the underlying agenda which can be causing problems in learning

b) raises the awareness of the teacher to this basic issue, possibly by confronting the teacher with the problem as they see it

c) seeks a resolution to the problem with the teacher

10.2.2 Personality factors

As well as being sensitive to the learning style of the teacher, the advisor must also be keenly aware of and sensitive to the personality of the teacher. The discussion and differentiation of different personality types is a complex subject and one which we do not have the space to go into in great detail in this book, but we offer the following taxonomy as a framework for considering the way of approaching the subject. Whilst there may be relationships between overall personality types and learning styles as discussed above, there is also a complex relationship between personality types and the types of intervention possible in feedback sessions. As with all interventions, there is no simple one-to-one relationship between any personality type and an intervention strategy. Any personality trait such as 'energy' will be a factor in the use of a number of different interventions. In the following table we have listed the interventions which are most likely to be affected by the given personality trait. Different interventions thus appear more than once and under different personality traits. A typical taxonomy of personality traits is given by Brand (1984) and can be mapped on to different interventions and strategies:

Traits	Dimensions	Intervention issues
Energy	talkative–silent sociable–unsociable adventurous–cautious	catalytic tool kit, empathy, listening, building trust, action research
Affection	trusting–suspicious affectionate–hostile cooperative–uncooperative	catalytic tool kit, empathy, listening, building trust, confronting
Conscience	responsible–irresponsible persistent–quitting order–disorder	identification of the personal agendas involved
Neuroticism	calm–anxious composed–excitable poised–nervous	confronting–supportive
Intelligence	general intelligence cognitive ability analytical ability	action research of various kinds
Will	independent–dependent dominating–submissive strong-willed–weak-willed	catalytic–directive confronting–supportive confronting–supportive

Figure 33 Interventions affected by personality traits

The above is a list of easily-identifiable personality types and the advisor will need to consider the approaches which might be used with different teachers/trainees. For example, a teacher who tends to be anxious and who easily gives up, will need a lot more 'stroking' and supportive interventions than one who appears overtly calm and dominant. The latter may well require a more confrontational approach.

10.3 Cultural influences

10.3.1 Language and socio-pragmatics

Language competence

Even if both participants share the same first language background, the illocutionary force (the intended meaning of the speaker) and the perlocutionary force (the understood meaning by the listener) of different utterances is a major factor to be taken into account. We have seen that such misunderstandings can lead to degenerative interventions. Many of the tasks included in this book include linguistic data as the basis for role play or analysis. These tasks are not intended as models of language behaviour, but as data for the discussion of the interplay between language and function, between linguistic form and pragmatics, between the intentions of the advisor and the perception of this message by the teacher.

In a situation in which both participants do not share the same first language background, or more precisely, have different levels of competence in the language used for conducting the feedback session, the problems of effectively communicating intentions is made much more difficult. In many situations in the world feedback is conducted in English, which is the second language of the teacher and possibly also the supervisor. In such situations, the latter will often have a much higher competence in the second language than the teacher. On a simple linguistic level, this will mean that the intentions of the supervisor will not necessarily be received by the teacher in the same way as intended because of the differences in language competence. On a more psychodynamic level, this inequality will build into the situation an imbalance in which the supervisor will be the dominant partner in the relationship. In consequence, this may mean that the range of interventions available to the advisor is severely limited. For example, the perceived imbalance inherent in the second language context will lead to the most supportive interventions being 'read' as threatening by the teacher. It will certainly mean that it will be much more difficult to successfully create a truly collaborative atmosphere.

Socio-pragmatics

In addition to the issue of basic 'structural' language competence, the impact of culture on the way that different meanings are conveyed – socio-pragmatics – also needs to be taken into account. A recent piece of research on Japanese vs

British students' perceptions of tutorial moves (Turner and Hiraga 1996) indicates that there exist clear, different and culturally-specific socio-pragmatic rules which govern such interactions. In their research they demonstrated that question prompts provided by English native-speaking tutors which were designed to produce elaboration and extended discussion by students were correctly interpreted as such by British students, but were interpreted quite differently by Japanese students. The latter merely 'answered' the questions and did not elaborate, unlike their British counterparts. This indicates that socio-pragmatic rules are important because they help or hinder the process of building and developing relationships within the feedback session. Without common socio-pragmatic rules, interventions will become 'crossed'. An intervention which is intended to elicit reflection might only elicit information. This will create problems in developing awareness in the teacher of new aspects of the teaching/learning process, in scaffolding understanding of the underlying principles of the teaching process. (Task 5.3 specifically focuses on this issue, but Tasks 5.2, 8.1 and 9.2 can all be used to explore the differences involved in using the first or second language as the medium for discussion in feedback sessions.)

10.3.2 Cultural expectations

Different cultural profiles

When discussing the cultural dimension it is necessary to constantly bear in mind that 'it is persons not cultures that are in contact' (Agar 1994), and one of the major difficulties in discussing this area is the need to avoid the pitfall of relying on anecdotal observations and generalisations which lead to grossly simplistic stereotyping. Within the ELT profession there is a tendency to make sweeping generalisations about national groupings and to expect that each and every member of that culture or national group displays the same characteristics (e.g. Brazilians may be characterised as 'warm, friendly, tactile people', whereas Japanese are characterised as 'withdrawn, formal and reticent'). In recent research into the way that Malaysian and British students handled seminar groups on undergraduate programmes in Britain, we found that the differences between the participants within the two national groupings far outweighed the differences between the national groups (Randall & Lavender 1997).

However, our individual personalities and approaches to life are influenced by the cultures in which we live. Bourdieu describes the relationship between the individual and culture as a:

> common set of previously assimilated master plans from which, by an act of invention, similar to that involved in writing music, an infinite number of individual patterns directly applicable to specific situations are generated. (Bourdieu 1976 in Lago & Thompson 1997: 33)

Thus, although complex, the notion of cultural perceptions and cultural differences is one which must be taken seriously and the area of cross-cultural studies is a fast-developing area of study.

There will probably be fewer problems in this area if the advisor and the teacher share the same national/cultural background, although the existence of sub-cultures must not be ignored. Hofstede (1991) identifies six layers of culture: a national level, an ethnic affiliation level, a religious affiliation level, a gender level, a social class level and an organisational level. While we shall be primarily discussing the 'national' level (as characterised by Hofstede), such a model should alert us to the complexities of talking about culture in monolithic national terms. Within each 'national' culture there are many micro-cultures which need to be taken into account in any interpersonal exchange, the most obvious of which are perhaps gender and ethnic origin. Equally, some cultural influences transcend the narrow confines of national boundaries, the most obvious perhaps being those of perceived ethnicity (i.e. the notion of an 'Arab' identity which embraces a geographically hugely diverse number of national cultures) and religious allegiance (cf Islam).

Hofstede (1991) conducted research into different national characteristics in a global study from within one organisation (IBM). According to this research cultural differences in societies can be described according to five persistent dimensions; collectivism vs individualism, large power distance vs small power distance, strong uncertainty avoidance vs weak uncertainty avoidance, competition vs cooperation, and masculinity vs femininity. As he pointed out in an earlier article (Hofstede 1986) these cultural attitudes will have an effect on teacher–student and student–student interactions in the classroom. In a similar manner, these cultural attitudes can affect the roles and relationships of advisors and teachers in the following way:

Cultural profile	Implications for advising	Cultural profile	Implications for advising
Collectivism	strong commitment to group, wanting to save face, less likely to admit problems	Individualism	willing to act alone, less worried by losing face, more ready to 'open up' about problems
Large power distance	more hierarchical, more advisor-centred, prefers disciplined approach	Small power distance	more 'democratic', learner-centred, less disciplined, willing to take initiative
Uncertainty avoidance strong	unwilling to take risks, more resistant to innovations, inflexible	Uncertainty avoidance weak	more willing to experiment, willing to innovate, flexible
Competition	more ready to see comments as 'assessing' rather than developmental	Cooperation	more ready to accept comments in a neutral light, to collaborate in learning
Masculinity	less ready to accept criticism, comments likely to be seen as threatening to self-image	Femininity	more likely to respond to emotional tone of session

Figure 34 The effects of cultural attitude on advisor/teacher roles and relationships

It is tempting to see in the set of descriptors a dichotomy between the culture profiles of 'Western', 'developed', democratic societies and those of more traditional societies. For example, individualism, small power difference and weak uncertainty avoidance are all characteristics which one would associate with the ideology of developed democratic societies as against collectivism and large power difference which can often be seen as more central to the operation of less developed societies. However, the picture is much more complex than this. There are many East Asian societies, for example, which have many of the characteristics of a traditional society yet, in economic terms, one would want to describe them as developed. Japan is just such an example with strong collectivism, large power distances and strong uncertainty avoidance, yet is clearly a highly developed industrial economy. However, the dimensions devised by Hofstede are a useful way to begin to understand and discuss cultural differences.

Cultural beliefs and counselling theory

We have consistently alluded to the fact that the counselling theories described in this book derive from a common set of cultural beliefs located in western democratic societies. Lago and Thompson (1997), in their discussion of counselling theories, identify the following set of cultural beliefs which seem to underpin Western approaches to counselling:

■ The theories are based on the idea of the 'individual', defined as a belief that individuals are in charge of their own destiny
■ Humans are in a constant state of flux, of movement, of 'becoming'
■ There is a requirement to be active in one's life, not passive
■ The process of growth therapy is to throw off or shed the effects of parental, family and community influences that have perceived negative effects
■ The challenge is to live authentically in the social world, to be truly oneself
■ As human beings we have scientific/rational tendencies
■ The world is how we perceive it to be
■ The sanctity of personal authority is not questioned, which implies that:
■ All personal and cultural values are open to questioning
■ The concept of personal choice is highly valued

Lago and Thompson 1997: 78

If we consider the dimensions of collectivism/individualism and large/small power distance, humanistic counselling is clearly located within what we could loosely characterise as a 'developed' rather than a 'traditional' cultural context. Within such cultural contexts (although the heterogeneous nature of such contexts must always be borne in mind) the individual is given much more importance than society in general. The counselling processes which we have been describing, derived ultimately from the ideas of Rogers (Rogers 1969) can be described as 'client-centred' which is essentially a 'democratic' approach. To use an analogy from Transactional Analysis (Berne 1964), the 'ideal' interpersonal transaction is that of the adult to adult. Such ideas seem to sit more comfortably within the philosophical framework of post-industrial Western democracies. In post-industrial societies the family unit is much less important than the social or work-placed unit. Many in such societies would be as likely to turn to a work colleague / close friend for advice as to a close family member. Within less industrially developed societies, such as those found in the Middle East, close family members such as a brother or sister, mother or father, mother-in-law are much more likely to be sought after for advice. As with all discussions of cultural differences, this is not to suggest that people from 'developed' societies never seek advice from family members – many obviously do – it is merely that, taken as a whole, family membership is seen as more important in some societies than others or, to put it another way, in some societies individualism is more highly regarded than collectivism.

Such basic cultural beliefs need to be taken seriously when we consider the approaches to be taken in giving advice. The models and metaphors we use may not be understood from different cultural perspectives (for a discussion of this issue see Randall and Lavender 1997). Lee (1991) argues that democratic counselling techniques may be dysfunctional when counselling Korean Americans by undermining the established patterns of authority. In the same way, if advisors use a culturally alien model of individual responsibility as the basis for trust in a society which does not value this, then they may not be respected. Advisors need to work within, or certainly be sensitive to, the culturally-accepted patterns of authority which are accepted by the teacher and the metaphors such patterns produce. To use the concept of 'validity claims' devised by Habermas (for a discussion of such claims in an ELT context, see Gieve 1995), in a humanistic view of counselling the advisor is saying 'you can believe what I am saying (you can trust me) because I am your friend, I am an equal, sincere and caring adult'. This claim is more likely to be successful if the teacher comes from a culture which places high value on individualism and has small power distance in its social organisation. However, as we discussed earlier when considering Heron's prescriptive/catalytic gradient (Chapter 5), trust can also be based on other validity claims. The advisor can say 'you can believe me because I am older than you and I have the experience' or 'you can believe me because I am your manager/supervisor and you must obey me'. Each of these may be as acceptable, if not more acceptable, to teachers from more collectivist cultural backgrounds or from cultural backgrounds where there are large power distances in social organisations. Indeed, advisors need to be aware of the confusion which the 'democratic' counselling techniques may cause to teachers from cultural backgrounds which place a high value on collectivism and authority.

(For an exercise to explore different aspects of cross-cultural communication, see Task 10.1.)

10.4 Different agendas in the feedback session

In earlier chapters we have discussed the different 'agendas' which may inform the way that advisors approach giving advice. Much of the discussion in those chapters has centred on various 'technical' agendas – the provision of advice on how to carry out the specific process of teaching (Chapter 5). We have also mentioned the importance of recognising other agendas, such as the interpersonal and emotional agendas when dealing with feelings of anxiety and defensive reactions (Chapter 7). Furthermore, in Chapter 1 we identified 'institutional setting' as an important influence on the advisory process. In this chapter we have identified two other major areas which will have an effect on the process, individual differences and cultural background. These three areas – the cultural background, the institutional setting and the individual differences – map on to the six major agenda types identified by Heron in the following way:

Culture	Global agendas	Issues to do with level of development, economic and political issues. These issues often overlap and strongly influence cultural agendas.
	Cultural agendas	Issues to do with the roles and status of individuals within the wider society and the structuring of the wider society. Issues to do with traditional vs 'developed' social norms. They pervade all aspects of behaviour, and particularly affect the types of organisation.
Institutional setting	Organisational agendas	Issues to do with the way that people act together in organisations, their roles and styles of operation within organisations. They can have strong effects on the way that individuals react in groups.
	Group-dynamic agendas	Issues concerned with the way that individuals interact with each other in groups. Influenced by the above, but also influenced by strictly interpersonal and intrapsychic agendas.
Individual differences	Interpersonal agendas	The way that individuals act towards each other and the way that such actions may cause offence to or hurt others. They may be related to the intrapsychic agendas, but are also related to all of the above agendas.
	Intrapsychic agendas	Issues and behaviours which derive from the uniqueness of the individual, from the personal history of the particular individual as distinct from the influences of society.

Figure 35 Heron's six agenda types and their relationship with culture, institution and individual

Heron's use of the term 'agenda' is interesting. It suggests strongly that the issues contained in these agendas can and should form the basis for discussion between the advisor and the client and that one of the roles of the advisor is to be aware of such factors and to bring them to the advisory session to be discussed. Implied within his description of agendas is a belief that such underlying agendas may lie at the root of the client's problems. Although we have indicated earlier that the identification of the underlying agenda (such as anxiety) may cause problems for the teacher, we feel that the main value of the idea of different agendas lies in the power they have to enable us to understand what is happening in the feedback session. They provide an explanation of the difficulties which can occur in a feedback session when an advisor and a teacher do not appear to be effectively communicating.

10.4.1 Crossed intentions

We discussed earlier in this chapter the socio-pragmatic problems involved in making sure that the intentions of the advisor are accurately communicated and perceived by the teacher in the way they were intended by the advisor. In such a situation there is a breakdown in effective communication. Such a breakdown can be characterised as having 'crossed' intentions (Berne 1964), or as Heron styles them, 'degenerate interventions'. However, this lack of communication of intent is not solely a language problem. Each of the areas we have discussed in this chapter may play a part in causing such a breakdown in communication.

In an interesting paper given at the Polish Teacher Trainer Conference in Krakow, tutors from International House noted a reluctance on the part of their native English speaker teachers to seek advice from the non-native English speaking trainers and vice versa (Adams and Markiewicz 1995). The reasons given for the reluctance on the part of the Polish staff included such things as the fact that the native speakers never seemed to solve their problems, that they seemed to want to discuss the problem, rather than give a solution, and from the Polish trainers, that their British counterparts did not seem to have a clear problem. Similar reasons were given by the English native speakers of their Polish trainer colleagues, for example, complaints that the latter did not want to discuss their problems. In a subsequent piece of research into the way that the advice was perceived by the two groups, their responses to specific pieces of feedback (such as 'The role play went quite well') were recorded on a scale of degree of threat/support perceived by them. It was noted that in general the Polish teachers perceived the feedback as more threatening than did their British counterparts (for an adapted version of the research task, see Task 5.3).

If we assume that the intent of the advisor in making the intervention about the role play was to provide a supportive intervention – valuing the teacher's work – then we have a situation of crossed intentions as it was not perceived in the same light. In order to understand what happened in this situation, we need to look at the part different 'agendas' played in the process. A teacher may perceive the intervention as threatening because:

• they generally expect feedback to be critical	a cultural agenda relating to the roles and status of individuals within their society
• the feedback was part of a teacher training programme	institutional setting – organisational agenda
• the teacher is lacking in confidence	interpersonal/intrapsychic agenda

- the teacher knew that part of the lesson had gone badly

an issue to do with the uniqueness of the situation and the particular individual and their lesson

The influences of the different factors on this situation can be represented diagrammatically:

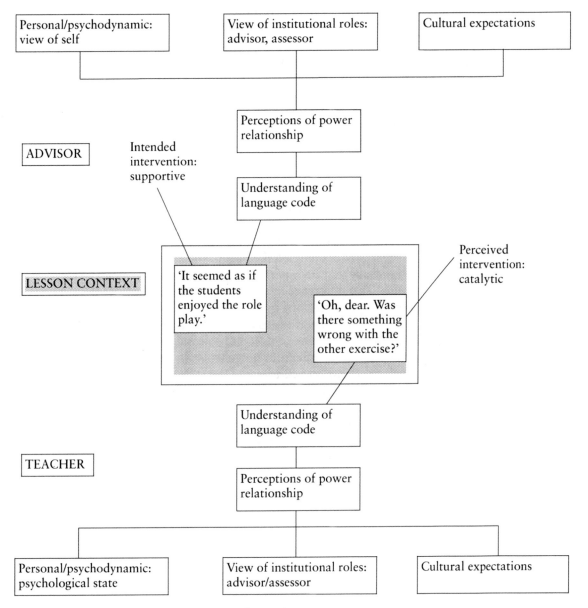

Figure 36 Different agendas causing crossed intentions

The above diagram represents the situation so graphically described by Adams and Markiewicz (1995). In the teacher advice sessions the advisor makes an apparently neutral statement to the teacher about the role play. The intention was one of positive feedback through personal interpretation. Such an intention derived not only from the advisor's knowledge of the English language and the way to express praise in English, it was also based on the advisor's view of their cultural expectations – a 'democratic' style of dealing with teachers; their role within the institution – as an advisor not an 'inspector'; and their own view of themselves – as open, friendly and approachable. However, the teacher's view of the situation is equally coloured by their cultural, institutional and personal views. Their views of the situation derive from a more hierarchical view of society, from a perception of the institutional role of the advisor as critic and assessor, and from a view of themselves as less than equal to the advisor. Seen through the lenses of these cultural frames, the advisor's message gets perceived in quite a different light, as a catalytic intervention.

10.4.2 Maximising understanding

Figure 36 indicates a situation in which messages can get perverted by different viewpoints of what is happening on the part of the advisor and that of the teacher. It is important that both parties to the feedback are aware of each other's viewpoint. This difference of viewpoint of the teacher and the students in the classroom is aptly described by Holliday (1994). He demonstrates how the set of methodological expectations of the classroom teacher and the students derive from a hierarchy of different cultural sources. From the students' point of view, the influences range from the individual view of learning through the classroom culture and the culture of the school, through to the socio-political culture of the region and nation. He highlights the lack of congruence between this and the professional–academic cultures, allied to international–educational related cultures of the teaching profession, or of advisors on teaching. We can use the same technique to describe the expectations of the advisor and the teacher in the feedback session:

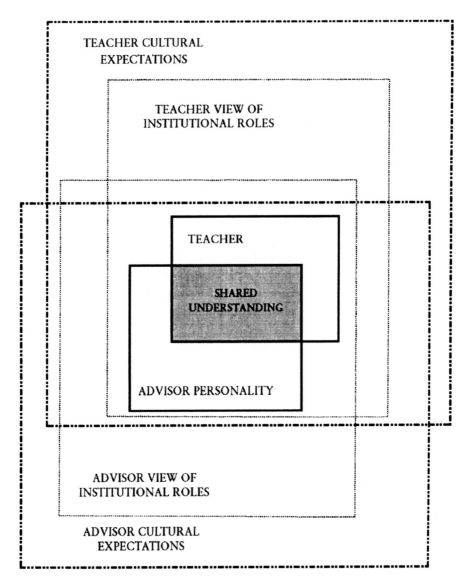

Figure 37 Factors affecting the feedback session

10.5 Conclusion

We started this book with the institutional contexts within which advisors work and now we have come full circle and examined the wider cultural contexts within which they operate. This may seem odd for a book which deals centrally with the ways that individuals communicate in feedback sessions and the way that new understandings are created. However, all such learning encounters take place within a wider context. All social practices are situated within a wider social context and it is important that while we explore the feelings and expectations which we all, as individuals, feel in interpersonal encounters, we are also aware of the wider canvas within which we work. Nowhere is this more pertinent than in advising within ELT. By its very nature, our profession brings us into contact with people from widely different cultural backgrounds. As we stated in the introduction, many of the ideas involved in the learning and counselling theories discussed in this book are contained within a particular intellectual paradigm, largely one which is associated with the humanist principles highly valued in democratic societies. That we have found these techniques and principles to have worked in a number of different advisory situations is perhaps testimony to their effectiveness, yet it is always important to bear in mind the different cultural and philosophical traditions which all individuals bring to the learning process. All interactions are socially located and we must take account of these differences when we undertake the process of guiding teachers to new understandings and professional growth – the ultimate aim of the process of giving advice.

Task 1.1 An inspector calls

Aim: To encourage participants to reflect on their feelings when they
            were first watched and to relate these feelings to the different
            contexts in which they were first observed.

Rationale: The first visit or observation is often the most daunting. By asking
            participants to reflect on this experience, many of the effects of the
            advisor's institutional role on the feelings of teachers will be revealed.

Procedure:
1. Ask the participants to write an essay for homework entitled 'An Inspector
    Calls'. In it, ask them to try to describe their first experience of being
    watched, either as a trainee or as a teacher. Ask them to write as honestly as
    possible their feelings and reactions to things that happened on that day.
2. Next day, put the participants into groups and ask them to tell the rest of their
    group about their experience. Ask them to list the things which upset them /
    made them nervous and the things which were good about the experience.
3. In plenary, discuss the common points with the groups and try to relate the
    points they make to the different contexts in which they were advised.

Notes for guidance: This activity is often a good one to start a course with. It
'sets the scene' for giving advice in teaching.

    Not all participants will have negative feelings towards their first
observation. If you have a chance to look at the written essays first, it may be
an idea to set up the group work by mixing those who had a positive
experience with those who had a less positive experience.

    Although the discussion is designed to raise issues of the importance of
institutional roles and expectations on the advisory process (see Chapter 1),
many aspects of successful (and unsuccessful) advice-giving will be brought up.
A useful discussion of what makes advice successful (see especially Chapters 4
& 6 and Task 4.2) can be extracted from this session.

    It is suggested that this is carried out as a written homework task, but it is
also possible, time permitting, to carry out the activity in the class, putting
participants in groups to think about their experience and then put them in
groups to tell the others as in the above procedure.

    NB 'An Inspector Calls' is a famous play by J. B. Priestley and one which is
often performed in schools.

Task 1.2 Case studies in advising

Aim: To sensitise the participants to the way that systems deal with the issue of assessing teachers.

Rationale: The issue of assessment and its effect on the advisory process is important and different systems have various ways of trying to separate developmental help from evaluation. By examining different systems, advisors will be more aware of the way that their own system deals with the issue.

Procedure: As a jigsaw activity:
1. Divide the participants into five equal groups, for example five groups of five.
2. Give each group one of the case studies (*Photocopiable resource 1* on pages 212–213).
3. Ask them in groups to discuss the situation described in the case studies and to answer the questions:
    How is developmental advice provided in this context?
    How is assessment carried out?
    What are the strengths and weaknesses of this separation?
4. Tell them they can refer to their own experience, or compare the system to their own, if relevant. They could also be asked to apply a SWOT analysis to each situation (see Task 1.3) if this will help.
5. After they have discussed the advantages and disadvantages of each system, they can then be rearranged into new groups in which each member has looked at a different case study. Each member of the group discusses their case study with the rest of the group.
6. If necessary, hold a plenary session to draw together the points which have been discussed and compare what has been discussed to their individual situation (if appropriate).

Notes for guidance: The primary aim of this exercise is to sensitise participants to the problems involved in separating their assessment function from their developmental function, but also to make them aware of ways in which this can be done through institutional structures. This is the main theme of Chapter 1, and such an exercise can be used as a way to 'present' the discussion provided in that chapter.

However, there are other issues which these case studies bring up, most notably that of the use of competencies, and it might be worth drawing teachers' attention to the issue of using competency schedules which is discussed in Chapter 2, and Task 2.3.

It is important to emphasise through the exercise the implications that these contexts would have on the relationship with the teacher in the feedback session and to get the advisors to imagine the personal/emotional implications which arise.

Case Study 1	Note here the attempt to separate development issues (second year TP) from final assessment (third year TP). Note also that in the second year the trainees are watched by one tutor, but in the third year they are watched by different tutors. It is worth discussing the issue of grading 'improvement' rather than 'achievement'. How can improvement be measured? What is the implication for a trainee who starts highly competent? See here the discussion of ipsative scales in Chapter 1.
Case Study 2	This brings up the issue of the use of 'critical friends' (Chapter 1) and peer observation. How appropriate is peer observation and feedback at this level of a course? Are trainees with so little experience able to reflect on their own or others' performance in any meaningful way? (See Chapter 2 for a discussion concerning a novice teacher's understanding.) What is the function of the tutor's written comments in the discussion as against the peers' comments? There is a lot of self-development in this context, but is the assessment aspect dealt with adequately?
Case Study 3	Note the way that the three-way conference divides the issue of assessment from that of development in an institutional way (see Chapter 1). What are the other advantages of the three-way input to the assessment session? What is the role of the trainee's own evaluation in this process, or in development? (See ideas on the reflective teacher, Chapter 2.)
Case Study 4	Note the way that this system makes the assessment aspect 'transparent', both by use of the general competencies, and the preparation of the lesson before the inspection visit. Many inspection systems in the developing world depend on random visits – trying to catch the teachers acting 'normally' – a monitoring function. This context has a developmental role – explaining how something should be done and then going to see if it has been achieved. Does this also allow the inspector to effectively carry out the monitoring function?
Case Study 5	This again raises the issue of the use of the 'critical friend' (Chapter 1). It also raises the issue of the appropriacy of using a checklist, especially one used for assessment purposes, in an essentially developmental process (again, see competencies, Chapter 2).

Task 1.3 SWOT analysis

Aim: To encourage participants to look critically at the context in which their advisory role is situated.

Rationale: We have found that participants are frequently working under very difficult circumstances with little recognition of the role they are fulfilling. Under such conditions it is easy to feel that difficulties are insurmountable and that little can be achieved. This exercise gets participants to focus on the strengths of the context in which they are working and to work within those weaknesses they have no power to change.

Procedure:
1. Point out that a SWOT analysis is a planning tool which helps us to get a picture of the overall situation in which we are working by analysing the Strengths, Weaknesses, Opportunities and Threats in each situation.

2. Ask participants to look at the SWOT analysis (*Photocopiable resource 2* on page 214).
3. Go through the SWOT analysis with them. This particular analysis was made by a group of Polish trainers discussing the merits of introducing a mentorship scheme for pre-service training in Poland.
4. Ask the participants to consider the context in which their advisory work takes place.
5. In groups, ask them to draw up their own SWOT analysis.

Notes for guidance: Some introduction to the use of this tool is necessary. You may need to give an example of a TP supervisor working with a college. They might find the following questions helpful:

Strengths	What are the positive aspects of the system?
	In what ways does it work well?
	Why does it work well?
Weaknesses	What are the negative aspects of the system?
	What problems are there for teachers, advisors, administrators?
Opportunities	How can the system be made to work better?
	What would need to be done?
	What changes in legislation, administration or training might be needed?
Threats	What might prevent the system from working properly in the future?

The resulting discussion should bring up many of the points raised in Chapter 1 about the operation of different systems for advice. The discussion of the grid from the Polish trainers is also a useful tool to analyse the strengths and weaknesses of mentor systems in general.

Task 1.4 Problems in supervision: lessons from the research

Aim: To explore problems inherent in many supervision contexts.

Rationale: By looking at problems revealed through research in Britain, participants are encouraged to examine provision in their own contexts and come up with possible solutions.

Procedure:
1. Ask participants to look at the list of problems (*Photocopiable resource 3* on page 215).
2. In pairs, ask the participants to discuss the following questions for each extract:
   Do you have any experience of such a problem?
   Have you ever encountered such difficulties yourself either as a trainee teacher or as a supervisor?

Have you worked in educational contexts where such problems existed? Have you ever encountered a situation in which such a 'problem' exists but is not viewed as a problem at all?

What solutions might you come up with to solve the problems?

3. When they have completed the task, discuss the issues with them in a plenary group.

Notes for guidance: The list of problems identified are common to many teaching practice situations. They are not all easily solvable, but they need consideration. Below are some possible solutions based on suggestions by McIntyre (1988).

a Providing trainees with structured support in the university for the tasks which they are asked to undertake in schools, through a jointly planned programme which carefully matches school and university tasks. See Chapter 2 on theory and practice.

b Using a school mentor (see Chapter 1). Note also the importance of liaison between the school and the university (link tutors).

c By giving trainees a clear indication of the range of teaching abilities they are expected to acquire, as a set of goals to structure their work in the earlier part of their year; these abilities being defined in terms of the tasks which face one in teaching, not in terms of behaviour which must be demonstrated. See Chapter 2 on observing teachers and apprenticeship schemes.

d Mentorship programmes can overcome this problem. Also by pairing them with another student teacher with whom to share their responsibilities and problems and to provide each other with feedback (Chapter 1).

e Again, the value of mentors is that they have this recent experience. It is also important that tutors from colleges spend some time back in the school to renew their experience (Chapter 1).

f Trying to ensure that each student teacher has a secure personal relationship with an advisor.

g By giving them effective diagnostic feedback in relation to those specified teaching abilities and the use of competencies (see Chapter 2).

h By giving them effective diagnostic feedback in relation to those specified teaching abilities.

i The use of individual schedules to define where the student teacher is and by initially only giving them very limited teaching tasks in lessons and only gradually increasing their responsibilities. The pace at which such demands increase can vary according to the perceived needs of individuals. See Chapter 2 on skill learning.

An early version of this activity was first used with a group of Czech mentors in collaboration with Tom Whiteside.

Task 1.5 Who wants to be my critical friend?

Aim: To sensitise participants to the issues involved in using peers to
            provide feedback.

Rationale: Peer group observation and feedback are used on a number of
            different training programmes, often as if they are going to work
            'naturally'. This exercise provides an opportunity for participants
            to examine the likely difficulties which can be faced by using peer
            observation and gives them a chance to think about how to prepare
            trainees/teachers to undertake peer observation.

Procedure:
1. Write 'critical friend' on the board and ask the participants to discuss what
   they understand by the term.
2. Then ask them individually to think of a person in their workplace who
   they would like to come in and watch them teach and give them feedback
   on their lesson. Ask them to list the reasons why they chose the person they
   did.
3. Put them in groups to discuss the attributes they would look for in a 'critical
   friend'.
4. If any of the group have ever participated in peer observation, ask them to
   discuss with their colleagues the positive and negative points about being
   observed / observing a friend or colleague.

or

4. Ask groups to look at the comments from teachers (*Photocopiable resource
   4* on page 216) and draw up a list of the problems which might derive from
   observing colleagues.
5. In plenary discuss the advantages and disadvantages of using peer
   observation/feedback and discuss the implications for the preparation of
   trainees/teachers to watch each other.

Notes for guidance: This is essentially a chance for the group to discuss the
advantages and disadvantages of using critical friends for providing advice. An
alternative way of approaching the task could be to use a SWOT analysis (see
Task 1.3).

The term 'critical friend' encapsulates the need to offer advice in a manner
which does not alienate the person you are advising.

By asking the participants to relate the idea to their own situation, it is
possible to explore exactly what is required from the process of getting advice
on teaching and the personal characteristics of someone who can provide good
advice (see Tasks 4.2 & 4.3 for a further exploration of this issue). The
selection of a particular person may also bring up some of the problems which
can be involved.

If some of the participants have experience of peer observation/feedback,
then they can be used to provide their own feelings about the system, but the

comments on the photocopiable page from MA students also highlight the difficulties of getting critical comment from colleagues.

The following comments can be made about the extracts:

Teacher A	Notice the conservative choice of 'critical friend' considerably reduces the critical value of the comments. This teacher also notes the problem of their own learning style (see Chapter 10) – suggesting that not everyone will find a peer observation beneficial.
Teacher B	This teacher had just listed a number of criticisms which he felt were unfair and offers an 'explanation' for the criticisms, suggesting that the criticisms were not actually taken on board. This teacher appears to be discussing learning styles and cultural differences, but actually sounds very 'defensive' (see Chapter 7), suggesting that the experience was not successful.
Teacher C	This teacher comments on the initial perceived artificiality of the situation, but notes that the situation is one which many will encounter in their career – a useful reason for using the technique.
Teacher D	This teacher refers to the problems which can arise from the collaborating teachers being poorly matched and of the problems involved in advice being misinterpreted, which is a major problem in offering advice (see Chapter 5 on 'degenerative interventions').

In discussion with the group it is important to emphasise that teachers and trainees will need to be sensitised to many issues of providing advice for peer observation to be effective.

Task 2.1 Characteristics of successful learning

Aim: To reflect on positive and negative learning experiences in order to highlight characteristics of successful learning.

Rationale: This is a well-known activity applicable to many training situations. In the context of learning about teaching, it is useful to reflect on features which characterise successful learning and then re-examine implications for teacher education in the light of these features.

Procedure:
1. Ask the participants individually to think of one thing they have learnt successfully and one thing they have not managed to learn successfully.
2. Ask the participants to describe their experiences of successful and unsuccessful learning to a partner.
3. Still working in pairs, ask the participants to extract features of the two learning experiences which they feel made the experiences either successful or unsuccessful. Ask them to list these in two columns on a sheet of paper:

Characteristics of successful learning	Characteristics of unsuccessful learning

4. To aid their thinking, give them questions which they might like to answer in deciding on the features:
   - What was the nature of the subject/skill you were trying to learn? Was it theoretical/practical?
   - Did you try to learn it by yourself or with a teacher?
   - If you learnt it with a teacher:
     To what extent did the teacher show you what to do?
     Did the teacher use explanation?
   - Did you use a book or guide to learn the subject?
   - How important was practice to you in learning the new subject/skill?
   - Did you get any feedback on your learning? Where did it come from?
   - To what extent do you both agree on the characteristics of a successful and unsuccessful learning experience?
5. When they have completed the discussion in pairs, pull the discussion together in plenary session to discuss what they have found.
6. Relate their points to learning about teaching by asking the following questions:
   What implications does this have for:
   a) teacher education in general?
   b) the supervision of teaching practice?
   c) your own particular advisory context?
   d) how could you incorporate the successful characteristics and minimise the unsuccessful characteristics when advising teachers?

Notes for guidance:
1. One of the problems often encountered with this type of exercise is deciding what a learning experience is. Participants will often only think of academic subjects as learning or, if they are more mature, they cannot think of anything they have learnt recently or cannot remember how they learnt at school/college. Encourage them to think about learning in a broader sense. There are many situations in which we learn things. We learn
   - how to use new equipment (e.g. computers, video recorders, cars)
   - how to do new things (e.g. play instruments/sports, cook for ourselves)
   - how to operate new systems (e.g. new procedures in schools, fill in different forms)
   - how to perform new duties (e.g. counsel students, be a head of year / form tutor)
2. Participants may have difficulties in deciding what the general

characteristics or features are of the learning experiences they have described. Here, direct their attention to the questions they can ask about the experiences.

3. It is probable that the participants will not agree on the general features of successful and unsuccessful learning. During the group discussion the following points can be made:

There will be differences of learning styles.	Participants can be referred to the discussion of learning styles in this book (Chapters 3 & 10).
There will be differences due to the nature of the learning task. Is it a practical skill or a theoretical subject?	The debate about the learning of practical skills vs theoretical knowledge is an important area to consider (Chapter 2).

4. One of the central issues discussed in Chapter 2 is the nature of learning involved in learning about teaching and the difference between the knowledge involved in more theoretical subjects compared with that involved in learning a skill. Thus, during the plenary feedback session it is important to cover the following issues, all discussed in Chapter 2:
    *   The differences between knowledge about teaching and the practical aspects of learning skills
    *   The importance of practice to the learning of new skills
    *   The importance of having someone to help/guide/coach the teaching practice
    *   The feasibility of being able to independently reflect on teaching
5. This awareness-raising activity feeds directly into discussions of successful teacher learning and the role of the advisor in facilitating success.

Task 2.2 Beliefs about teaching

Aims: To examine the views that the participants have about what is involved in being a successful teacher.
            To examine how training can be approached in view of the qualities of a successful teacher identified earlier.

Rationale: There are many commonly-held beliefs about teaching which participants need to be aware of. This is a discussion-based activity which attempts to bring these beliefs out into the open and to examine their implications for giving advice to teachers.

Procedure:
1. Ask the participants individually to look at the statements (*Photocopiable resource 5* on page 216), and then to say if they agree with them / disagree with them or if they wish, modify them so that they agree with them.
2. Once they have done this, ask them to pair up with another group member

and try to reach agreement. Ask two pairs to team up to form a group of four and repeat the process. The aim should be to reach consensus. This may mean modifying the statements so that all group members agree.
3. Plenary feedback using the notes for guidance below.

Notes for guidance:

As commonly-held views about teaching, many of these statements contain a degree of truth about them and they relate to many of the issues discussed in this book. It is important to get trainers to explore their feelings about these issues and to discuss the implications of these views for providing advice. Although there are no 'right' answers to any of these statements, the following are areas which are important to bring out during the discussion.

Teachers are born not made.	This question relates to the belief that the personal qualities of a teacher are the most important aspect of teaching, that these are innate and fixed and suggests that there is an 'ideal' teacher personality. Although personal skills are very important, innate or intuitive behaviour may not be ideal (see the discussion of Schön's reflection in/on action, Chapter 2) and can be altered by discussion and reflection. Also, a belief in one fixed solution runs counter to the idea of allowing the individual to construct their own solutions (see Chapter 4). And it is very difficult to advise someone to do something which is impossible (see SMART, Chapter 8).
Teachers need to have excellent English before they learn how to teach.	This issue relates to the knowledge/skills divide in teacher education (Chapter 2). It is also very important in deciding the agenda chosen in the feedback session and the type of intervention strategy used (see Chapter 5). And it can seriously affect the relationship between the advisor and the teacher (see Chapter 8, informative interventions).
The first thing teachers need to learn is sound classroom management skills.	There are two issues involved here. The first concerns the importance placed on 'surface behaviours' as against deeper understandings of teaching (Chapter 3) and the second concerns the types of knowledge required by teachers at different stages of their development (Chapters 2 and 3).
The best way to learn how to teach is by observing and copying an experienced teacher.	The relative advantages and disadvantages of apprenticeship schemes are discussed in Chapter 2. Most would agree that observation of mature professionals is an important factor, but that this observation needs to be 'coached' (see Schön's 'practicum', Chapter 2) and new awareness needs to be 'scaffolded' by a more knowledgeable guide (Chapter 3).
It is impossible for teachers new to the profession to reflect on their own teaching.	Again, this relates to the different needs of teachers at different points in their career (Chapter 2). It also relates to the importance of a guide in the early stages of learning (Chapter 3), and the importance of the feedback session as a template for training the reflective practitioner (Chapter 2, independent teacher development).

Task 2.3 Good teachers and better teachers – multi-level teaching competencies

Aims: To examine the usefulness of competency descriptors.
To look at the feasibility of devising a system of competencies at two levels.

Rationale: It is helpful to see an example of what competency descriptors actually look like and asking participants to write their own competency descriptors is helpful in reviewing the difficulties involved in establishing descriptors for teaching performance.

Procedure:
1. Divide the participants into pairs or groups.
2. Cut out the cards (*Photocopiable resource 6*, page 217) and distribute one set of cards to each group of participants.
3. Point out that these competency descriptors of classroom management were drawn up for a state educational system in the Middle East where the teachers teach from a set textbook. Ask them to pair competencies that deal with the same topic and then to divide them into two levels:
    a) Basic level i.e. this is the minimum level of competency a teacher would need in order to achieve qualified teacher status
    b) Level one competency – typical of a confident beginning teacher
4. Ask the participants to list other competency areas which they would want to use to evaluate a teacher (e.g. handling of errors, personal qualities, interpersonal skills, lesson planning etc.).
5. Ask the participants in their groups to choose one of the competency areas they have listed and to devise descriptors for the competencies. They should again try to think of two levels of competency descriptors.

Competency Area _____

BASIC LEVEL	LEVEL ONE

6. Discuss with the participants how useful such descriptors would be in their own advisory context. Who would they be they useful for? How would they use them?
7. Ask the participants what difficulties they would envisage with actually interpreting and using such descriptors.
8. If possible, try to use them on a real or video-taped lesson.

Notes for guidance:

1. These descriptors were drawn up with a typical non-native speaker teacher working in a state educational system in mind. The basic competencies are really very basic, yet they are designed to be realistic and achievable. The following competencies all relate to aspects of classroom management and are divided into the basic and more advanced levels (see Chapter 2).

BASIC LEVEL	LEVEL ONE
Teacher follows activities in Teacher's Book carefully and carries them out efficiently	Teacher plans and carries out activities appropriate to the class and the aims of the lesson
Teacher gives clear simple instructions for pupils to carry out coursebook activities and checks they are understood	Teacher uses a range of methods appropriate to the level of the class to give instructions and check these are understood
Teacher maintains good discipline to enable pupils to work effectively	Teacher is able to combine periods of whole class control with periods of individual work while maintaining overall class control
Teacher monitors pair and group work activities	Teacher closely monitors pair and group work activities and acts on the information gained in an appropriate manner
Teacher is able to open and close activities in an orderly fashion	Teacher is able to manage transitions between activities smoothly and competently including cases where learners are completing a task at different times
Teacher has the necessary aids to teach the lesson and uses them efficiently	Teacher provides extra aids and uses other physical resources efficiently to achieve the goals of the lesson
Teacher is aware of the overall purpose of the lesson	Teacher is aware of the overall purpose of the lesson and how individual activities contribute to the general aim

2. In drawing up competencies for their specific contexts, participants may well wish to be much more ambitious in their descriptions. However, it is important in this area to make sure that they do not become too idealistic and describe an impossibly ideal teacher. The following is an example of competencies drawn up by inspectors in Oman on the Handling of Errors:

Level I	Level II
Teacher shows awareness of errors and facilitates correction	Teacher shows the ability to differentiate between serious and less serious errors and deals with them appropriately
Teacher corrects him/herself most of the time but does allow students to peer- or self-correct some of the time	Teacher has a range of techniques for error correction and prompts genuine self-awareness in the pupils

3. In discussing the use of competency descriptors, it is helpful to emphasise the use of competencies as a tool for personal development (see Chapter 2) as well as one for external assessment (for the assessment/development debate, see Chapter 1).
4. It is also worth pointing out the importance to teachers and trainees of knowing the basis on which they are being assessed. Therefore procedures need to be in place to ensure shared understanding of competencies.
5. Participants should be aware that competencies and competency descriptors are known by other names in other contexts. So participants may see references to teacher standards and performance criteria when reading about this area, particularly in the American context.

Task 2.4 Hot slips: training for reflection

Aims: To consider ways in which reflection might be facilitated on pre-service training courses.

Rationale: There is a great deal of discussion as to the importance of training teachers to be reflective, even at relatively early stages of their career. A number of techniques have been suggested to facilitate this. One such technique is the use of 'hot slips'. Immediately after teaching a lesson or part of a lesson, the teacher is asked to write down their first reactions to a number of questions about aspects of the lesson they have just taught and their feelings about it. These slips are given to the advisor and used as a basis for discussion in the feedback session.

Procedure:
1. Tell participants that hot slips are one technique which is often used on courses to help teachers reflect on their teaching. With this technique, the advisor sets a number of questions for teachers to answer privately in writing immediately after they have taught a lesson.
2. Ask participants individually to look at teachers' responses to questions (*Photocopiable resource 7* on page 218). Ask them to work out the questions which they think were asked to prompt the responses in each box. Tell them to write the question on the dotted line in each box.
3. Get a participant to share their answers then to reflect on the following:
   What are the advantages and disadvantages of this technique?
   Why were those particular questions chosen?
   How effective were the questions in getting the trainees to reflect on present classroom performance?
   What other purposes might some of the questions serve?
   What follow-up questions could an advisor ask to prompt further reflection?

Notes for guidance: While these questions are a useful starting point for reflection, they can also be a source of invaluable information to the advisor on

the developmental stage of the teacher (see Chapter 2) which in turn will
influence the type of advice given to the teacher. This can be seen from the
variety of responses to the questions, some of which focus on discrete teaching
techniques (Question 5 Teacher B); some deal with the effect on learners (e.g.
Question 4 Teacher B); while some of the respondents focused only on their
personal feelings about the lesson (Question 1 Teacher B). Once the questions and
responses have been matched, one useful issue to discuss is the degree to which
such an approach can be used to prepare for teacher autonomy (Chapter 2).

The following are the questions which were actually asked and some
discussion of the way that the question can be interpreted and followed up.

Question 1	How did you feel?	It may be that this question is phatic since it does not really help the trainee to reflect on classroom performance as is evidenced in the examples above. However, it can serve a useful cathartic function (Chapter 7). Teachers in training can find teaching, particularly in front of an audience, quite nerve-racking. The experience can provoke a number of reactions from exhaustion through to elation. It may be useful for advisors to acknowledge these feelings and possibly to adapt their feedback to take any sensitivities into account (see identifying agendas, Chapter 5 and anxiety, Chapter 7).
Question 2	How did the lesson go?	A question such as this helps to focus on the teacher's overall perceptions of the lesson. Some teachers will nevertheless still tend to comment on individual aspects of the lesson from a negative point of view. It is then up to the advisor whether to explore these specific issues further ('following', Chapter 9) or whether to bring the discussion back to more global issues through prompting with questions relating to achievement of general aims ('leading', Chapter 9).
Question 3	What were you pleased with?	It is useful to encourage teachers to look at positive features of the lesson since in many cultures and advisors within these cultures tend to focus on the negative (Chapter 10). A follow-up to be explored by the advisor can then be how the positive features can be built on and further improved. (supportive interventions, Chapter 6). It is interesting that at this level most of the responses focus on individual aspects of teaching with only one response looking at the lesson from the learners' point of view. Again this area can be probed through follow-up questions by the advisor.
Question 4	What were you unhappy about?	This question aims to get teachers to reflect on parts of the lesson they were not pleased with. It is interesting that again there is a split between those teachers focusing on their own teaching techniques and those who view the lesson from the learners' point of view. Although at pre-service level it is questionable whether trainee teachers have sufficiently well developed criteria to self-evaluate their lessons, the trainee's perceptions are an obvious starting point for the advisor to work from. Further probing can take place to see what actions teachers might take to remedy the perceived defects in their lessons.

Question 5	What would you do differently next time?	The aim of this question is to help trainees think of positive actions they could take to improve on performance (devising new understanding, Chapter 4, action planning, Chapter 8)). With more able teachers it enables them to see how their perceptions of the lesson would feed in to future planning. Again if a teacher produces a very general response to this question, the advisor may have to guide the trainee teacher to parts of the lesson which might have been conducted in a different fashion.

Task 2.5 Being a catalyst

Aims: To reflect on the way that an advisor can comment on a lesson in order to lead a trainee to evaluate their lesson.
To discuss the possible ways in which the advisor can prompt the trainee into being self-critical.

Rationale: The purpose of the comments made by an advisor are not solely to point out to a trainee the things which are good or bad about the lesson, but to provide the trainee with the framework for being able to evaluate their own lesson and to become an independent reflective practitioner.

Procedure:
1. Ask the participants to look at the questions asked by a TP supervisor (*Photocopiable resource 8* on page 219).
2. Ask them to identify the issue which the supervisor wanted to discuss in each case.
3. Ask them to consider the following:
    • What steps did the advisor take to encourage the trainees to reflect?
    • To what extent do the questions encourage collaboration between the advisor and the trainee?
    • To what extent do the questions lead the trainee towards autonomy?
    • Could the questions be modified or improved in any way?
4. If appropriate, ask the participants to relate these to the concept of critical questioning (Chapter 9).

Notes for guidance: These questions were asked by a TP supervisor during feedback sessions to first year undergraduate students on their first block teaching practice experience.
   The aim of this exercise is to get participants to think about how they might comment on something which happens in a lesson. The point to extract from this is the way that theoretical issues such as the use of metalanguage (number 2), motivation and assessment (number 8) can be raised and discussed in the feedback session through the use of strategic questions which focus the teacher's attention on aspects of the lesson. Such questions are the 'probing'

questions suggested by Schön (see Chapter 2), or they can be described as 'catalytic' interventions (see Chapter 9). It is worth pointing out that the purpose of both types of intervention is to 'elicit self-discovery' and to discuss the degree to which the group feel that these questions do in fact do this effectively. However, the dangers of the questions becoming 'inquisitorial' (Chapter 9, effects of different question types) must also be borne in mind. Here are some possible interpretations of the interventions made by the advisor. The labels are not as important as the discussion of the possible intentions of the advisor and their likely effect on the trainee.

Question	Issue(s) discussed Comment	Intervention type(s) (see Chapters 5–9, especially 9)
It was a nice idea to dictate the definition of the leader article to the students but what was the language purpose of giving them the definition?	planning; the importance of having a language aim	positive, supportive comment + probing question to check on their understanding
You said they understood the explanation of the past perfect. Do the students have the structure in their own first language? Is there a difference between what the teacher should know and what the student should know?	use of metalanguage: student knowledge and teacher knowledge	simple echoing: progressive focusing. Advisor is 'leading' the trainer
You said you were not happy with the initial comprehension exercise. You asked the students 'Can you understand this passage?' What does that question tell you as the teacher?	text comprehension & questions	advisor following: direct question about T's behaviour
When you asked someone to read out the sentence, what happened? What could/should you have done? What was the consequence of moving on?	non-correction of student error	direct question about T's behaviour + encouraging T to analyse consequences (closed questioning)
Did you notice how they worked in pairs? Did some work individually? What do you feel about this?	classroom control	asking about the T's feelings (open questioning)
It seems you weren't sure what time to set them to do the task, is that right? Should you have been worried? What criteria are you going to use for deciding how long an activity should be, the clock or the student progress?	timing	advisor interprets T's actions (empathetic divining) and challenges T to devise rules

| How do you want the students to see you? As a guide, as an examiner, as a teacher, as a helper? During your monitoring of their group work, how will the following reinforce or conflict with the role you want them to see you as:
• Using a red pen to correct what they do?
• Squatting down to be at their eye level?
• Walking around the class looking over their shoulders?
• Only intervening if asked by a student?
• Asking them about their work? | Correction techniques | advisor asks T to establish general principle and then examines classroom behaviour in the light of these principles: logical marshalling |
| Can we think about the following questions about the comprehension passage: Do you want to test the students' comprehension or do you want to teach them to read? What is the difference between testing and teaching reading? What do you mean by 'read the passage silently'? How can you tell if it has been carried out effectively? | the purpose of a reading comprehension exercise | advisor proposing: logical marshalling through closed questions |

Task 3.1 Implementing the teaching practice cycle

Aim: To examine and evaluate the way that teaching practice and observation are organised in the contexts in which participants work and to evaluate this procedure.

Rationale: Many contexts are far from ideal in terms of physical resources available (e.g. a quiet place to talk to a teacher/trainee) and time available to talk things through properly. By examining their advisory contexts in the light of the functions TP is supposed to perform, participants may be able to take steps to improve the situation.

Procedure:
1. Ask the participants to make a list of the stages which are used in the teaching practice cycle in their current context.
2. Introduce participants to the functions and steps in the teaching practice cycle:

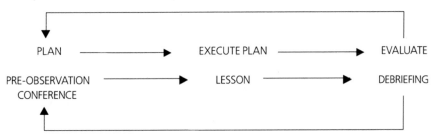

3. Ask them to compare their context with the ideal context. Ask them to concentrate on the way that the three 'functions' (i.e. planning, teaching and feedback) are carried out in their contexts and the role the advisor plays in helping to successfully achieve the aims of the teaching practice.
4. Ask the groups to make a list of the problems advisors face in carrying out the three principle functions and to provide suggestions as to how the situation might be improved.

Notes for guidance: One of the problems which can often be faced by advisor trainers is that the contexts in which trainee advisors are destined to work often make the implementation of the full teaching practice cycle highly problematic.

If this exercise is being carried out with experienced advisors, then it is likely that they will raise many problems about implementing the complete cycle. Sometimes these problems may be an excuse to reject any new innovations and to retain the present system.

However, many of the problems are real. It is important that the trainer listens to the problems that the advisors face and empathises with their situation. Some of the possible solutions to the problems are outlined in Chapter 3, but it is probable that experienced advisors have come up with their own solutions, and these solutions can be shared and discussed.

This exercise may also bring up 'structural/institutional' issues and reference may be made to the case studies presented in Task 1.2.

However, it is unlikely that advisors will have the power to change the macro system which is used, and therefore it is better to concentrate the discussion on features which the advisor can change, e.g. location, making sure that feedback looks forward to the next session as well as backwards to the one taught, using written feedback, etc. (For issues to do with creating a relaxed and productive feedback session, see Chapter 3 and Chapter 7, dealing with anxiety.)

Task 3.2 The roles of the advisor and the teaching cycle

Aim: To examine the role of the advisor at the various stages of the teaching cycle.

Rationale: An advisor may need to play a number of different roles at the various stages of the teaching cycle. Identifying these will help to raise awareness of the roles involved and could be used for further individual work on the particular skill areas advisors would like to develop.

Procedure:
1. Ask participants individually to look at the roles (*Photocopiable resource 9* on page 220) and to decide how important the roles are in their context.
2. Ask participants to compare their ratings with those of a colleague.
3. Then compare these roles with the pedagogic functions of the advisor in Chapter 3.

4. If appropriate, get participants to decide which of the areas they would most like to work on for their own personal development.

Notes for guidance: This is a very wide-ranging activity and brings up a whole range of issues which are discussed in different parts of the book. It can be usefully used as a spring board for the introduction of a series of issues. It can also be used as an 'inventory' to enable teachers to think about the particular skills/competencies which they need to develop as advisors.

In Chapter 3 a number of pedagogic functions of the advisor at different stages of the teaching cycle are discussed. Chapter 1 also gives a number of functions of a mentor. The literature in this area has identified a further number of roles in the affective and organisational domains and these are listed on the photocopiable resource. These will inevitably vary according to context as well as the stage of the teaching cycle.

The following points can be made about the roles identified and the place in the TP cycle where they are likely to occur:

(P = Pre-lesson conference, L = Lesson, F = Post-lesson feedback/lesson debriefing)

Role no.	Comments	Stage
1	This role is very important in the mentorship context (see Chapter 1).	F
2	Although not a strictly pedagogic function, this role is important in the adaptation of the specific contexts to make sure all the functions of TP are met (see Task 3.1 & Chapter 3).	F, L, P
3	Again, this relates to the mentor contexts. It also relates to the personal, professional dimensions discussed in Chapter 1 and to the 'stance' taken by the advisor (cf the coach, Chapter 2).	F
4	See the discussion in Chapter 3 on lesson observation. The observer role is also discussed in Chapter 4.	L
5	See comments in Chapter 3, but also the place of listening in the teaching cycle (Chapters 4 & 6).	F
6	See Chapter 4 on helping and 6 (supportive interventions) for the importance of being supportive.	F, P
7	See Chapter 3 on the collection of data for a discussion of the role of the advisor in bringing information to the feedback session. See also Chapter 8 for a discussion of informative interventions.	F, P
8	See Chapter 7 for a discussion of managing conflict. It is also an important institutional role as a manager of TP in schools (see Chapter 1 on institutional roles).	F
9	This is perhaps an all-pervasive function and could be related to any part of the teaching cycle.	F, L, P
10	This is a vital part of any feedback process. See Chapter 4.	F (P)
11	This is probably most closely related to a mentorship context (Chapter 1).	
12	This is an important function as outlined in Chapter 3. See particularly the discussion about Experiential Learning, Vygotsky and the integration of theory into practice.	F

Task 3.3 Observation scenarios

Aim: To look at difficulties which may arise at the various stages of the teaching cycle and identify strategies for dealing with these.

Rationale: There are a number of difficulties which can arise during observation which are less to do with personality but more to do with the conduct of the observation. Below are three situations which we have experienced. Other similar case studies could be made up dealing with typical problems experienced in a particular advisory context.

Procedure: Ask participants in groups to look at the case studies (*Photocopiable resource 10* on page 221) and to discuss their responses to each scenario.

Notes for guidance: This is a wide-ranging activity. Whilst it raises some of the issues about the teaching practice cycle and particularly the pre-observation conference and planning (see Chapter 3), it also raises a lot of issues about the relationship which may be created between the advisor and the teacher (see Chapter 4).

This activity can be extended by using other similar scenarios more closely related to the context in which the participants are working. The following are points to consider when discussing each scenario. They are not offered as 'ideal' solutions:

The new lesson plan

It is very easy as an advisor to take over the planning of a lesson so that the lesson is yours rather than the teacher's. In this sense, John has ownership of the lesson he has planned. The fact that he has spent so long on it should also be borne in mind. Perhaps John should teach his new lesson, but hold some activities from his old lesson in reserve in case he has insufficient material.

The 'safe' teacher

Observation can be a stressful experience, so much so that some teachers will only want to be visited during safe lessons with safe classes. One way of building up trust is to ask the teacher to choose the areas the observer will comment on. It has been claimed that whereas teachers might initially focus on safe areas, as confidence in the advisor grows, they will ask for feedback on issues of real concern to them. However, it may be that some teachers will be unwilling to expose their perceived weaknesses in this way. In this case, the advisor should initially focus on the areas requested by the teacher, but other targets should be negotiated as part of an ongoing process for future lessons.

Do I interfere?

This issue is one of the 'chestnuts' of advising. It is often an issue which is brought up by inspectors and in general, most commentators would suggest that it is wrong to intervene. However, this is another area in which there is no one right answer. By interfering it is easy for the class to lose confidence in the teacher and for the teacher to lose confidence in herself. On the other hand, it has been suggested that it is appropriate with beginning teachers to adopt a 'driving lesson' approach to teaching practice. Just as a driving instructor would not allow their pupil to crash the car, if advisors can see that the trainee is heading for disaster, then they should intervene. In the example above, a team-teaching approach might work with the class teacher taking on a minor role, such as monitoring and helping those students who are in difficulties.

The fatal mistake

This is an additional scenario relating to intervention vs. non-intervention in a lesson, included because an informal survey seemed to suggest that it is when teachers teach wrong language to their students that inspectors feel most tempted to intervene. In fact, this scenario was given to us by an inspector from the Middle East. A number of imaginative ways of dealing with this were suggested including holding up a flashcard to alert the teacher to his mistake and turning the board work into a correct the mistake activity. The effect of intervention on the self-confidence of the teacher is probably more harmful than letting a mistake go by.

Task 3.4 'Objective' observations

Aim: To explore the effect of the observation instrument on the impression gained of a lesson.
To evaluate the use and usefulness of various observation instruments.

Rationale: The type of observation instrument used will inevitably have an effect on perceptions of a lesson. The extent to which an observation instrument can be truly objective is doubtful. It is interesting to note that even with supposedly objective low-inference forms, results between observers can vary.

Procedure:
1. Put the observers into three groups A, B and C, and give each group an observation form. If you wish, you can use the observation forms provided (*Photocopiable resource 11* on pages 222–225) or take forms from Wajnryb (1992) or Malamah-Thomas (1987).
2. In groups, evaluate the forms against the following criteria:
   Ease of use
   How easy or difficult do you think the form would be to use as you are watching a lesson?
   Subjectivity
   Is the form subjective or objective? Does it involve the observer in making value judgments about the lesson at the same time as observing?
   Usefulness
   What information would this form give you?
   How useful would the information be to a teacher?

Would the teacher be likely to accept this information, i.e. does the form have face validity?

In what context might you use this form?

High inference vs low inference

Does the form require you to infer information?

This information can then be shared, either through discussion or through being included on a poster.

3. Choose a video extract of a lesson and rearrange the group so that nobody is sitting next to somebody with the same form.
4. After watching the video, put the participants into groups containing one A, one B and one C and ask them to compare the overall picture of the lesson they got.
5. Discuss with the whole group the way that the instruments affected the way they viewed the lesson.

Notes for guidance: This activity is a useful one to explore issues involved in observation.

Make sure that the instrument chosen is possible to operate with the video extract. Some information (e.g. pupil reactions) are difficult to see on most videos. A good source of classroom extracts is Bampfield (1997).

If observation instruments are chosen carefully (e.g. one which concentrates on pupils, one which concentrates on the teacher and one which is a checklist) a number of issues can be explored. Among them are:

The value of a competency-based checklist approach (see Chapter 2 & Tasks 2.3 and 8.4). Do such forms provide a valid picture of the lesson?

The way that instruments extract different data from the lesson (e.g. the teacher or the student; correction or teacher talking time?) (See discussion in Chapters 2 & 3 on the way that trainers and teachers view lessons).

How do high inference and low inference forms compare? For example, a question such as 'Are the students motivated?' requires you to infer levels of motivation from student behaviour and as such falls within the high inference category. A question such as 'How many times does the student put up his hand?' requires simple counting and is therefore low inference.

How do different observers use the same forms? Is there such a thing as 'objective' evidence? (See Chapter 4 for a discussion of objectivity vs subjectivity in observing.)

Task 3.5 Designing observation forms

Aim: To design observation forms which can be used to bring data about classroom practice to the feedback session.

Rationale: Teachers are often unaware of their current practices and often need evidence of what they are currently doing before they can move on. Classroom observation forms that concentrate on collecting data rather than evaluating performance are one way of doing this.

Procedure:
1. Put the participants into groups and either:
2. Use the three situations (*Photocopiable resource 12*, page 226), giving each group one situation.

or

2. Ask the participants to think of their own teaching and design an instrument to collect data on the way they teach a particular area.
3. Having designed the instruments, mix the participants so they can share the instrument they have designed with the rest of the group.
4. A good extension for this exercise, for in-service programmes, is to ask the participants to get a colleague or critical friend to use the instrument on one of their lessons.

Notes for guidance: This exercise is useful, both for a discussion of the importance of having a purpose for observation (see Chapter 4 and Task 4.4), and to raise consciousness about the use of such instruments for teachers to use as part of an action plan following the feedback session (Chapter 8, providing action plans).

There are many books offering suggestions of instruments which can be used to gather data on different areas. Perhaps the most user-friendly is Wajnryb (1992). An adaptation of this task would be to allow the participants to select instruments from Wajnryb or Malamah-Thomas (1987) to fulfil the functions required by the task.

Some suggestions of instruments to fulfil the requirements of the situations:

Teacher A

A map of the class on which the number of responses are charted is the obvious way of doing this. The movement of the teacher around the class can also be included. Many books contain examples of such instruments (e.g. Wajnryb 106–109).

Teacher B

The form below would make teachers aware of the fact that they overuse one particular technique when nominating students to answer a particular question, as well as alerting them to the fact that there are a number of other strategies which could be used which might improve levels of participation.

Nomination Strategies
Make a note of every time the teacher uses each nomination strategy.

Strategy	Frequency	Total
Teacher names or identifies student and then asks question		
Teacher asks question, then names or identifies student		
Teacher asks question, then selects one of the students who offers to answer		
Teacher asks question then anybody answers		
Teacher asks question then asks for chorus response		
Some other nomination strategy is used		

Teacher C

As with the previous chart, a simple record of the errors made by the student and the responses made by the teacher is a good way to approach this. For an example, see Wajnryb 1992, 103–104.

Task 3.6 What's important?

Aim: To look at the way in which advisors take observation notes.

Rationale: One of the most common observation instruments is the blank sheet of paper. This does not however mean that the observer has no criteria in mind, merely that these are internalised. In the end, the areas the advisor chooses to focus on are based on subjective judgments.

Procedure:

1. Explain that the lesson notes (*Photocopiable resource 14* on page 228) were made by an experienced observer to give them an overall picture of the lesson. The information was later transferred to a form. The purpose of these notes was an aide-memoire to the observers. The notes were not shown to the trainees.

2. Ask participants to look at the lesson observation notes, and for each one, note:

   What aspects of teacher performance were commented on in the areas of personality, planning, classroom management, language awareness and teaching techniques?

   Were the comments evaluative in either a positive or negative sense, or merely descriptive?

   The table (*Photocopiable resource 13* on page 227) could be useful for participants to use.

3. What does this tell you about the criteria the observer had in mind?

4. Consider the language which is used by the observer to signal the negative

points of the lesson. What does this tell you about the observer and his agenda?
5. How do these notes compare to those you make when observing teachers?
6. Transfer the information contained in these notes to a sheet which could be given to the teacher.

Notes for guidance: As discussed in Chapter 3, one of the functions of the advisor in watching a lesson is to bring evidence to the feedback session for discussion with the teacher. The observer makes notes on the lesson using a time framework to chronicle what is happening.

However, the actual notes are far from 'objective'. Most notes start with an evaluation (good to . . ., or problem with . . .). This clearly shows that the advisor is basically evaluating the performance. Does this reveal the institutional role of the advisor (Chapter 1)?

Note the use of questions – showing the advisor's isolation of issues to be raised in the feedback session and the approach which will be used. Are these questions useful to 'scaffold' learning (Chapter 3) or to act as a catalyst (Chapter 9 and Task 2.5)?

In discussing the way that the participants provide written feedback to the teacher, reference could be made to Tasks 8.2 and 8.3.

Task 3.7 Scaffolding learning

Aim: To examine an extract from a feedback session to see how an advisor engages in a dialogue with a trainee to raise new awareness.

Rationale: The concept of scaffolding learning is a very powerful one and it is important that advisors think about how this can be operationalised in a feedback discussion.

Procedure:
1. Ask the participants to look at the extract from a pre-service feedback session (*Photocopiable resource 15* on pages 229–230). The student teacher was at the end of her first year on a BEd programme.
2. Ask them to consider the following questions:
   What are the two issues ('deep structures') that the advisor is trying to discuss?
   What are the conclusions he wants the student to make?
   How does the supervisor 'scaffold' the knowledge of the trainee?
   How do the questions help the trainee to arrive at the understanding the advisor wants?
   To what extent is there a dialogue happening here?
   Would it have been more efficient to just tell the trainee what to do? (Would the deep structures have been revealed?)
   Are there any alternative ways this could have been approached?
3. Following the discussion of their answers, ask them to look at the two

situations in the boxes and, in pairs, choose one of the situations and write down prompting questions which could be used to scaffold understanding of the issues indicated. The pairs may like to then role play this and discuss the effectiveness of the questions.

Notes for guidance: This is a useful exercise to get the participants to look at actual data of a feedback session. It raises a whole host of issues. In many ways, it is similar to Task 2.5, except that in this extract both the questions and the replies can be seen. As well as allowing discussion on scaffolding, it raises other issues such as the interventions used (see Chapter 9 on catalytic interventions and scaffolding) and the style of supervision (see Chapter 4 for a discussion of directive versus non-directive styles).

One important point to make about scaffolding is that it is dialogic in nature and thus the participants should be engaged in a discussion about the issues. This extract is heavily dominated by the advisor, but by getting the trainee to describe and explain what she was doing, the advisor is able to relate the general theoretical points to her actual classroom experience.

Points to consider:

Lines

1–24 The issue is that demonstration is a better way to explain an activity than giving instructions.

Note that this was based on something which the teacher did well, but the advisor uses this to explore the deep reasons for this rather than just praising the surface behaviours.

11–16 Note the way that the advisor brings his observation of the lesson procedure to start the discussion. The trainee was not aware of the actual procedures she had followed, but the advisor was able to bring the data of what happened to the discussion.

25–45 The issue here is concerned with the principles involved in monitoring groups – the criteria used for selecting which group should be visited first.

Note that in this case the teacher probably did the 'right' thing, i.e. going to the weakest group first, but for the 'wrong' reason – the natural right-to-left spatial organisation of Islam.

In this case there is perhaps more of a genuine dialogue taking place between the trainee and the advisor as the reason for the selection was rather surprising.

The reasons for actions are more important than the surface features.

Task 4.1 Personal constructs of feedback roles

Aim: To explore personal feelings regarding different ways of intervening
            in sessions by looking at extracts from feedback sessions.

Rationale: By examining different extracts and by separating the extracts into
            different constructs we can see what elements of the interactions are
            most important. By comparing this with others we can be aware of
            different views of the same event.

Procedure: Divide the participants into groups of four to six.
1. Cut up the extracts (*Photocopiable resource 16* on pages 231–232) and give
    one complete set of extracts to each member of the group.
2. Explain to the groups that you are going to call out three letters and you
    want each person to select the three extracts which you have called out.
3. Then ask each participant to *individually* select two of the situations which
    they feel have something in common. This will leave one extract which is
    different in some way.
4. When they have done this, get them in groups to discuss their selection and
    to say why they have selected the two situations in the way that they have.
    Get them to compare their selections.
5. Then read out another three letters at random, get the participants to select
    another three extracts and repeat the procedure in 3 and 4.
6. Continue with this until all the extracts have been selected and compared,
    or until you judge that no new ideas are emerging from the discussions. The
    following letter sequences will allow for the extracts to be mixed and
    discussed in different combinations:
    ACG
    BDE
    ABF
    BCF
    CDG
    ADE
7. Discuss the common elements found with the whole group.

Notes for guidance: The technique used in this exercise is known as 'triadic
sorting' and is one of the essential techniques used in the elicitation of personal
constructs using 'Repertory Grids' (for those interested in following this up, see
Kelly 1955 and Pope and Keen 1981).
    This exercise can be used to sensitise participants to different ways of
intervening in feedback sessions and to probe their own feelings about different
feedback styles.
    By allowing them to decide on their own 'constructs' they can see what they
think is important in each exchange and how this compares to the views of
others.
    Although there will be differences of views (implicit in the Personal
Construct Theory approach) there is also likely to be a degree of agreement

about what is going on in each exchange, although people's *attitude* to what is happening will be different. Thus, one of the constructs which should emerge is that of the Directive / Non-directive / Alternatives approaches to feedback (see Chapter 4).

There are also a number of other interventions used by the advisors, and these extracts can also be used to further explore these:

A	Directive/Alternative. Offering an alternative (Chapter 4)
B	Non-directive / Empathetic divining (Chapters 4/9)
C	Non-directive /Following (Chapters 4/9), Disclosure (Chapter 8), Owning the feedback (Chapter 8)
D	Directive. Confronting, Holding up a mirror (Chapters 4/8)
E	Directive/Supportive interventions (Chapters 4/6), Disclosure (Chapter 8)
F	Directive/Commanding prescription (Chapters 4/5)
G	Directive/Action Research (Chapters 4/5)

As well as using the extracts for triadic sorting, the elements have also been used by groups to 'rank' the different interventions from those which they think are most effective to those which they think are least effective. Again, this allows for discussion on the extent to which advisors 'direct' the feedback or leave it open for the trainee to set the agenda.

Task 4.2 **Effective advice**

Aim: To elicit the general factors which affect the giving and receiving of advice.
            To get participants to reflect on factors which contribute to the success of the advice-giving process.

Rationale: Although participants may not have studied counselling, they have a lot of built-in intuitions about what constitutes good advice and how to give it. By making use of this experience of giving and receiving advice, it is possible to pull out the factors which are important in any advisory situation.

Procedure:
1. Ask participants to think of one situation in which they either received or gave advice successfully, and to think of one situation in which they either received or gave advice which they considered was not successful.
2. Ask them to describe their situations to a partner. Tell them to be as concrete as possible about the situation and try not to make generalisations.
3. Once both partners have described their successful and unsuccessful advice

situations, ask the pairs to think of reasons why the situations were either successful or unsuccessful.

4. When the pairs have finished, elicit from the group the factors which they feel affect the giving and receiving of advice. It might be worth gathering together the factors under the following headings:

The people involved	The setting	The topic / type of advice	The relationship between the advisor and the advisee

Notes for guidance:

1. When asking the participants to describe the two situations it is important that they describe the situations in detail and try to be as specific as possible. Emphasise that the situations do not need to be restricted to teaching. In fact, for the purposes of the exercise, try to get them *not* to think about their professional situation. The general procedure is that used for describing Critical incidents (Brookfield 1995 and Chapter 9). It may also be worth using the 'present tense account' (Heron 1990 & Chapter 9).

2. This exercise can produce a lot of different advice situations, from the simple offering of information through to the discussion of emotional and personal problems. It might be worth using Heron's concepts of Agenda types (Heron 1990 and Chapter 5).

3. The factors which make advice effective will vary from person to person, but there are usually important areas which are shared by effective advice and are not present in ineffective advice. Whilst the detailed accounts are important for the advisors to make the situations real, the purpose of the discussion is to pull out from these specific incidents general principles concerning advice. Again, the critical questioning suggested by Brookfield (Chapter 9) can be useful here.

Some of the points which often come up and are worth emphasising:

Effective advice	Ineffective advice
led to a solution	wasn't taken up
was specific	had no particular action involved
was 'owned' by the receiver	was 'imposed' from the advisor
was given by a person who was trusted	was offered by someone who wasn't trusted
was given by a person who had more knowledge of the situation	was given by a person who didn't have any real knowledge of the situation

Task 4.3 Exam cheat role play

Aim: To examine the verbal and non-verbal behaviour which contributes to and detracts from successful advice-giving.

Rationale: This activity also looks at advice-giving outside the context of teaching. The situation is one which transfers easily to any culture. The role play helps to highlight personal reactions to common features of any advice-giving situation. The debriefing can provide a wide range of points for discussion.

Procedure:

Role Play:

1. Choose five individuals to play the parts in the role play and take them outside the room. The remaining members of the group are the observers.
2. Give out the role cards (*Photocopiable resource 17* on page 233) to the five participants, instructing them not to show them to each other.
3. Give out the observation form (*Photocopiable resource 18* on page 234) to the observers and make sure all parts of it are understood.
4. Call the medical student (Decision Maker) and flatmate into the room – let the medical student explain the problem and allow the role play to continue for about 3–5 minutes. Do not allow any feedback after this stage but repeat the role plays with the president of the students' union, the tutor and the doctor. As the advice-givers finish they can join the group of observers.

Debriefing:

5. Ask the student how they felt about the advice given and which advice they would take. Was any advice felt to be particularly helpful or unhelpful?
6. Ask the observers for feedback on the behaviours they observed.
7. Cross-reference behaviours with feelings.

Notes for guidance: This can be a very interesting role play. The reactions of the different characters will differ according to the interpretations of the different advisors playing them. There may also be cultural differences in both reactions to the situation itself (some cultures may not view the cheating situation in the same light as in the West) and in the way that advice is given (especially factors such as body posture etc.). However, it is surprising how often the doctor, when realising that there is nothing physically wrong with the student, reacts by saying something like 'Well, why have you come to see me then?' – it seems that the stereotypical lack of attention to people as individuals which characterises doctors is quite universal!

 However, the characters are designed to elicit certain types of feedback which may or may not emerge during the role play:

the flatmate As a friend we might expect more empathy with the decision maker. There may be more emotional help given and maybe there will be more listening involved. This may be indicated by more nodding and back-channelling, although this is by no means the preserve of the flatmate. There may also be more relaxed body

the S.U.
President

language and closer proximity in this situation (see Chapter 6 and Task 6.1 on non-verbal communication and body language). The relationship between the President and the decision maker is more 'official'. We might expect the President to provide more 'information' than the flatmate or the doctor (informative interventions, Chapter 8). The President can help by providing the information needed by the decision maker to make the decision.

the tutor

As a person of higher status and experience, this person may well offer more solutions and be more 'authoritative' (see Chapter 5) in the way advice is given.

the doctor

Apart from the observations made above about doctors, this character is likely to take a more moralistic stance to the issue and thus we might expect more 'prescriptive' advice (Chapter 8) from the doctor.

Although the role play is designed to produce different styles of advising, it is important to work with the situation as produced and experienced by the advisors. The examination of the feelings of the decision maker towards the different styles used by the advisors is a very important phase.

It is worth examining in detail the micro-skills of creating empathy, active listening and active attending (see Chapter 6) and the specific 'interventions' which foster them (see also the 'catalytic tool kit', Chapter 9).

It can also be a forum for discussing the macro-strategies of the three-stage model of helping (Chapter 4).

The different role play situations will also produce different examples of non-verbal communication (Chapter 6), which can be further explored through Task 6.1.

Task 4.4 Role play

Aim: To examine the conduct of the pre-lesson discussion through role play.

Rationale: A pre-lesson discussion, if properly conducted, can facilitate shared understandings of both the purpose of observation and the conduct and content of a lesson; it is important to allow participants to 'try out' different techniques for creating the right atmosphere in a pre-lesson discussion.

Procedure:
1. This activity is designed for groups of three: the advisor, the teacher and an observer.
2. Give out the cards (*Photocopiable resource 19* on page 235) and allow participants 5 minutes or so to prepare themselves.
3. Allow 10–15 minutes for the role play.
4. Ask the participants to 'debrief' each other in their groups by discussing the following questions:

Advisors:

What difficulties did you encounter?

Were you able to get all the information you needed?

Teachers:

How did you feel?

Did you feel reassured about the presence of the advisor in your lesson?

Observers:

Are any generalisations possible with regard to:

- the types of questions which are the most / least productive in terms of the response they elicit?
- the effect on the teacher of body language and posture etc.?

5. Feedback from the groups in plenary.

Notes for guidance: In these role plays it is important for the participants to explore their feelings and reactions to the situation. They should therefore be able to discuss situations in a non-judgmental manner and to give honest feedback to one another without letting the situation deteriorate. Thus, in some ways step 4 is as important as the actual role play itself.

One of the problems with such a role play is creating a situation which is real to both the advisor and the teacher. It might be an idea for you to produce an actual lesson plan for the teacher to work from. This can be especially useful in situations where there is a standard coursebook with a detailed teacher's book to which most teachers adhere.

The discussion of the role of the advisor in this stage of the lesson is given in Chapters 4 & 6 and it might be worth discussing the sort of questions which lead to a genuine sense of interest and attention rather than any idea of challenge or confrontation (see Chapter 9 for a discussion of different types of question).

It is also worth considering the non-verbal communication which is associated with anxiety and how anxiety can be dealt with (see Chapter 6).

Task 4.5 Crossed/uncrossed

Aim: To establish the importance of having a shared understanding of the criteria by which a lesson is being evaluated.

To explore feelings relating to judgmental feedback.

To demonstrate the importance of focused observation.

Rationale: Through the use of a parlour game the following points can be established and emphasised:

- it is not necessarily helpful to be told that you are doing things well or getting things right if you do not know why
- it is very frustrating to be told to look carefully without knowing what you are looking for
- the emotional effects of negative feedback and different reactions to it

Procedure: This activity is based on a party game where a pair of scissors is passed round a circle of players. The players have to pass the scissors round from one to another saying 'I received the scissors crossed/uncrossed and I pass them on crossed/uncrossed' as they pass them on to the next person in the circle. The aim of the game is for the participants to learn the 'rule' about when the scissors are crossed or uncrossed and then to act correctly. Most people assume that it is the position of the scissors which determines whether crossed or uncrossed is the correct response. In fact, it is whether the person who is passing the scissors on is sitting with their legs crossed or uncrossed.

1. Seat the participants in a circle. The game works well with up to 10 players. If you have more than 10 in your group, it is a good idea to use the 'goldfish bowl' technique with some playing the game and others watching and taking notes – this can nicely increase the tension and will perhaps allow more to come from the debriefing.
2. Tell the participants that this is a game and that you want to test their powers of observation, so they must watch everything you do very carefully.
3. Begin the game by demonstrating what you want. Receive the scissors from the person to your left saying either 'I am receiving the scissors crossed' or 'uncrossed' (depending on the way you are sitting), perform some kind of action with the scissors e.g. open or close them, turn them over several times etc. and pass them on to the person on your right saying 'and I pass them on' either 'crossed' or 'uncrossed', again depending on how you are sitting.
4. Wait for the next person to pass the scissors on and give them feedback on whether the response was correct. Be lavish in your praise if they were right e.g. 'Good. Well done! That was really excellent!' and fairly cool if they got it wrong.
5. Continue passing the scissors round the circle four or five times. By this time some of the participants should have worked out the rule, and others will begin to show a high degree of frustration.
6. Stop the game and facilitate reflection on the activity using the following questions:
   - How did you feel?
   - Did being told you were doing things right help you to produce the right response?
   - Did being told you were doing things wrong help you to produce the right response?
   - Did being told you were doing things wrong help you to produce the wrong response?
   - What application does this activity have for teaching practice and feedback?

Notes for guidance: This is a very powerful game and it can be great fun, although it can also lead to a high degree of tension – especially when more 'senior' members of the group are still in the dark and other 'juniors' have worked out the system and are laughing at those still struggling. In most cultures this embarrassment is released as laughter (a cathartic reaction – see Chapter 7), but reactions can vary immensely both between cultures and depending on the composition of the group.

Thus, the facilitator needs to be sensitive to these emotions and the debriefing plenary needs to be handled very carefully and should not be rushed.

Typical responses to how they feel are uncertain, insecure, annoyed, feeling that others were 'cleverer' than they were.

Participants often report that being told they are doing things right without knowing how or why actually exacerbates feelings of insecurity and uncertainty.

At the end it is usually agreed that:

- there is little point in observing carefully without knowing what you are looking for (see Chapter 4 on observation).
- it is important that the rules – the evaluation criteria – are made clear and are shared by all concerned (see Chapter 3 & the role of the pre-lesson discussion).
- it is not enough to be told you are doing well without being told specifically what it is that is good and why it is good.
- it is not enough to be told that you are doing something badly without being given an indication of how you might put it right.

Task 5.1 Facilitative or authoritative?

Aims: To look at a transcript of a feedback session and to examine the way that a mentor provides advice to a novice teacher.

Rationale: By examining the actual interventions made by a mentor it is possible to see the range of options which are available to the advisor. In particular, by looking at the large number of authoritative interventions and their different manifestations it is possible to have a balanced view of the term 'authoritative' and to see that they can be very useful interventions.

Procedure:
1. Ask the participants to look at the feedback transcript (*Photocopiable resource 20*[1] on pages 236–238). Ideally, as this is a long transcript, ask the participants to read the transcript before the session. Ask them to think about:
   - the areas where the student is having difficulties
   - the general 'tenor' of the feedback session
2. After they have read the transcript, put them into pairs to decide on the type of intervention made by the mentor. Ask them

---

[1] This data (although not the interpretation) was collected by Richard Wallace and formed part of his MA(Ed) dissertation 'Interaction Styles and Mentoring', University College Chichester, 1998.

- to categorise each intervention as either authoritative or facilitative
- to try to decide which type of authoritative or facilitative intervention each is

3. Bring the participants together to discuss what they have found.

Notes for guidance:

1. Point out that this is the second session for a novice teacher with this mentor, although this is her second 'block' of teaching practice. She has had a previous 'block' of some ten weeks before this. The class she is teaching is the mentor's normal class, thus comments about last Christmas refer to work the mentor has done with the class when the student was not present. It is a mixed ability class in a government secondary school with about 25 students. 'Differentiation' (23 & 24) refers to designing lessons to cater for a range of different abilities.
2. The student clearly seems to be having problems with discipline (especially one boy, Ashley), and with other classroom management problems such as homework collection (not unusual for a novice teacher – see Chapter 2).
3. The student is generally not very happy about the way that the class went and is somewhat lacking in confidence. Note the way that the discipline problems made it difficult for her to 'teach' and she 'lost direction' (4). This is again what one would expect from a novice teacher (Chapter 2).
4. During most of the feedback session the mentor is offering fairly prescriptive advice, although these prescriptions and directions are generally 'benevolent' (Chapter 5) and follow sections where he is being catalytic (Chapter 9) and probing the student to reflect on the lesson. However, these catalytic interventions are generally 'leading' (Chapter 9). Note the way that the mentor finishes with an action plan (Chapter 8) for the student to work on (39/41).
5. This is quite a long transcript and it may not be possible (or desirable) to go through it all in the plenary discussion, but there are a number of points which can be extracted from it. Perhaps the most important to discuss is that although the mentor's 'style' is quite authoritative, the overall tenor of the session is reasonably consultative and the student commented after her TP that she often valued the direct advice being offered by the mentor.
6. What follows is a *possible* interpretation of the feedback session. You will need to point out that a lot of the interpretation will depend on the way that things are said, and it is a good idea to ask the teachers when they are working in pairs to 'act out' sections to try to arrive at an interpretation of what was happening.

			Intervention Type
1.	M	//So how do you think things went?//	F: CATALYTIC (Leading)
2.	S	PAUSE (student puts hands to face in mock despair)	
3.	M	//Well, were you happy with the way things progressed . . . generally.//	F: CATALYTIC (Cathartic)
4.	S	Err. . . well I find that last group quite difficult to handle and like when Ashley decided to play up,	

I somehow lost the direction of the lesson and
became worried that he was going to start up again.

5. M //He is a difficult pupil who is obviously aware of
your status as a trainee.//
We will need to look at strategies for coping with
that . . . maybe later.//
But firstly, the lesson as a whole . . . tell me the
good points and . . . bits you feel you need to
work on.//

> A: INFORMATIVE
> (personal
> interpretation)
> A: PRESCRIPTIVE
> (benevolent
> prescription)
> F: CATALYTIC
> (proposing)

6. S Err . . . discipline. I don't think that they respect
me. Some do. They work really well but I tend to
focus all my teaching on them, I know I shouldn't,
but all I get from the boys is like sarcastic
comments and a load of lip.

7. M //You must be careful not to generalise.//
There are some hard working boys in the group//...
and you could be ignoring them because of this
kind of sweeping categorisation.//
What about the good points, let's focus on them
first?//

> A: PRESCRIPTIVE
> A: INFORMATIVE
> A: INFORMATIVE
> (personal
> interpretation)
> F: CATALYTIC
> (leading)

8. S Some of the homework I got in from them last
week was quite good. I've given some of them
merits and asked them to make copies on paper,
so that we can make a board display.

9. M //Good.//

> F: SUPPORTIVE
> (valuing)

They would like to do something like that.//
We did a huge collage for last Christmas, with all
the different areas of France and Germany on it.//
They loved doing it and genuinely felt proud of
the product.//
Good.//

> A: INFORMATIVE
> A: INFORMATIVE
> A: INFORMATIVE
>
> F: SUPPORTIVE

10. S Some haven't given me homework now for two
weeks. What do I need to do with those?

11. M //Have you confronted them about this?//

> A: PRESCRIPTIVE
> (consultative)

12. S Yes. I think that may have been the start of
Ashley's tantrum.

13. M //Well, maybe after the lesson would be best to
speak to him.//
//He loves an audience,//
so beware of challenging him in front of
the group.//

> A: PRESCRIPTIVE
> (benevolent)
> A: INFORMATIVE
>
> A: PRESCRIPTIVE

14. S OK. So do you think I should speak to him at the
end of the lesson or in tutor time or something.

15. M //Yes.// It is less confrontational and he'll probably listen if he is on his own.//

A: INFORMATIVE (personal interpretation)

16. S And what about the others? I am still missing . . . err . . . six pieces of work.

17. M //I bet I could guess the names too.// Let me look at your register.// Yes. I will speak to these boys and warn them that the work needs to be handed to you by the next lesson or they can have an after-school detention. Can you jot those down on a piece of paper for me?//

A: PRESCRIPTIVE (commanding)

18. S Yes. Thank you. I'll speak to Ashley tomorrow as well.

19. M Hmmm . . . //I think I'll catch up with him too on this occasion. It may seem a bit unfair otherwise.// You know, like you singled him out.//

A: INFORMATIVE

20. S I would like to be there though so that they don't think I am unaware of the chat you are going to have with them.

21. M Yes. //Any other point about the lesson that you feel needs discussing.// What about the timing for instance?//

F: CATALYTIC (leading/proposing)

22. S It started off OK, but then when I set them the shopping list task I don't think I really gave them enough time to complete the answers, which meant that half the group couldn't understand the next task which I wrote on the board.

23. M //I agree. Things went a bit too quickly after the vocabulary opening.// You could have differentiated the shopping list to enable those who can work quicker to complete the work and continue with the task that you wrote on the board. It would have also meant the slower individuals in the group could have been given more attention and help in completing what was set.//

A: INFORMATIVE (personal interpretation / negative feedback)

A: PRESCRIPTIVE (benevolent)

24. S Yes. The differentiation in the lesson worked well for the girl groups, who were working well. They are quite talented and the two girls at the front completed all the questions and the question boxes in the textbook. That detail of lesson planning really worked well for them. That made me really pleased. Although I feel they are the sort of pupils who would complete any task well.

25. M //I think some of the group were more on task than last week, certainly.//

A: INFORMATIVE (personal interpretation)

26. S It didn't feel like that. It was like I was teaching two groups in one class. Most of my attention was

directed at the disruptive lot at the back. I didn't
feel that I was 'teaching'. . . not getting the
opportunity to.

27. M //Well, you need to think about ways not only to   A: PRESCRIPTIVE
impose sanctions upon them but also ways in   (directive)
which you can create opportunities to praise them.//

28. S I did say to them that they did really well in the
quiz last week and that I hoped they would behave
themselves well enough in order for us to play the
game again. But by the end of the lesson, there was
no way I was going to allow that to happen.

29. M //Retrospectively, do you think that was the best   F: CATALYTIC
way to end the lesson?//   (leading)

30. S I didn't feel I had much choice. I had warned them
last week that if their behaviour wasn't acceptable,
we wouldn't play the game. And their behaviour
was anything but acceptable!

31. M //Not all of them though.// You finished the lesson   A: INFORMATIVE
by sitting them all in silence.//   (feedback)

32. S Yes. I was concerned about letting them out to
the next class in the silly mood they were in.
Particularly as the other student has them next!

33. M //But it was a punishment for the good ones in   A: INFORMATIVE
the group as well as the naughty ones.//   (personal
                                                        interpretation)

34. S But it seems that there are just so many of them.
If I played the game with the good ones it would
end up with only four or five playing it! And I
wouldn't know what to do with the naughty ones
whilst I was playing with the others.

35. M ///I think it would be more than that.//   A: INFORMATIVE
Again you must be observant to the whole group   (personal
and not be too black and white in your   interpretation)
judgments.// If the ringleaders are isolated, the   A: PRESCRIPTIVE
rest of the group could be warned about the   (directive,
actions you will take.// Then introduce the games   benevolent)
even to a reduced number at the end of the lesson.
They will soon learn to respond to the threat of no
games, if it is approached more subtly.// Use
rewards too. Merits or even a chocolate prize for
the highest scoring house at the end of the term.//

36. S Do you think they would respond to making
them jealous, you know what I mean, that
they are not included.

37. M //You saw how much they enjoyed it last week,   A: INFORMATIVE
it may very well work.//

38. S	Yeah. Even Ashley seemed to get quite motivated, though he always spoils it by going over the top.	
39. M	//Well, I think that you have got a lot to consider there.// I don't think that content, manner, planning etc. seem to be causing any real concern.// And at the moment, probably you've got enough to focus on in getting the group working without the added worry of other professional concerns.//	A: INFORMATIVE (feedback)
40. S	Yes. Unless there is anything that you think would help the group in settling and behaving themselves.	
41. M	//I think the strategies we have discussed today need to be the immediate focus for the next lesson.// Ensure that these are indicated on your plan and don't forget to implement them for the next lesson.// Run through this strategy through your mind a couple of times so that it happens quite naturally.//	A: PRESCRIPTIVE (directive, benevolent, action planning) A: PRESCRIPTIVE (directive, benevolent)
42. S	And the report slips we will go through tomorrow?	
43. M	//Yes. Cheer up!//	

Other points:

Line 1. Is the mentor's question a genuine request for self-evaluation or an ice-breaker? (See Chapter 6, Active listening).

Lines 10–11. Note the way that the mentor does not respond immediately with a solution to the student's question but uses a question. This question is however, not an 'open' question (Chapter 9, Question types).

Line 23. Note the way the mentor gives negative feedback by offering quite directive advice, but this does not lead to defensiveness on the part of the student.

Lines 31–34. Note how the mentor provides information which is clearly designed to probe the student's thinking and is 'heard' as critical by the student, who produces a defensive reaction (Chapter 7).

Task 5.2 What you say is not what I hear

Aims: To explore the meaning of different interventions.
To explore the difference between the intentions of the speaker and the perceived meaning.

Rationale: By working in pairs on such an exercise participants can explore the differences between illocutionary and perlocutionary force and linguistic form in providing feedback and can begin to explore the way that different interventions can provide different ways of giving advice.

Procedure:
1. Put the participants into pairs and ask them to try out the statements (1–10) (*Photocopiable resource 21* on page 239) with their partner, substituting a sensible phrase for the blanks.
2. First, one member of the pair says one statement and the partner notes down their feelings about the statement. Then the pairs discuss what was intended by the speaker and what was felt by the receiver, expressing what they felt in their own words. They can then be asked to categorise what they felt using the list of intentions provided (a–l).
3. Next reverse the roles with the other partner reading the statement and their partner noting down their feelings.
4. When they have finished all the statements, ask the pairs to work out alternative ways of conveying the same message and write them in the blank spaces. Try to make the alternatives more or less threatening than the originals.
5. Discuss the findings with all the participants. Discuss with the group the things which made the interventions less threatening. What factors made them more threatening?

Notes for guidance: This exercise is designed to allow participants to explore their own feelings with regard to set phrases which can be used to perform different interventions in the feedback process. The exercise can lead to a useful comparison of what they felt with what was intended by the speaker and what was signalled in the linguistic form used (see also Task 5.3).

The matching of the intentions with the statements provides a chance for the participants to think about the intervention types used by Heron (see Chapters 5–9). Note that there are different interpretations of the interventions. The following are the most probable interpretations:

1	i or k	6	d or b
2	e or h	7	l or f
3	h or e	8	k or l
4	a or j	9	g or k
5	a or j	10	f or b

The second half of the exercise also gives the participants a chance to experiment with different forms which are more or less threatening.

Note the importance of

- the context in which the intervention is made
- the manner in which it is made (i.e. intonation, gesture, body posture etc.)

in the way that the message is interpreted (see Chapter 6 for a discussion of different features of non-verbal communication).

The different interventions and their reference:

a)	Inviting self-evaluation	see Chapter 9, sequencing interventions
b)	Consultative prescription	see Chapter 5
c)	Empathising	see Chapter 6
d)	Personal interpretation	see Chapter 8
e)	Confronting	see Chapter 8
f)	Feedback	see Chapter 8
g)	Directing	see Chapter 8
h)	Benevolent prescription	see Chapter 5
i)	Providing alternatives	see Chapter 8
j)	Disclosure	see Chapter 8
k)	Focusing attention	see Chapter 9, critical thinking
l)	Providing reinforcement	see Chapter 6, supportive interventions

Task 5.3 What did you intend?

Aim: To sensitise participants to the difference between intended meanings and perceived meanings in feedback situations.

Rationale: By exploring personal feelings about comments made in a feedback session we will be better able to judge the effect that our own statements may have on others.

Procedure:
1. Give out the table (*Photocopiable resource 22* on page 240).
2. Introduce the task by reading out the example:
   'Why didn't you ask the pupils to repeat the dialogue?'
3. Then get the participants to mark on the grid, select a context and establish the intention which they heard in the way that you asked the question.
4. Discuss the answers with the group.

5. Then read out the following, getting the group to fill out the sheet for each one in the same way.
   A I was not sure if all the students followed your explanation.
   B Did you plan what explanation you were going to give of the vocabulary?
   C Tell me about the role play.
   D You had good class control during the pairwork phase.
   E I felt there were some problems during the pairwork. Do you agree?
   F Can we talk about the pairwork exercise?
   G What about using mime for giving instructions?
6. When you have finished, read the sentences again (trying to use the same intonation) and discuss with the group what they 'heard' and the contexts in which they placed the statement/question.

Notes for guidance: This exercise is based on an idea given in a paper by two trainers from International House, Krakow.[2] It is useful to explore with the group the way that individuals differ in the degree to which they hear such statements in a threatening or non-threatening manner.

It is important to bring out to the group the interplay between the context in which the utterance is made and the resulting perceived intention (see catalytic vs confronting interventions and context, Chapter 8).

It can also be used to explore the differences in intonation patterns which will make one statement more or less threatening.

Again, the intervention types used by Heron (see Task 5.2) can be used to describe the intentions as perceived by the speaker.

It is an advantage if the utterances can be tape-recorded so that the actual way in which they were said can be analysed and discussed in Step 6. It can also be useful to bring in other voices, particularly male/female and different nationalities (if advising is taking place in a cross-cultural situation) to see how these factors may affect the way interventions are interpreted.

As an extension, it is useful to get non-native English speaking participants to try out the exercise in their own first languages to see if the reactions are different.

For a discussion of the cultural implications see Chapter 10.

[2] Adams, K. and Markiewicz, M. (1995) 'Cross-cultural problems in teacher training', paper given at the Polish Teacher Training Conference, Krakow.

Task 5.4 Who's in charge?

Aims: To examine extracts from two feedback sessions in order to examine the way that role relationships are signalled by different intervention types.

Rationale: By examining extracts from two different feedback sessions in which the same teachers act in different roles, the effects of status and feedback role can be explored.

Procedure:
1. Put the participants into pairs and ask them to look at the transcripts of the two feedback sessions (*Photocopiable resource 23* on pages 241–242).
2. Ask them to discuss the following questions:
   1. What can you tell about the status of the two teachers from these extracts?
   2. What points are the two observer/mentors trying to raise in the two sessions?
   3. What are the reactions of the teachers to the points raised?
   4. Can you explain why the teachers reacted in the way that they did?

Notes for guidance: These transcripts derive from an action research task in which trainee mentor teachers were paired as 'critical friends' for the purpose of observing each other and then providing feedback to each other on the lessons watched. They were asked to record the feedback session and come along with two 'critical moments' from each session transcribed, along with a commentary.

The two teachers who produced these two extracts are very different in experience and status. Teacher A is a reasonably inexperienced locally-qualified teacher in only his third year of teaching, whereas Teacher B is a very experienced teacher with several years of experience and a BEd qualification from the UK. Thus Teacher B perceives himself and is perceived by Teacher A as having much higher status as a teacher.

It is useful to examine the two sessions to see the way that the different roles in the feedback session either amplify or reduce the status differential between the two. It is also useful to examine the prescriptive nature of the comments made by both advisors and the reactions which these interventions produce in the teachers.

After examining the transcripts, partcipants can then be encouraged to produce alternative suggestions as to the way that the points could have been raised.

Session 1   A begins by praising B and highlighting the positive points of the lesson, which is a standard way of beginning a feedback session (see Chapter 6, Validation).

A then makes an observation, l. 3 (informative intervention, Chapter 8) which is clearly perceived as a criticism or negative evaluation by B, l. 4.

A then asks (probes) B by asking him what he thinks, l. 5.

B is clearly somewhat flustered by this, l. 5, and shows his discomfort with the perceived criticism of his teaching leading to a defensive reaction (Chapter 7).

A focuses the discussion by asking about B's voice, l. 7.

B is not sure of the reason for this. Again, he is perhaps unsettled by being challenged by a less experienced teacher. It is worth noting here the problems of making comments on something which the person is unable to do anything about – the 'A' in SMART (Chapter 8).

A appears to be trying to seriously and non-judgmentally discuss the issue of voice, l. 9, 11, but the implied self-criticism of 'weak' is quickly rejected by B, who appears to accept the 'criticism', although offers a justification, again being defensive, l. 12.

A 'reads' this defensive stance and counters with a positive, valuing comment, l. 13.

Session 2 B certainly assumes control of the session. He asks A for his opinion/ view of the lesson, but 'before I say my opinion'. He clearly sees himself as the authority – benevolent prescription (Chapter 5). Note also the use of 'should', l. 7, and 'would have been better', l. 9.

A is generally quite defensive by justifying his actions according to the Teacher's Book, l. 4.

B appears to feel free to be critical using the textbook aims to justify his criticisms, l. 5 – commanding prescription (Chapter 5).

B's approach is characteristic of probing for 'testing' rather than exploration (see Chapter 9 on open and closed questions).

A has not been led to a new understanding but has been told what to do, note the only superficial acceptance of the ideas in l. 10.

B does praise A's teaching, l. 11 (validating intervention, Chapter 6), but immediately counters with two informative interventions which are intended and understood as negative evaluation and confronting (Chapter 8).

It is interesting that A counters the criticism with a reason which is not defensive but informative, a reason which is accepted by B.

Task 6.1 Communication through body language[1]

Aims: To raise awareness of the ways in which body language contributes to the message being communicated.
To compare interpretations of common gestures and body language.

Rationale: While interpretations of body language may give rise to some discussion in the sense that there is no one-to-one correspondence between body language and attitude, it is useful to see how gestures and posture are interpreted by others.
Lack of awareness of how body language may be interpreted can mean that wrong signals are unwittingly sent out or that incorrect messages are read from the posture or gestures of participants in a communicative encounter.

Procedure:

1. Put the participants into four groups (A, B, C & D) and give each group one of the four sketches (*Photocopiable resource 24* on pages 243–244); you will need to make enough copies of each sketch to make sure that each member of the group has one. Ask them to discuss their interpretations of the emotions and feelings which each of the people in the sketches are projecting. They can also discuss what they feel is the context which is being depicted in the sketches.
2. After the groups have discussed the sketches, regroup the participants into new groups of four with one participant from each of the original groups. Thus the new groups will consist of one from A, one from B, one from C and one from D. Ask each member of the group to describe the feelings of the people in their sketches to the others.
3. Give out the explanation of the sketches (*Photocopiable resource 25* on page 245) taken from Pease (1981) and get the groups to compare their impressions with his interpretations.

Notes for guidance: There is much discussion about the meaning of non-verbal communication (NVC), its applicability in cross-cultural communication and the degree to which certain ways of sitting and gesturing are culture-specific (see Chapter 6 for a discussion). It is likely that you will have differences between the participants in the way that the different sketches are interpreted, but it is also likely that there will be degrees of agreement about the interpretation of the sketches. It is important to emphasise the importance of being sensitive to the effects that body posture and gesture may have on intended messages, and to draw attention to the intentional and unintentional messages which can be conveyed by NVC (see Chapter 6). However, the following often seem to be agreed by many from different cultures as being somewhat 'universal':

---

[1] The pictures from Pease have been used by a number of people. In particular, they are used in Edge 1992.

Mirroring	See sketch 4. Mirroring gives the impression that the listener is engaged – see also Task 6.2.
Crossed arms/legs	This is often interpreted as defensive (see sketch 2).
Eye contact	This is interpreted as engagement (see sketch 4).
Body pointing towards/away from the listener	This is interpreted as lack of concern (see sketch 3).
Open gesture with palms upward	Person on left in sketch 4 would be interpreted as honest, interested and open. (cf S-O-L-E-R, Chapter 6).

Task 6.2 Investigating listening behaviour[2]

Aim: To investigate helpful and non-helpful listening behaviour.

Rationale: This activity helps participants become more aware of the ways in which interest, attentive listening, boredom, impatience etc. are signalled through verbal and non-verbal behaviour.

Procedure: See the role play cards (*Photocopiable resource 26* on page 246).
1. Choose three situations to use.
2. Split the group into threes: As, Bs and Cs. Give out one of the role play cards. Allow 5–10 minutes for this stage.
3. Do not feed back on the role play at this stage but assign new roles e.g. As become Bs: Bs become Cs; Cs become As. Give out the second role play cards, again allowing 5–10 minutes for completion of this stage.
4. Repeat the procedure for the third role play.
5. Get the students to compare notes in threes. Then feed back in plenary, coming up with a list of behaviours which indicate poor listening and behaviours which facilitate active listening.

Notes for guidance: There are five situations on the photocopiable page. You should select three which highlight the particular points you wish to make.

   This can be a very enjoyable exercise even though it is very simple. The body behaviours which facilitate listening quickly become obvious during the group discussions. Again, this exercise can be combined with Task 6.1 to explore the types of body language which enhance good listening. Note Egan's acronym S-O-L-E-R (Chapter 6).

[2] A similar series of exercises appears in Edge 1992.

Behaviour which enhances listening	Behaviour which indicates poor listening
leaning forward, proximity	leaning away
maintaining eye contact	avoiding eye contact
back-channelling – 'Hmm', etc. Encouraging person to continue in breaks	no response to what person is saying
not doing things, no 'fidgeting'	making notes, even though they are notes of what is said (see effective attending in lessons, Chapter 4)
mirroring the posture/gestures of the speaker (see Task 6.1)	
repeating and paraphrasing what is said	lack of verbal response to what is said

Task 6.3 The pre-lesson discussion[3]

Aim:　　　　To examine the uses and usefulness of the pre-lesson discussion stage.

Rationale:　The benefits of effective observation can be lost if the teacher is unclear about the purposes of the observation or if the observer misunderstands key aspects of the lesson.

Procedure: Look at the transcript (*Photocopiable resource 27* on pages 247–248) and consider the following questions:
1. What can you say about the relationship between the observer and the teacher?
2. What are the observer's aims during this stage of the teaching practice cycle? Do you think the approach taken by the observer is one that provides for a supportive atmosphere? Why / why not?
3. What are the main concerns of the teacher? Does the observer pick them up?
4. What aspects of the lesson do you learn about from this conversation? Do we know what the aims of the teacher are?
5. Why does the observer ask if the teacher wants to use Czech or English (line 1)?
   What advantages and disadvantages are there to carrying out the conversation in English when:
   a) both observer and teacher are non-native speakers (as in this case)?
   b) the observer is a native speaker and the teacher is a non-native speaker (as is the case in many aid-funded contexts)?

---

[3] We would like to thank Ingrid Wisniewska who collected and transcribed the original version of this feedback encounter.

Notes for guidance: Background Information

The purpose of this particular observation is assessment. The observer has a form to fill in, not all of which can be filled in from watching the lesson (e.g. the reference to the report on line 29). The observer is a junior member of academic staff from a university, relatively new to supervising. The teacher is a qualified teacher of Russian who is in the process of qualifying as a teacher of English. The observer has clearly been trained in what she should do during this stage of the teaching cycle and does her best to show solidarity with the teacher by empathising with what she feels is the low level of motivation in technical schools.

Some points in answer to the questions:

1. Although the power differential is not particularly evident, there are some signs that the teacher may feel a little insecure in what she is doing (line 10). However, although the observer on the surface asks questions about the teacher and the lesson, the whole session is rather 'inquisitorial' and it appears as if the observer is testing the teacher's knowledge (cf lines 13, 21, 23, 25, 31). There definitely appears to be a tutor–student relationship assumed by both parties.

2. In some ways the observer is trying to 'find out' about the teacher, she clearly has agendas which she wants to talk to the teacher about. Note that in lines 31/32 an innocent (?) enquiry about writing leads to an anxious reaction from the teacher, which is then countered by a supportive reaction from the observer (line 33).

3. The teacher appears to have concerns about the speaking of Czech and the observer only partly deals with this. She gives her line on the situation, but does not really listen to the teacher. The teacher appears to be really pleased with the group / pair work, yet the observer only introduces a negative point (confronting – see Chapter 8).

4. Note that we don't learn about the aims of the teacher from this conversation. There is an attempt to find out the concerns of the teacher and an attempt to allow the teacher to set the agenda for the lesson observation (line 35); this is done very clumsily, the teacher is unprepared for the question and nothing gets done.

5. The issue of the language in which advice is given is an important one, especially in setting the 'power/status' parameters (see Chapter 8, informative interventions and Chapter 10, for a discussion of the different effects of first or second language supervision).

Some other points to notice:

line 3   Open invitation to talk about the class, get T's viewpoint

line 7   Empathising with the T? (see also line 41). Is this an open Q? (see Chapter 9).

line 9   The observer 'interprets' what the teacher has said, 'empathetic divining' (see Chapter 9).

line 13   This would not appear to be an 'open' question (See Chapter 9).

line 15   Challenging question. Is there another way to express this which is not so confrontational?

line 19   Is this confronting intervention? (See Chapter 8.) Is the pre-lesson
           stage the right place for confronting?

line 23   The observer has her own agenda, not that of the teacher; 'leading'
           not 'following' (See Chapter 9.)

line 32   Note the anxiety which the teacher has as a reaction to the observer's
           question.

line 33   The observer reacts by supporting the teacher by 'valuing' what she is
           doing (see Chapter 6).

line 39   This sounds a little like a 'police caution'. The intention is laudable
           but how could it have been improved?

Task 6.4 Giving oral feedback

Aims: To examine two transcripts of oral feedback given after a lesson.
             To look at the ways in which advisors provide scaffolding for their
             teachers during oral feedback.

Rationale: The post-lesson feedback session is the most crucial arena for
             providing feedback to teachers and it is important to examine in
             some detail the different ways in which feedback is given in this
             session. This exercise compares two different ways of providing
             advice.

Procedure:
1. Divide the participants into two groups and give each group one of the
    extracts from post-lesson discussions (*Photocopiable resources 28 and 29
    on pages 249 and 250*).
2. Ask each group to discuss the following questions about their extract:
    1. What was important in this trainee's mind?
    2. What was the supervisor's agenda?
    3. What techniques does the supervisor use to establish what happened in
        the lesson?
    4. Look at the ways in which the supervisor tries to elicit alternatives from
        the trainee. How successful is the supervisor?
    5. Find an example of an evaluative comment by a) the trainee b) the
        supervisor.
    6. How successful is this supervisor in leading the trainee to a new
        understanding?
    7. What impression do you form of this trainee's ability to reflect on her
        own teaching?
3. When they have finished discussing them put the participants into groups
    with equal numbers of those who have looked at Extract A and those who
    have looked at Extract B in each group. Get them to share with the others
    what they have found out about their extract.
4. Discuss the findings in plenary.

Notes for guidance: Note that Extract A appears to have a much more relaxed atmosphere. Note the atmosphere allows a cathartic release (see Chapter 7) when the trainee laughs. The supervisor listens to the trainee and there is a lot of active listening (Chapter 6) by using back-channelling and empathetic divining (l. 25) (see Chapter 9).

Extract B, in contrast, appears inquisitional. The supervisor does not appear to be listening to the trainee. There are a lot of probing questions but these follow the supervisor's agenda and do not connect with what the trainee says. Here are some notes on the possible answers to the questions set.

Q	Extract A	Extract B
1	Trainee is concerned by lack of class response to her questions.	Trainee is concerned with getting students to do writing/homework.
2	Supervisor is concerned to get the trainee to talk about the problem and explore alternatives.	Supervisor appears to want to get the trainee to use dictation and not to use copying.
3	Qs: What happened next? Being specific: What about the girl by the window?	None. Supervisor tells the trainee what happened and then asks the trainee to justify her actions.
4	Asking questions about what the trainee thinks (l. 3). Asking questions, 'drawing out' the trainee by rephrasing (l. 9), asking trainee to evaluate (l. 13), interpreting, 'empathetic divining' (l. 17, l.25) (Chapter 9).	Supervisor uses many direct questions which seem not to be truly 'open' despite their form (see Chapter 9). Supervisor appears to interpret and re-phrase what the trainee says (ll. 7, 11 & 13), but the impression is that the supervisor has an 'agenda' which she is following.
5a	Maybe it was just too difficult (l.8); I felt a bit bad about that (l. 12); Wrong (l. 14) . . .	None
5b	None	Although a series of instructions to think about the way to do it, l. 17 would appear to be an indirect evaluation of what happened. This is a good example of the surface 'form' of the speech having quite a different function and interpretation in context (see Tasks 5.2 & 5.3).
6	Highly successful. Uses prompts to get the trainee to evaluate and explore the problem.	Not really. Supervisor asks a lot of probing questions which intend to scaffold the trainee's thinking (see Chapter 3), but the trainee never really seems to 'own' the solution (Chapter 4).
7	Trainee appears highly reflective.	Trainee does not seem to be very reflective.

Task 8.1 Feedback role play

Aims: To allow participants to experience giving and receiving negative
               feedback in a supportive atmosphere and to allow for reflection on
               the way that this feedback was given and received.

Rationale: By acting out the process of giving difficult feedback with a
               colleague in a low-risk situation and by then working on the
               responses with a partner, participants can be given the space to
               explore alternative ways of providing feedback and thus develop a
               range of responses.

Procedure:
1. Divide the participants into pairs. Ask each pair to decide on one person to
   be the teacher and one to be the advisor.
2. Give out Role cards A (*Photocopiable resource 30* on page 251).
   Demonstrate with the whole group what is required by acting out the first
   situation with one of the participants.
3. Allow the pairs to continue with the other three situations and complete the
   discussion points at the end of the role card.
4. When they have finished, give out Role cards B (*Photocopiable resource 31*
   on page 252) with the roles reversed.
5. Pairs then continue with the exercise until both Role cards have been
   completed.
6. Discuss with the group the responses that were written down – both the
   immediate responses and the considered responses.

Notes for guidance: This task allows the participants to try out techniques
involved in giving negative feedback to each other. It involves the participants
working in pairs, one as a teacher and the other as an advisor with roles
assigned to them on separate role cards.

It is important to emphasise the necessity of being spontaneous and of noting
down exactly what was said in the first instance.

It also involves a technique which is very useful in skills training; the
reflection on what has been said and joint reconstruction of alternative ways of
putting the same idea across. It is particularly useful for the exploration of
different intervention types such as personal interpretation (Chapter 8), self-
disclosure (Chapter 8), and direct questioning (Chapter 9) and various
prescriptive interventions (Chapter 8) as alternatives to negative feedback.

Other issues which can arise: commanding prescription vs negotiation
(Chapter 5); feedback on language issues (Chapter 8); degenerative
interventions (Chapter 5).

When working with non-native English speaking participants, it can also be
useful to get the group to do one of the role plays in English and the other in
their first language and to compare the results (see Chapter 8 & Chapter 10 for
a discussion of use of first vs second language in feedback).

Task 8.2 **Written feedback**

Aims: To look at the notes which an observer might make during a lesson. To examine the effect of the written feedback form on the type of feedback given.
To look at ways in which written feedback can be made more helpful.

Rationale: A written lesson report is required within many formal teacher training programmes. They do have a strong influence on the trainee because of their permanence, so it is important to examine any documents from the point of view of both their usefulness and their potential effect on the trainee.

Procedure:
1. Give out the completed observation sheet, Part A (*Photocopiable resource 32* on pages 253–254).
2. Ask participants in groups to consider the following questions:
    a) How does the observer take notes of the lesson? What aspects of the lesson are noted?
    b) What do you think the advantages and disadvantages are of this way of making notes on a lesson?
    c) Are these notes primarily for the teacher or the observer?
    d) As a teacher, in what ways might it help you to be given such a document?
    e) Can you suggest any modifications to the sheet which would make it a more helpful instrument?
    f) Based on these lesson notes, what comments might you make to the teacher after the lesson?
3. Discuss the group answers in plenary.
4. Next ask the groups to look at Part B (*Photocopiable resource 33* on page 254) and to discuss the following questions:
    g) As a teacher how helpful would you find it to be given these notes?
    h) Which of the items work best? Why do you think so?
    i) Write three more sentence completion items which you could use to give a teacher feedback after a lesson.
5. Again, discuss the answers. Then, ask the group to consider the overall document. Does it:
    j) provide a written record of what went on in the lesson that teacher and observer could use as a basis for discussion?
    k) make the teacher aware of her own strengths?
    l) make the teacher aware of weaknesses in her teaching?
    m) help the teacher focus on areas to work on in the future?
    n) give the teacher suggestions for improvement?
6. Based on this, discuss with the participants:
    Are there any aspects of the document you would like to change?
    Is there any feedback which doesn't seem very helpful?

Notes for guidance: This form is a fairly typical one which can be used by an observer to note down what is happening in the lesson. As such it is a useful tool for an observer to use to bring data to the feedback session for discussion with the teacher (see Chapter 3 for the role of data in the feedback session). The technique of making a chronological record of the lesson is one which is used by many advisors (see also Task 3.6). In many ways, it is an observer's view of the lesson plan and can be compared with the lesson plan prepared by the teacher. Apart from the issue of selectivity (the record is what the observer has chosen to record) there is little evidence of any judgment or interpretation of what is going on in the notes on the lesson. The detailed description of the lesson would seem to be more useful to the observer for use in the feedback session than to the teacher as a record.

The following comments might be made on the questions:

a) Uses time frame and develops a chronological record. T actions noted without comment.
b) This has the advantage of being apparently non-judgmental in approach, but the disadvantage as a record for the T of not indicating any questions or challenges which the T might consider.
c) The observer.
d) It might be useful to see what you actually did, and to compare your lesson plan with the actual performance. It could help to consider aspects of timing.
e) A larger section on comments and suggestions, or a column where the advisor could raise questions about activities carried out. A section for the T to comment on the lesson. A section on agreed actions which can be negotiated with the T after the feedback session.
f) The questions of level of difficulty and ways to help students understand are central issues which need discussion.
g) These notes help to focus and give effective feedback to the T about the most important aspects of the lesson.
h) Point 3. This shows the importance of 'looking with' rather than 'at' the T (see Chapter 3 for a discussion of this).
    Point 9. The inclusion of points for action is very important (Chapter 8 and Task 8.3).
i) Allow for comments from the group. Perhaps comments could be added focusing on issues like: 'I think you should think about . . .' or encouraging reflection: 'What did you think about . . .?'.
j) Yes. This is perhaps its main strength.
k) To some extent.
l) This is probably more prevalent than indicating her strengths.
m) Not really. The action planning aspect appears weakest.
n) Again, not really.

Task 8.3 Formal reports

Aim: To look at samples of written feedback produced by inspectors in
                order to determine what features of this feedback are effective.

Rationale: In many situations advisors are asked to produce a written
                statement for both the teacher's own reference and for official
                records. This activity examines some actual samples of feedback
                written by inspectors following inspection visits and allows
                participants to look at the effectiveness of different styles of written
                feedback and to comment on the effectiveness of different features.

Procedure:
1. Ask the participants to look at the written reports (*Photocopiable resource
    34* on pages 255–258). Ask them to individually pick out:
    *   the reports they would most like to get as a teacher
    *   the reports they would least like to get
    *   the reports which they feel would be most useful to them as a teacher
2. Ask them to share their findings in pairs.
3. Still working in pairs, ask them to look at all the reports and discuss the
    following questions for each one:

		Recommendations for good practice
A	Who is the intended audience for the report (the teacher / school / education authority / records)? Does this make a difference to your interpretation of the remarks?	
B	How are the positive points expressed? Are they effective?	
C	How are the critical points expressed? Are they effective?	
D	Is there a clear action plan? Are there clear indications of what the teacher should do to improve?	

4. When they have answered these questions, put the pairs into groups of four
    and ask them to prepare a series of recommendations for good practice
    about the writing of a lesson report on a teacher.
5. Finally, if necessary, pull together all the comments from the groups into a
    plenary discussion.

Notes for guidance: These reports were written by inspectors of English in the
Middle East.[4] The inspectors come from a variety of different national
backgrounds (British, Indian, Sri Lankan and Arabs). They are providing advice
to teachers from a similar variety of national and linguistic backgrounds. Thus

---

[4] We would like to thank Nicholas Parsons, the Chief Inspector in the Sultanate of Oman in
1989, for collecting these reports, and the anonymous inspectors to whom they belong.

there is an interesting cross-cultural situation involved here (Chapter 10). They work in a school system which has three levels, Elementary (9–11), Preparatory (12–14) and Secondary (15–18).

The following are points which may be brought up about the different forms of feedback:

Most of the reports are written directly to the teachers as forms of advice, but Report 4 is written in the third person as a report to an outside agency. Although this is a very positive evaluation it is disturbing to read such a report as a teacher. In other reports (cf Report 2, point 3) there is a mixture of descriptive third person and direct instructions to the teacher. Third person accounts seem much less personal and are possibly less effective as advice. Many of the reports use the technique of using the first person 'I', to 'talk' to the teacher as 'you' and this makes the report much more personal. Advice, suggestions, praise and directions seem much more effective when the inspector 'owns' the feedback (see personal interpretation, Chapter 8).

Notes on the specific reports:

Report 1	This report mixes positive and critical points (see sequencing, Chapter 9) both overall and within individual comments. It uses questions to get the teacher to reflect (cf point 2), but this is not an 'open' question; it is in fact, a suggestion (Chapter 9). It provides reasons for the suggestions and it uses a lot of informative interventions (Chapter 8). It provides a clear, limited, set of general points as an 'action plan'. It is organised clearly.
Report 2	This report begins and ends with positive comments (sequencing, Chapter 9). It also uses the 'good news – bad news' strategy. Point 2 is a positive evaluation but clearly signalled as personal interpretation (Chapter 8).
Report 3	This clearly lays out the good points and suggestions and ends very nicely with a personal message to the teacher. However, overall tone is authoritative (Chapter 5). The suggestions contain a number of different ways of prescribing (Chapter 8). Some use commanding prescription (i, ii, viii), prescription and information/feedback (iii), simple negative feedback (iv, vi), benevolent prescription and action research (v) and holding up a mirror (vii).
Report 4	This is clearly written as a report to an institution and the tone is that of assessment. It uses the good news – bad news strategy quite extensively. Alone of the reports, it refers to previous visits and action plans from a previous report. It provides a clear piece of advice as an action plan for the teacher. However, despite these positive features the third person style probably makes it ineffective as a piece of advice to a teacher.
Report 5	This report mixes statements about the content with comments on the way the lesson was carried out. It is very authoritative and has the sense of commanding prescription (Chapter 5). It uses different prescriptive devices, some personalised (I recommend), some using a simple directive (Try to include . . .), statements of principles (This is a reading lesson for the pupils not for the teacher) followed by negative feedback (you should have . . .) and explanation of the reason for a problem.

Report 6	This report is extremely negative and the inspector makes no attempt to scaffold or help the teacher. All of the statements consist of simple directives and there is little reference to the actual lesson. All the directives consist of generalised rules.

Task 8.4 Self-assessment and target-setting

Aim: To examine a self-evaluation profile questionnaire as a means of providing an individual action plan.

Rationale: Action planning is one tool which may be used in an attempt to encourage habits of positive reflection and target-setting. The process seen below helps to provide a framework for the review and planning stages of the teaching practice cycle. Such formal systems are often included in institutional teaching practice situations.

Procedure:
1. Give out the self-evaluation sheet (*Photocopiable resource 35* on pages 259–261) and ask participants in groups to consider the following questions:
   1. Consider the areas in which this trainee lacks confidence. How could she be helped to develop in the areas where she has given herself a low evaluation? e.g.:
      a) given advice during a pre-lesson stage
      b) given guidance during post-lesson feedback
      c) advised to work on the area independently
   2. If you were this trainee's supervisor, what specific developmental targets might you set for her in the early stages of her teaching practice period?
   3. What are the possible advantages and disadvantages of using this particular profile questionnaire? Could it be improved in any way?
2. Discuss the answers that the groups give you to these questions.

Notes for guidance: The completed sheets are parts of a document developed by Wasyl Cajkler, which is used at the University of Leicester School of Education as part of the ongoing Action planning process. The profile questionnaire forms part of an initial review to provide an audit of a student teacher's strengths and areas for development. The idea is that such a profile offers an opportunity for a phased development of classroom skills.

This questionnaire would be completed by a modern language trainee on an initial teacher training course.

Section 1
Note that NCATs and PoS refer to the National Curriculum guidelines in use in the UK.

It is noticeable that the trainee's self-assessment is low in the area of classroom skills, as would be expected. However, her confidence in other areas may be misplaced. Her areas for development are still quite wide.

General

This pro-forma raises a whole range of issues about the use of competency lists (Chapter 2), the value of self-evaluation versus tutor evaluation (Chapter 3) and could usefully be compared with discursive advice provided by supervisors (see Task 8.2).

Task 9.1 Leading or following?

Aim: To investigate the way that an advisor can lead trainees to discuss issues.

Rationale: By examining a transcript of a session it is possible to see the interventions that an experienced advisor can make to focus trainees' attention on certain aspects of a lesson.

Procedure:
1. Ask the participants to look at the dialogue between a mentor and two trainees (*Photocopiable resource 36* on pages 262–264).
2. Ask them to read through the discussion individually and to make notes in the last column about the interventions made by the advisor. Ask them to particularly consider:
   - the intention behind what the advisor says
   - whether the advisor is following on from what the trainees say or is leading them to consider new aspects
   - the 'issues' which the advisor wishes the trainees to consider
3. Put the participants into pairs or groups of three to discuss their interpretations.
4. Discuss in plenary the way that the advisor 'scaffolds' the trainees' ideas about the lesson.

Notes for guidance: This is a particularly skilled advisor working with two young trainees. The trainees have just team taught in an English middle school with English children. There was a range of abilities among the children, and they were grouped according to their abilities. The lesson consisted of a role play in which the children had to devise and act out a radio interview.[5]

The feedback transcript shows the advisor giving a lot of 'space' to the trainees to talk about their lesson and there is a lot of evidence of the advisor using the active listening and attending strategies (see Chapter 6). This is the start of the feedback session and the advisor speaks less than the trainees and provides encouragement for them to give their view of the lesson. Thus, initially, this is an example of Egan's first stage of helping (Chapter 4), although the advisor uses the input from the trainees to begin to focus on issues, to 'develop new understandings' (Chapter 4). It also illustrates good examples of

[5] We would like to thank Diana Mitchene of University College Chichester, for collecting the data on which this exercise is based.

the advisor 'following' the client – one of Heron's catalytic interventions (Chapter 9).

The central issue which the advisor wants the trainees to consider concerns the value of writing out dialogues when doing a role play. The advisor wants the trainees to 'explore' the issue and does not offer prescriptive solutions to the problems she poses.

The following interventions can be seen in the feedback transcription:

Turn no.	Comment / intervention type	Reference
1–11	Advisor elicits from the Ts the situation.	Chapter 4
12	Confirming/checking.	Chapter 9, 'catalytic tool kit'
16	Advisor 'follows' S1 comments in turn 12. Paraphrasing and asking for more information.	Chapter 9
18	Agreeing. Personal interpretation ('it seems to me') plus providing relevant information about the lesson.	Chapter 8
27	Following. Catalytic 'open' questions.	Chapter 9
29	Providing feedback.	Chapter 8
32	Following. Focusing on one aspect. Paraphrasing and summarising. Providing relevant information.	Chapter 9 Chapter 8
34	Catalytic question. Note the way the advisor avoided the direct Q (Why . . .) which might have been 'heard' as threatening, preferring to produce a 'personalised' statement for comment.	Chapter 9
38	Checking, paraphrasing.	Chapter 9
40	Catalytic questioning / scaffolding. Posing a problem. Generalising (abstract conceptualisation?). Asking the T to evaluate. Advisor begins to 'lead'.	Chapter 9
44	'Closed' question about real world which is non-threatening because it does not refer to the classroom *per se*.	Chapter 9, types of question
47	As above. Advisor is now 'leading' the Ts.	Chapter 9
49	Valuing what the T says. Providing an explanation.	Chapter 6
51	Advisor re-interprets what the Ts have told her. Provides information from the lesson about the Ts' behaviour and provides a principled explanation.	Chapter 8, personal interpretation Chapter 9 logical marshalling.
54	Benevolent prescription. Providing alternative.	Chapter 5
56	Advisor acknowledges what the T offers. Offers further explanation of supporting	

reasons for not reading aloud (abstract   Chapter 3
conceptualisation).

59 & 66 Advisor 'closes' episode with general   Chapter 6
praise (supportive intervention). Asks Q
about the lesson, inviting evaluation, which
again finishes with a supportive 'closure'.

Task 9.2 Feedback role play

Aims: To allow participants the chance to conduct a full feedback session
and to put into practice the different skills that are involved in a full
feedback session in the 'safety' of a simulation.

Rationale: By acting out a role play, then recording it and analysing it in
groups, participants can examine the way that different
interventions work in different situations and can explore the
effects that their interventions have on each other.

Procedure:
1. Select a video of a lesson and show it to the whole group. Tell them that
   they should watch the video and make notes so that they can then give
   advice to the teacher on the lesson. If possible, select a lesson where you
   have the teacher's lesson plan as well.
2. Then divide the participants into groups of three and give each member of
   the group a letter, A, B, or C.
3. Give each member of each group one of the role cards (*Photocopiable
   resource 37* on page 265). Tell them not to show their role card to the other
   members of the group. Tell them that they should take on the persona of the
   teacher on the role card when it is their turn to be the teacher.
4. Tell the teachers that, as a group, they are going to give each other feedback
   in three stages, with each member of the group taking the role of the
   advisor, the teacher and an observer in each stage. The three stages are to
   be: Exploration, New Understanding and Action. They should assume roles
   in the following manner:

	ADVISOR	TEACHER	OBSERVER
STAGE 1: EXPLORATION	B	A	C
STAGE 2: NEW UNDERSTANDING	C	B	A
STAGE 3: ACTION	A	C	B

If possible, get the groups to record their role plays, with each advisor
recording their advice session on their own cassette.

5. Get the groups to role play the full feedback session with the observer making notes on the way that each advisor gave feedback.
6. If the role play has been recorded, get the advisor to listen to their own piece of feedback and to transcribe any section of the feedback which they felt was interesting/important.
7. Ask the groups to discuss the feedback with the 'observer' leading the debriefing and the 'teacher' in each case giving their feelings about the way the feedback was conducted.
8. Alternatively, if it has been possible to make transcripts, ask the groups to work from the transcripts, again with the observer and the teacher giving feedback to the advisor.

Notes for guidance: This is a very good activity to use near the end of a course on advising. It should bring up a lot of the issues which have been covered in the book. To do it properly needs a lot of time. It is worth considering planning it to cover more than one day, with the participants having the chance to listen to their tapes and transcribe their feedback overnight.

It is important to choose a good lesson to watch. The lesson should not be too 'perfect', but neither should it be too bad. A good lesson from the end of a pre-service course, taught by a reasonably competent teacher/trainee, is ideal.

When handing out the role cards, try to suit the card to the personality of the participant – it will make it easier for them to fulfil their role.

There is clearly a degree of artificiality in the situation, and the splitting of the feedback into 3 'stages' can cause problems. Emphasise that you want them to examine the way that each advisor handles the feedback on a micro-level, and that the participants should not worry too much about 'following on' from the previous advisor, but that they should concentrate on fulfilling the main goals of their stage (see Chapter 9, sequencing the interventions).

Some of the points that can arise from the feedback to the different 'teachers':

Teacher 1	There may be difficulties in getting this teacher to talk. She may be classified as 'introverted' (Chapter 10). There may be a need for a lot of supportive interventions (Chapter 6). However, informative interventions (Chapter 8) may well suit her style of learning.
Teacher 2	The problem with this teacher is to get them to consider their teaching and be critical of what was done (see critical questioning, Chapter 9). It may be necessary to use confronting interventions (Chapter 8) and even commanding prescription (Chapter 5) may emerge.
Teacher 3	Again, it may be difficult to get this teacher to evaluate her lesson and the use of different prescriptions may emerge, especially benevolent prescription (Chapter 5).

Task 9.3 Is this your problem?

Aims: To allow participants to discuss likely problems they might face and
to suggest possible interventions which might be appropriate.

Rationale: By discussing the situations in groups the participants can share
ideas and offer different possible courses of action based on
different intervention strategies.

Procedure:
1. Divide the participants into groups of four or five. Give out the list of
problems (*Photocopiable resource 38* on page 266). Ask them to discuss the
problems and to come up with solutions.
2. Allow the participants plenty of time in groups to come up with
explanations for the situations described and solutions which they think
might work in each situation.
3. When they have finished discussing the problems, give out the possible
solutions (*Photocopiable resource 39* on pages 267–268) and get them to
compare these to their own.
4. Discuss the solutions with the whole group.

Notes for guidance: This task works better with participants who have had
some experience of advising. If you have a mixture of experienced and less
experienced participants, then it is a good idea to mix the two groups. This task
allows the participants to discuss problems which they may have giving advice
to teacher/trainees. It is a useful activity to review many of the issues brought
up in this book. They are problems which have come up in the course of
different mentorship programmes. Some possible solutions which have been
brought up on different courses are offered after the task sheet. They are not
designed as definitive answers, but raise some issues which are likely to come
up in the real advisory situation. However, the following discussions in this
book deal with some of the problems and the solutions which have been
offered:
Problem

1 Stage of development (Chapter 2). Defensive reactions (Chapter 7).
Personality factors (Chapter 10).
2 'Owning the solution', negotiating the problem (Chapter 4).
3 Stage of teacher development (Chapter 2). Guiding teachers to new
awareness (Chapter 8).
4 Creating a collaborative environment (Chapters 4 & 6).
5 Confrontation (Chapter 8).
6 Age and cultural differences (Chapter 10).
7 Dealing with emotions, cathartic interventions (Chapter 7).

Task 10.1 Exploring cultural differences[1]

Aim: To raise awareness of the factors which can affect communication
           between two people from different cultures.

Rationale: By allowing participants to brainstorm different factors on a
           general social level, they can become aware of the complexities of
           the situation which can exist when giving feedback and advising
           teachers from different cultures.

Procedure:
1. Draw two stick figures on the board and ask the participants to brainstorm
   as many barriers to communication that they can between two people from
   different cultures.
2. Collect their suggestions as they provide them.
3. Then carry out a further brainstorm in which the two figures are actually a
   teacher and advisor from racially and culturally different groups.
4. Finally, get the group to use the factors thrown up by the brainstorming
   session to consider the following situation:
   > The advisor is a tall, blonde female from the UK, who has worked most
   > of her life in tertiary private language teaching in the UK.
   > She is advising a shorter, male primary school teacher in the Middle East.
   > (NB This scenario can be changed, depending on the situation of the
   > participants.)
5. Discuss the difficulties which the advisor and the teacher might face in
   effectively communicating in such a situation.

Notes for guidance: The diagram below, taken from Lago and Thompson
(1997: 40), illustrates the range of factors which can be thrown up in the initial
brainstorm. In addition, during the more focused brainstorm on the advising
and teaching situation, many of the issues which we have discussed in this book
such as institutional role, beliefs about teaching and learning, professional
status, and experience should also emerge. Reference can be made to Holliday's
views of local, national and international ways of looking at teaching methods
(Holliday 1994) and its adaptation to the advising situation given on the Venn
diagram (page 147, Figure 37) in Chapter 10.

   The transfer of these factors to a specific situation allows participants the
chance to discuss issues in a concrete situation. In addition to the philosophical/
methodological differences between a teacher from tertiary private ELT and
state school primary teaching implicit in the situation (and this is the essential
tension discussed by Holliday 1994), it is also useful to spend some time
examining the implications of simple factors like height, especially in a cross-
gender context.

---

[1] This activity appears in Lago and Thompson 1997, 39–41

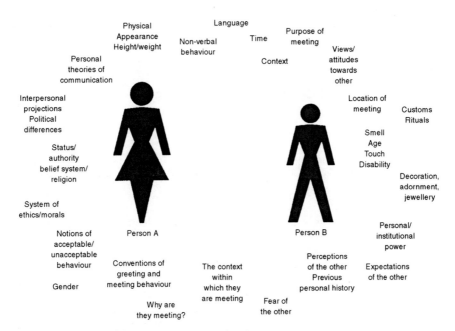

Figure 38 Cultural barriers to communication

Photocopiable resources

Photocopiable resource 1 (Task 1.2, page 150)

Case Study 1 Pre-service
In the Sultanate of Oman, pre-service trainees from the Intermediate Teacher Training Colleges were provided with two periods of teaching practice. In the second year of their studies, trainees were sent out for one term on a 'serial' teaching experience in which they went into a particular school for one day a week and taught 2 or 3 classes per week in that school. This was followed by a 'block' teaching practice of four weeks in their third year. During both teaching practice placements trainees taught different classes, replacing the normal English teacher. In the first practice each trainee was visited four times by a tutor from the college. The aim of this period was to provide help and guidance and each lesson was not separately assessed, but the tutor provided guidance notes for the trainee. The grade awarded for this period was an overall assessment based on the degree of progress the trainee had made during the placement. On the second, block practice, each trainee was visited four times by different tutors from the college and each lesson was separately assessed using a standard assessment schedule, and the overall grade for this period was based on an aggregate of the separate assessed lessons.

Case Study 2 Pre-service
On a Cambridge RSA CELTA course, trainees taught special classes of volunteer students for periods of between 20 minutes and 40 minutes. The trainees were divided into groups of three, team teaching classes in the shorter teaching periods, and all the trainees watched each other teach. The sessions were also attended by tutors from the course who made notes on the lessons taught. After each experience, the trainees were given notes made by the tutor and then put into groups to discuss the lessons they had observed each other teach, using the notes provided if necessary. They were asked during this period to extract common 'themes' which had arisen during the lesson. Following this, the tutor discussed the lessons with the group in a plenary session. There were also one-to-one tutorial sessions with each participant to chart progress and to discuss issues specifically related to individual progress. The lesson notes and the individual tutorial sessions were used by the tutor to arrive at an overall grade for that teacher's teaching.

Case Study 3 Mentorship

On a pre-service undergraduate programme at a College of Education, teachers were placed in specified schools and each was allocated a mentor, the class teacher with whom they worked for the whole placement. A group of four mentors with their trainees was assigned a 'Link Tutor' from the college. The role of the mentor was to provide help to the trainee on a daily basis in all aspects of teaching, from preparation through to performance, and to provide feedback to the trainee on a regular basis. Three times throughout the placement, each trainee was observed teaching by the Link Tutor, who provided a written evaluation of the lesson seen. Each evaluation was based on a common schedule of competencies drawn up by the college. Trainees were also required to keep a teaching log, in which they wrote down their own evaluation of the lessons. The final grade for the teaching practice was decided at a three-way conference of the mentor, the trainee and the tutor, again based on the schedule of competencies.

Case Study 4 Inspection

In the Sultanate of Oman, the inspection of English teachers was organised around a series of training workshops. The one-day workshops were based on a series of 'themes' and were closely related to the material the teachers were using in their schools. The sessions involved both introductions to the topics (such as carrying out a listening lesson) and lesson planning sessions. All teachers from a particular area were invited to attend the workshop and at the workshop an appointment was made to visit the teacher within the next two weeks, who undertook to teach a lesson using the skill/area which had been discussed and prepared during the workshop. The inspector visited the teacher and gave written feedback in the teacher's Inspection Book as well as oral feedback. The Inspection Book also included a generic schedule of competencies which all teachers were expected to meet.

Case Study 5 Internal Appraisal

In a language department of a college, all teachers had to be observed teaching at least three times per year. The information arising from these visits was used as a part of the annual appraisal interview with the Head of Department at which each teacher and the Head of Department reviewed the year's work and identified areas for staff development. The teachers were also asked to self-evaluate their work and to identify their own areas for staff development. The observations were carried out by a colleague nominated by the teacher, who wrote a report on the observations to be used in the performance review. This department was periodically reviewed by an outside agency which had a specific checklist of competencies which was used to grade the work of the department. It was decided to use this schedule for the internal observations of lessons.

Photocopiable resource 2 (Task 1.3, page 151)

STRENGTHS	WEAKNESSES
• the approach emphasised practice rather than theory • the training was more relevant to the trainees • the trainees had close contact with schools as well as the language classroom • supervision of the trainees could be continuous rather than the intermittent visits of a supervisor • support and ideas are provided by a current practitioner	• who would provide the link between theory and practice? • only one view of teaching would be supplied by the mentor • difficulty of identifying suitable mentors with both experience and tutorial skills • difficulty of explaining to mentors the standards required by the college • difficulties of ensuring that the experience is the same for all trainees if they are in very different schools supervised by very different mentors
OPPORTUNITIES	THREATS
• allows trainees time to develop practical skills with support from a teacher • teachers in schools are in contact with current curriculum and regulations • mentorship provides a professional development route for classroom teachers other than administration • brings training institutions and schools closer together	• separates theory from practice: trainees may develop coping skills without knowing why they are doing them • may lead to concentration on delivering the present curriculum rather than learning generic techniques • mentors may feel threatened by their lack of up-to-date theoretical knowledge compared to supervisors • supervisors may feel threatened by their lack of knowledge about current curriculum issues • problem of incompatibility between mentor and mentee

STRENGTHS	WEAKNESSES
OPPORTUNITIES	THREATS

Photocopiable resource 3 (Task 1.4, page 152)

The extracts a) to i) below are taken from an article on teacher education by Donald McIntyre (1988) which describes some of the endemic problems relating to teaching practice in Britain which have been revealed by research.

a) **The problem of theory vs practice**
'Student teachers frequently find the "educational theorising" they encounter in their courses irrelevant to the practical tasks which confront them in schools.'

b) **The problem of the unsupported teacher**
'Student teachers sometimes find little opportunity or support in their schools for trying out even the practical advice they have been given in their courses at the university.'

c) **The case of the unobservant observer**
'Student teachers generally do not learn much, although there is a great deal to be learned from their observation of the practice of experienced teachers. This is because the student teachers do not know what to look for and because the teachers being observed often do not recognise how much there is to be learned from their own teaching.'

d) **The dilemma of the overworked supervisor**
'Visiting supervisors are generally seen as authoritative assessors. They may be too busy to visit student teachers sufficiently often for their visits to be much more than tests for the student teachers to pass, sometimes with the collusion of the school staff.'

e) **The case of 'those who can't teach teach others how to teach'**
'Visiting supervisors may have insufficient recent school experience to provide credible assistance in that context to student teachers.'

f) **The problem of unsystematic supervisors**
'There is a great variation in the extent to which supervisors are able to conduct systematic diagnostic appraisals of student teachers' teaching, or to conduct coherent and helpful discussions about their teaching.'

g) **The problem of unclear criteria**
'The criteria for the assessment of student teachers' teaching competence and of their professional knowledge and understanding often lack clarity and may appear to be insufficiently related to one another.'

h) **Learning to teach**
'A great deal of student teachers' learning about teaching is at a level of semi-conscious trial and error learning, with 'correct' responses being shaped and reinforced by the reactions of pupils. Therefore their patterns of teaching behaviour are not generally easily accessible to their awareness for critical examination.'

i) **The dilemma of the individual vs the system**
'The developing agenda of concerns of each individual student teacher is not necessarily closely related to the official and non-individualised agenda of the teacher education programme.'

Adapted from:
McIntyre, D. (1988). 'Designing a teacher education curriculum from research and theory on teacher knowledge', in Calderhood, J. (ed.) *Teacher's Professional Learning*, 97–115

Photocopiable resource 4 (Task 1.5, page 154)

The following are comments from teachers on an MA course who had recently been through research procedures employing critical friends.

Teacher A
'. . . in reality, most of my associates within the group wanted to "play it safe" and work within the confines of their own area of educational experience, thus choosing an appropriate and like minded "critical friend".'

'I must admit to not perhaps being the sort of person who reacts well to this suggested approach where my own work on a course is the focus – something I would willingly criticise myself for.'

Teacher B
'I have to ask whether there was a cultural difference between mine and [my critical friend's] preferred learning styles.'

Teacher C
'The fact that my feedback partner is also a colleague had initially led me to believe that it would not be a "real" situation but in terms of my career future it will be just as likely, if not more likely, that I will receive feedback from a colleague rather than a friend.'

Teacher D
'I thoroughly enjoyed and benefited from working with a critical friend.'

It has also alerted me however to the potential problems of a collaboration where one's partner is not so well matched, and I can see many pitfalls in such a scenario. Having had my advice quite unintentionally misrepresented by both colleagues and students I know how frustrating this can be, and would therefore bear in mind that a partner who inspired less confidence than [my critical friend] did in this instance, would need a more restricted brief and more structured activity to perform.

Photocopiable resource 5 (Task 2.2, page 157)

1. Teachers are born not made.

2. Teachers need to have excellent English before they learn how to teach.

3. The first thing teachers need to learn is sound classroom management skills.

4. The best way to learn how to teach is by observing and copying an experienced teacher.

5. It is impossible for teachers new to the profession to reflect on their own teaching.

Photocopiable resource 6 (Task 2.3, page 159)

Teacher follows activities in Teacher's Book carefully and carries them out efficiently	Teacher uses a range of methods to give instructions and check these are understood in a manner appropriate to the level of the class
Teacher maintains good discipline to enable pupils to work effectively	Teacher monitors pair and group work activities
Teacher is able to open and close activities in an orderly fashion	Teacher has the necessary aids to teach the lesson and uses them efficiently
Teacher gives clear simple instructions for pupils to carry out coursebook activities and checks they are understood	Teacher is able to manage transitions between activities smoothly and competently including cases where learners are completing a task at different times
Teacher is aware of the overall purpose of the lesson	Teacher provides extra aids and uses other physical resources efficiently to achieve the goals of the lesson
Teacher plans and carries out activities appropriate to the class and the aims of the lesson	Teacher is aware of the overall purpose of the lesson and how individual activities contribute to the general aim
Teacher closely monitors pair and group work activities and acts on the information gained in an appropriate manner	Teacher is able to combine periods of whole class control with periods of individual work while maintaining overall class control

Photocopiable resource 7 (Task 2.4, page 161)

Question 1	Question 2
. . . .	. . . .
Teacher A	Teacher A
I don't really feel I'm improving very much this week. The first two weeks I felt I was getting better with every lesson, but I can't see any improvement at the moment.	I made loads of mistakes, but I managed to pick up on some of them.
Teacher B	Teacher B
Just pleased it's all over and depressed things didn't go the way I intended. I just feel exhausted.	I don't think it was as good as last time. I thought they'd know the words but they didn't so they couldn't do the reading exercise properly or answer the comprehension questions.
Teacher C	Teacher C
I feel a bag of nerves. I found having everybody sitting at the back of the room made me much more nervous than when they sat at the side like last time.	I don't think they understood the passage despite the fact that I checked by asking them if they understood everything.
Teacher D	Teacher D
Great! At the end two of them came up and thanked me.	Fine! It went just as I intended and I didn't change anything in the plan. I achieved my aims.

Question 3	Question 4
. . . .	. . . .
Teacher A	Teacher A
I managed to slow down the speed of my speech. I didn't gabble like I did the last time.	I'd like to have had more time to check the exercise. I've no idea if they got it right or not.
Teacher B	Teacher B
I'm glad I dictated the definition of the leader article so they all had it.	They found it really hard to use the new words I'd taught them in the exercise.
Teacher C	Teacher C
I felt that by the end of my slot they actually understood when to use the present perfect.	They didn't seem to work very well in pairs.
Teacher D	Teacher D
I was pleased with the fact that they actually seemed to enjoy the lesson.	It took me a really long time to go round checking their answers to the reading comprehension questions. They made so many mistakes!

Question 5
. . . .
Teacher A
I must stop trying to repeat everything they say.
Teacher B
I should have given them more practice in saying the form and taken longer over explaining it.
Teacher C
I'd change the whole thing. They found it all too difficult.
Teacher D
I think I'd cut the last activity.

Photocopiable resource 8 (Task 2.5, page 163)

Question	Issue(s) discussed Comment	Intervention type(s)
It was a nice idea to dictate the definition of the leader article to the students but what was the language purpose of giving them the definition?		
You said they understood the explanation of the past perfect. Do they have the structure in their own first language? Is there a difference between what the teacher should know and what the student should know?		
You said you were not happy with the initial comprehension exercise. You asked the students 'Can you understand this passage?' What does that question tell you as a teacher?		
When you asked someone to read out the sentence, what happened? What could/should you have done? What was the consequence of moving on?		
Did you notice how they worked in pairs? Did some work individually? What do you feel about this?		
It seems you weren't sure what time to set them to do the task, is that right? Should you have been worried? What criteria are you going to use for deciding how long an activity should be, the clock or the student progress?		
How do you want the students to see you? As a guide, as an examiner, as a teacher, as a helper? During your monitoring of their group work, how will the following reinforce or conflict with the role you want them to see you as: • using a red pen to correct what they do? • squatting down to be at their eye level? • walking around the class looking over their shoulders? • only intervening if asked by a student? • asking them about their work?		
Can we think about the following questions about the comprehension passage: Do you want to test the students' comprehension or do you want to teach them to read? What is the difference between testing and teaching reading? What do you mean by 'read the passage silently'? How can you tell if it has been carried out effectively?		

© Cambridge University Press 2001

Photocopiable resource 9 (Task 3.2, page 166)

How important are these roles in your own particular advisory context? Grade each one on a scale of 1 to 5.

   1 = unimportant – this role is redundant
   5 = extremely important – this is a key part of my role

An advisor is:

   1) **A good role model**   5 4 3 2 1
      Someone to be respected through
      professionalism / experience / willingness to learn /
      communication skills etc.

   2) **An organiser**   5 4 3 2 1
      Well organised, able to impose structure etc.,
      meet deadlines, organise others, both in and
      out of the classroom

   3) **A nurturer**   5 4 3 2 1
      Someone who is interested in the
      professional development of others /
      gives energy to the progress of others,
      encourages others to develop ideas

   4) **An observer**   5 4 3 2 1
      Someone who is familiar with a range of observation
      techniques

   5) **A listener**   5 4 3 2 1
      A good listener, encouraging and accessible
      a sympathetic ear

   6) **A supporter**   5 4 3 2 1
      Possesses good counselling skills
      Good at giving feedback
      On your side, understands the difficulties

   7) **An informant**   5 4 3 2 1
      Willing and able to share knowledge and information
      Passes on tips and ideas

   8) **A manager of conflict**   5 4 3 2 1
      A good negotiator; aware of institutional
      politics; strong interpersonal skills; someone to turn to,
      able to deal with difficult situations

   9) **An enthusiast**   5 4 3 2 1
      Someone who is able to motivate,
      make teaching appear interesting, a catalyst

   10) **An action planner**   5 4 3 2 1
      Someone who is able to help the teacher/trainee identify
      areas for further development; to prioritise individual needs
      Good at setting tasks for gradual development

   11) **Teaching skills**   5 4 3 2 1
      Skilled at planning, preparation and execution
      of own teaching; good classroom management
      and organisational skills

   12) **A theoretician**   5 4 3 2 1
      Sound knowledge of the theoretical issues
      behind classroom practice

from: Smith and West-Burnham (1993) 12–14

Photocopiable resource 10 (Task 3.3, page 168)

Different Teachers

The new lesson plan

You are the Head of Department in a secondary school. It is the first lesson of the week and you are about to observe John. You spent a long time with him before the weekend talking through his intentions, talking through his lesson plan and ironing out difficulties. He now presents you with a completely new plan. He says he has thought about it a lot over the weekend and feels his new plan is better. He has clearly spent a great deal of time producing some beautiful professional-looking worksheets. You realise on quickly glancing through that there is insufficient work in the new plan to keep the class occupied and that they will find the worksheets quite easy. There is insufficient time for a lengthy consultation but you do have a few minutes to talk to John. What do you say?[1]

The 'safe' teacher

You are a school-based mentor who has been assigned to help Jane, a newly qualified teacher. Part of your role is to observe her and offer feedback. You have negotiated with Jane that when you observe you will give feedback only on those areas requested by Jane. So far, Jane has asked you to comment on very 'safe' areas, but you feel you are now starting to win her trust and hope you will be able to start to offer guidance on areas where you really feel she needs to improve, such as her instruction-giving and error correction techniques.

You are about to observe Jane and ask her what three areas she would like you to focus on in this lesson. She asks you to give her feedback on the following:

1. whether her board work is neat enough
2. whether her voice is loud enough to be heard at the back of the room

She says she does not really want feedback on anything else. What do you do?

Do I interfere?

You are the usual class teacher and Maria is a trainee who is using your class for her teaching practice.

Maria has planned some excellent information gap worksheets to be completed in pairs which are entirely appropriate to the class and their level. It is the first time she has tried out anything like this and you have done your best to reassure her that the activity is a good one. However, her instructions are rather muddled and although some of the class are working well, it is clear that others are not sure what to do and start messing around and speaking in the L1. One of the pupils shouts out to Maria that the activity is too hard and a pupil sitting next to you turns round and says 'Miss, I don't understand what she's saying. What are we supposed to do?' It is clear that Maria is starting to panic and is about to give up on the activity. What do you do?

The fatal mistake

You are an inspector observing Ahmed, a non-specialist teacher of English. The teacher is very nervous and keeps making mistakes in his English. At one point, he makes the students repeat: 'Did he went there yesterday?' He then writes this sentence on the board and asks the students to copy it into their exercise books. Would you intervene in this case? If not, what would you do?

© Cambridge University Press 2001

[1] This scenario comes from one described in Calvert, M. and Fletcher, S. (1994) *Working with your Student Teacher*, Cheltenham: Nelson Thornes.

Photocopiable resource 11 (Task 3.4, page 169)

OBSERVATION FORM A[1]

Teacher	Date
Class Grade	
Book	

Description of the classroom

Objectives as written on the lesson plan, stated by the teacher, or based on observations

   To what extent were these achieved?

Skills practised

Materials and aids used

Description of the lesson (continue on a separate sheet if necessary)

Time	Activities (what is happening)	Interaction pattern (e.g. T → SS; S → S

COMMENTS AND SUGGESTIONS (sentence completion by observer)

1. The best thing about the lesson was ....
2. Another thing I enjoyed was ....
3. The teacher really ....
4. The students were ....
5. There was a lot of ....
6. I would have liked to see ....
7. The hardest thing for me as an observer was ....
8. The next time I observe this teacher I would like to see ....

© Cambridge University Press 2001

[1] We would like to thank the teachers from the Sosnowiec cluster of training colleges, Poland for providing this form

OBSERVATION FORM B[2]
Focus on classroom management

PART A

Is there a clear point at which this lesson begins?   Yes / No

During the lesson, focus on *staging, instructions, organization*
Then answer these questions by ticking the appropriate box and adding comments as necessary.

	Always	Sometimes	Never	Comments
Were you clear when a new stage in the lesson began?				
Was the transition from one stage to another smooth and logical?				
Were the instructions to students clear / easy to understand?				
Were the instructions checked?				
Did the teacher manage changes of group activity well?				
Could students easily see and hear each other and the teacher?				
Did the teacher handle handle aids / respond to the physical environment well?				

PART B
How is the seating arranged – semi-circle / U-shape / rows
Draw a plan of the classroom below, marking on it males and females. Then each time an individual speaks mark it on the chart as in the example overleaf.

© Cambridge University Press 2001

[2] A variation of this form was first given to us by Roberta Allam

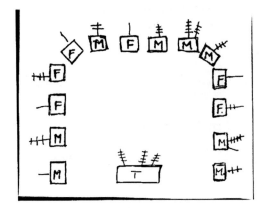
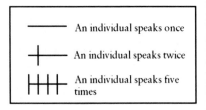

OBSERVATION FORM C
Use of questions

PART A

Complete the following form by keeping a tally of the results.

How many times does:

the teacher	In L1	In L2
ask a display question i.e. a question to which everyone knows the answer?		
ask a referential question i.e. a question to which s/he does not know the answer?		
say "Do you understand?", "is that clear"? etc.		
ask a question which really checks understanding?		
prompt a student to ask a question?		
ask a question to check what to do, understanding etc.?		
ask a question to practise the language?		

PART B

After asking a question, on average, how long does the teacher wait for an answer?

0–5 seconds	
5–10 seconds	
Longer than 10 seconds	

PART C

What does the teacher do when a student answers a question correctly?

If a student does not know the correct answer what does the teacher do?

Photocopiable resource 12 (Task 3.5, page 171)

Teacher A

This teacher is working in a secondary school and has a marked tendency to concentrate on the boys in her class at the expense of the girls. She directs more questions to boys, boys speak more and when working in groups she monitors groups of boys much more frequently and for longer than she does girls. She is completely unaware that she is doing this. Design an observation form which you could use to bring evidence to her of the way she is operating and make her aware of current practice.

Teacher B

This teacher asks a lot of questions in class but the same students always seem to answer. This is partly because when he asks the question only a small number of pupils put up their hands and he always chooses one of these. Design a form which would make him aware of current practice and alert him to other possibilities in this area.

Teacher C

This teacher is reasonably aware of learners' errors in the area of grammar and corrects these regardless of whether the activity is fluency- or accuracy-based, but completely ignores pronunciation errors. You are unsure whether this is deliberate. In terms of error correction techniques, the teacher tends to nominate another student to correct or corrects the mistake himself. Design a form which you could use to bring evidence to the feedback session of the types of errors which she selects for correction, as well as the techniques she uses to correct the errors.

Photocopiable resource 13 (Task 3.6, page 172)

Observer:

Area of comment	Aspect	P, N, or D
Personality		
Planning		
Classroom management		
Language		
Teaching techniques		

Photocopiable resource 14 (Task 3.6, page 172)

9.15 Good, confident attitude to class
Gave out handouts reasonably efficiently although
didn't check the instructions had been understood

Good setting up of pair work "Guess the Story"- again
didn't check understanding of instructions
Good monitoring of pair work. Responded to SS
questions

Why were there two sheets? The 2 sheets led to SS
creating separate stories

Good valuing of what students were producing

SS given no longer than four minutes to create story. Only
4 minutes? Why?

T misinterpreted Maxine's attempt to pronounce 'lay'

9.35 Nicely acted story

9.36 T asked the SS to think of the Q. she was going to ask
Why? Is T aware of the <u>reasons</u> for the activity?

Good acting and lively presence in the discussion.
Appropriate for adults

9.40 Good elicitation of the mistake 'For'

Problem with the presentation of <u>to</u> make /tuː meɪk/
  a) stress of TO
  b) incorrect explanation of ellipsis

9.45 Nice production of story in groups

9.50 Gave out cards
Good use of intonation and paralinguistics to liven up
this stage
SS responses to find and number

9.55 T introduces idea of people who travel regularly on a
plane

10.00 Cindy Crawford situation was not well presented.
Weakness about giving instructions

10.03 h/o given out and S asked to read introduction
Attention to individuals - pointed out the SS who didn't
use 'to'

Lesson showed good attention to phonology
Aim achieved, but were aims sophisticated enough?
Aids well produced and handled well?
Manner lively but is it entirely appropriate to students?

Photocopiable resource 15 (Task 3.7, page 173)

1. A: Tell me about what you did when the pupils started to work in groups.
2. T: I went to one group of boys.
3. A: Why?
4. T: I wanted to explain to them what to do.
5. A: Had they understood your instructions?
6. T: A bit.
7. A: Your written instructions which you gave to every group were very nicely prepared and they were quite long, but had the group fully understood them?
8. T: Not really.
9. A: So. What did you do?
10. T: I explained to them.
11. A: Did you? I'm not sure that is exactly what you did. Tell me exactly what you did.
12. T: I told them what to do.
13. A: That isn't what I saw. How did you tell them? Did you read the instructions to them?
14. T: Yes, I think so.
15. A: I thought you got them to pick up the cards and play the game. Isn't that right?
16. T: Oh yes.
17. A: Is that the same as giving them instructions?
18. T: No. Not quite.
19. A: So, what method did you use to 'explain' to them? Did you show them or tell them again in words?
20. T: Oh. I showed them.
21. A: Does that give you any ideas about the best way to explain complicated games to students?
22. T: Yes. Demonstration.
23. A: Right, it is much easier to demonstrate something than to try to explain it in words isn't it?
24. T: Yes.
25. A: Another point I'd like to discuss about that is, why did you go to that group of boys?
26. T: To see if they understood.
27. A: OK. Good. You wanted to check if your instructions have been understood, but why that group? Why not another group?
28. T: Because they were on my right.
29. A: Because they were on your right?
30. T: Yes. That is the Islamic way.
31. A: Interesting. You chose the right side of the class because that is the natural way to start in Islamic culture, is that right?
32. T: Yes.
33. A: OK. But is that a good pedagogic reason? Do you understand what I mean?

229

34. T: Yes. Is it a good reason for teaching.
35. A: Yes. What are the reasons from a teaching point of view for deciding which group to go to?
36. T: Should I start in the middle?
37. A: That's another reason based on the position of the group. Are there any reasons from the teaching point of view?
38. T: I don't understand.
39. A: What did we say is the reason for the first, quick monitoring of the group work?
40. T: To see if they know what to do.
41. A: So who should you go to first, those who can understand or those who you think will have difficulty understanding?
42. T: Those who are not understanding.
43. A: Yes. So, as the girls in this class are much better than the boys, you did not really need to go to the girls first because they quickly worked out what to do. But the boys were having more trouble.
44. T: So I should go to the pupils who are not understanding first, is that right?
45. A: Yes I think so. As it happens you did the best thing, but only because the boys were sitting to your right.

Devise a series of leading questions for a trainee in the following situations:

> Following a pairwork exercise, the trainee asks each student to stand up and read out the problem and another to stand up and provide the answer. No effective feedback is given by the trainee and many of the students cannot hear what the students are saying.

> The trainee asks the students to read a comprehension passage aloud round the class without any preparation for the reading of the passage. The trainee then proceeds to ask detailed questions about the vocabulary of the passage and finally asks questions to check on comprehension, which have to be written down in their exercise books.

© Cambridge University Press 2001

Photocopiable resource 16 (Task 4.1, page 175)

A
A: The student in the comer seemed to be having problems with the oral exercise.

T: Yes. Cheryl always seems to have problems speaking in the class when she is asked, but she is very good when I talk to her quietly.

A: Have you tried giving her enough time to think up her answer before she speaks?

T: I always try to give students as much time as I can, but it's really difficult when you've got other students who can answer much more quickly.

B
A: How do you feel it went?

T: They seem to understand the grammar work alright, but when it comes to using the grammar in their speech, they make all sorts of mistakes. I don't know why.

A: Yes, there is always a lot of difficulty getting students to put the rules into practice.

T: The open discussion was supposed to give them the chance to use the language, but I felt that they didn't really use the language we had been practising.

C
A: How successful do you think you were in achieving your objectives?

T: Parts of the lesson went quite well, but in others I felt less happy.

A: I would agree with you. I particularly thought the practice exercise was quite difficult for the children and your explanation did not really help that much.

T: Yes. I hadn't expected them to find the exercise so difficult. We've done other exercises like this before so I didn't expect them to have any problems.

A: I have often had the same problem. I've learnt from bitter experience to give too many explanations rather than too few.

D

A: What do you feel about the class?

T: I'm having a lot of problems controlling Denise. She always plays me up. She's a really difficult child.

A: Yes, she was being somewhat disruptive. Perhaps the way you approach her is not the best. If I say to you 'Please stop that noise! Act your age. You're supposed to be responsible at this age,' how do you feel?

T: I would feel angry and embarrassed.

A: And is that a positive feeling? How do you think Denise would act if she felt like that?

E

A: I liked the way you handled the reading comprehension. It really was an interesting passage and the questions were well thought through. What did you think about the punctuation exercise?

T: I can never find interesting ways to explain punctuation, and the class get very bored with endless exercises when they have to copy things out.

A: Yes, I've always found punctuation difficult to handle. There are times when it is necessary to do simple exercises. When I was a new teacher I used to get worried about boring the students. I now realise that there are times when the students will be bored, but it is necessary for them to do exercises sometimes.

F

A: Talk me through the lesson.

T: The listening stage of the lesson seemed to go quite well. Most of them seemed to follow what was on the tape.

A: Yes, but you had to play the tape several times. There was a lot of noise in the class. You will get their attention much better if you play the tape at a lower volume.

G

T: The blackboard is really useful, but the wet cloth which I use makes it difficult to write on afterwards. A dry cloth doesn't get the board clean enough. What we need is proper blackboard cleaners, but the head says we can't afford them.

A: Do all the other teachers have the same problems? It might be worth talking to other teachers about it. What do you think? Is that possible?

Photocopiable resource 17 (Task 4.3, page 178)

Exam cheat[1]

After photocopying the role cards the trainer should cut between them and distribute separately.

Role card for Decision Maker

You are a medical student in your final year and you have just taken the last paper in your final exams.

From where you were sitting during the examination you could see quite clearly that another student was cheating by continually referring to a small book. Term is at an end. You tried to find the student who cheated immediately after the examination but discovered that they had already left for home.

What should you do? Report a fellow student? Sit back and allow someone who has cheated enter as a fellow professional to a profession respected for its integrity?

Before coming to your decision you can talk to four people who may help you. They are: your flatmate, who is also a medical student; the president of the students' union, who is not a medical student; your tutor, with whom you can discuss matters such as this in confidence; and your own doctor. You will see them each in turn for about ten minutes. You must then reach a reasoned decision.

Role Card A – for Flatmate	**Role Card B – for the President of the Students' Union**
You are a medical student in your final year and have just completed your final examinations. Your flatmate is a medical student in the same year. He wants your help in solving a dilemma.	You are president of the students' union at university and in the last year of your course, reading law. A member of the union who is a final year medical student wants your help with a problem.

Role Card C – for Tutor	**Role Card D – for Doctor**
You are a university lecturer in medicine and part of your job is to act as a personal tutor to about 25 students throughout their course at the university. One of your students, who is now in his final year, wants your help with a dilemma. The confidentiality of the relationship between a student and his tutor is respected throughout the university.	You are one of three doctors attached to the university. One of your patients is a medical student, now in his final year. He has seen you for minor ailments over the last few years, but now needs your help with a different sort of problem.

[1] From *A Handbook of Management Training Exercises*, published in 1978 by the British Association of Commercial and Industrial Education, 16 Park Crescent, London W1N 4AP.

Photocopiable resource 18 (Task 4.3, page 178)

Exam cheat role play
Behaviour Observation Sheet

You are going to observe four role plays involving a medical student who has a problem. The student is going to ask four people in turn for advice.

Try to note down what each of the people giving advice is actually doing. Each time one of the advisors makes a comment which fits into one of the categories listed, place a tick in that category.

Also try to make a note of the non-verbal behaviour of each observer.

	Flatmate	S.U. President	Tutor	Doctor
Supporting				
Offering suggestions				
Giving opinions				
Giving information				
Asking for information				
Asking for views				
Asking for proposals				
Criticising				
Paraphrasing				
Summarising				
Asking questions for clarification				
Back-channelling				

Non-verbal Behaviour

	Flatmate	S.U. President	Tutor	Doctor
leaning forward				
sitting face to face				
mirroring speaker				
crossed arms				
relaxed but crossed arms				
eye contact				
nodding				
smiling				
other non-verbal responses (make a note of these)				

Photocopiable resource 19 (Task 4.4, page 179)

Role cards

Advisor

You are about to observe a new teacher. Your aim is to:

a) put the teacher at ease and reassure him/her about your role
b) find out about the context of the observed lesson
c) have a clear idea of the teacher's intentions for this particular lesson
d) see if the teacher has any particular concerns you may be able to help with
e) set targets for the observed lesson

Teacher

You are a new teacher and are quite nervous about being observed. You know the advisor wants to talk to you about the lesson. You have some lesson notes but are not sure about the 'correct format' for the lesson plan, so do not want to show these to the advisor. You are unsure about the exact purpose of the advisor's visit. Think of a specific lesson you have taught or use a lesson plan and class profile to talk through the lesson with the advisor.

Observer

Use the following notes to observe the verbal and non-verbal behaviour of the advisor and teacher.

1. How does the advisor sit in relation to the teacher? What posture does the advisor adopt?
2. How do you think the teacher is feeling? How can you tell?
3. How does the advisor try to put the teacher at ease? Make a note of the actual language that is used and any non-verbal behaviour you feel is helpful in this respect.
4. As an observer, do you have a clear idea of the lesson in terms of the overall aims and content?
5. Make a note of the questions which elicit the best response from the teacher.

Photocopiable resource 20 (Task 5.1, page 182)

Feedback session 2

A student on TP (S) has a second session with her mentor (M). She is an English MFL (Modern Foreign Language) teacher of French. Mark the type of intervention (A = Authoritative, F = Facilitative). Try to decide exactly which type of authoritative or facilitative intervention is used.

// = boundary between interventions

Intervention Type

1. M //So how do you think things went?
2. S PAUSE (student puts hands to face in mock despair)
3. M //Well, were you happy with the way things progressed . . . generally.//
4. S Err. . . well I find that last group quite difficult to handle and like when Ashley decided to play up, I somehow lost the direction of the lesson and became worried that he was going to start up again.
5. M //He is a difficult pupil who is obviously aware of your status as a trainee.// We will need to look at strategies for coping with that . . . maybe later.// But firstly, the lesson as a whole . . . tell me the good points and . . . bits you feel you need to work on.
6. S Err. . . discipline. I don't think that they respect me. Some do. They work really well but I tend to focus all my teaching on them, I know I shouldn't, but all I get from the boys is like sarcastic comments and a load of lip.
7. M //You must be careful not to generalise.// There are some hard working boys in the group// . . . and you could be ignoring them because of this kind of sweeping categorisation.// What about the good points, let's focus on them first?//
8. S Some of the homework I got in from them last week was quite good. I've given some of them merits and asked them to make copies on paper, so that we can make a board display.
9. M //Good.// They would like to do something like that.// We did a huge collage for last Christmas, with all the different areas of France and Germany on it.// They loved doing it and genuinely felt proud of the product.// Good.//
10. S Some haven't given me homework now for two weeks. What do I need to do with those?
11. M //Have you confronted them about this?//
12. S Yes. I think that may have been the start of Ashley's tantrum.
13. M //Well, maybe after the lesson would be best to speak to him.// //He loves an audience,// so beware of challenging him in front of the group.//
14. S OK. So do you think I should speak to him at the end of the lesson or in tutor time or something.

15. M //Yes.// It is less confrontational and he'll probably listen if he is on his own.//

16. S And what about the others? I am still missing . . . err . . . six pieces of work.

17. M //I bet I could guess the names too.// Let me look at your register.// Yes. I will speak to these boys and warn them that the work needs to be handed to you by the next lesson or they can have an after-school detention. Can you jot those down on a piece of paper for me?//

18. S Yes. Thank you. I'll speak to Ashley tomorrow as well.

19. M Hmmm . . . //I think I'll catch up with him too on this occasion. It may seem a bit unfair otherwise.// You know, like you singled him out.//

20. S I would like to be there though so that they don't think I am unaware of the chat you are going to have with them.

21. M Yes. //Any other point about the lesson that you feel needs discussing.// What about the timing for instance?//

22. S It started off OK, but then when I set them the shopping list task I don't think I really gave them enough time to complete the answers, which meant that half the group couldn't understand the next task which I wrote on the board.

23. M //I agree. Things went a bit too quickly after the vocabulary opening.// You could have differentiated the shopping list to enable those who can work quicker to complete the work and continue with the task that you wrote on the board. It would have also meant the slower individuals in the group could have been given more attention and help in completing what was set.//

24. S Yes. The differentiation in the lesson worked well for the girl groups, who were working well. They are quite talented and the two girls at the front completed all the questions and the question boxes in the textbook. That detail of lesson planning really worked well for them. That made me really pleased. Although I feel they are the sort of pupils who would complete any task well.

25. N //I think some of the group were more on task than last week, certainly.//

26. S It didn't feel like that. It was like I was teaching two groups in one class. Most of my attention was directed at the disruptive lot at the back. I didn't feel that I was 'teaching' . . . not getting the opportunity to.

27. M //Well, you need to think about ways not only to impose sanctions upon them but also ways in which you can create opportunities to praise them.//

28. S I did say to them that they did really well in the quiz last week and that I hoped they would behave themselves well enough in order for us to play the game again. But by the end of the lesson, there was no way I was going to allow that to happen.

29. M //Retrospectively, do you think that was the best way to end the lesson?//

30. S I didn't feel I had much choice. I had warned them last week that if their behaviour wasn't acceptable, we wouldn't play the game. And their behaviour was anything but acceptable!

31. M //Not all of them though.// You finished the lesson by sitting them all in silence.//

32. S Yes. I was concerned about letting them out to the next class in the silly mood they were in. Particularly as the other student has them next!

33. M //But it was a punishment for the good ones in the group as well as the naughty ones.//

34. S But it seems that there are just so many of them. If I played the game with the good ones it would end up with only four or five playing it! And I wouldn't know what to do with the naughty ones whilst I was playing with the others.

35. M //I think it would be more than that.// Again you must be observant to the whole group and not be too black and white in your judgments.// If the ringleaders are isolated, the rest of the group could be warned about the actions you will take.// Then introduce the games even to a reduced number at the end of the lesson. They will soon learn to respond to the threat of no games, if it is approached more subtly.// Use rewards too. Merits or even a chocolate prize for the highest scoring house at the end of the term.//

36. S Do you think they would respond to making them jealous, you know what I mean, that they are not included.

37. M //You saw how much they enjoyed it last week, it may very well work.//

38. S Yeah. Even Ashley seemed to get quite motivated, though he always spoils it by going over the top.

39. M //Well, I think that you have got a lot to consider there.// I don't think that content, manner, planning etc. seem to be causing any real concern.// And at the moment, probably you've got enough to focus on in getting the group working without the added worry of other professional concerns.//

40. S Yes. Unless there is anything that you think would help the group in settling and behaving themselves.

41. M //I think the strategies we have discussed today need to be the immediate focus for the next lesson.// Ensure that these are indicated on your plan and don't forget to implement them for the next lesson.// Run through this strategy through your mind a couple of times so that it happens quite naturally.//

42. S And the report slips we will go through tomorrow?

43. M //Yes. Cheer up!//

Photocopiable resource 21 (Task 5.2, page 188)

		Feelings	Int.
1	The . . . didn't go very well.		
2	It's always difficult to . . .		
3	I've always found . . . very hard.		
4	What did you feel about . . .?		
5	How did you feel the . . . went?		
6	Don't you think you should've . . .?		
7	I liked the way you . . .		
8	The . . . went very well.		
9	I thought the . . . was well done.		
10	Have you ever tried . . .?		

Intentions/Interventions (Int.):

a)	*Inviting self-evaluation*	b)	*Directing*
c)	*Consultative prescription*	d)	*Benevolent prescription*
e)	*Empathising*	f)	*Providing alternatives*
g)	*Personal interpretation*	h)	*Disclosure*
i)	*Confronting*	j)	*Focusing attention*
k)	*Feedback*	l)	*Providing reinforcement*

Alternatives:

1	
2	
3	
4	
5	
6	
7	
8	
9	
10	

© Cambridge University Press 2001

Photocopiable resource 22 (Task 5.3, page 189)

Listen to the statements read out by the tutor. As you hear each statement, mark along the line the degree to which you 'heard' the statement as supportive (the 'S' end) or threatening (the 'T' end) or neutral (in the middle).

In each case, imagine the comment being made in a specific context. Try to note down what you think the tutor's 'intention' was in making the comment in that context. For example, was it providing empathy, or was it challenging?

e.g. Listen to this:

'Why didn't you ask the pupils to repeat the dialogue?'

		Context	Int.
A	N S —————— T		
B	N S —————— T		
C	N S —————— T		
D	N S —————— T		
E	N S —————— T		
F	N S —————— T		
G	N S —————— T		

Intentions/Interventions (Int.):

m)	*Inviting self-evaluation*	n)	*Directing*
o)	*Consultative prescription*	p)	*Benevolent prescription*
q)	*Empathising*	r)	*Providing alternatives*
s)	*Personal interpretation*	t)	*Disclosure*
u)	*Confronting*	v)	*Focusing attention*
w)	*Feedback*	x)	*Providing reinforcement*

© Cambridge University Press 2001

Photocopiable resource 23 (Task 5.4, page 191)

Session 1

(B: Teacher; A: Observer/mentor)

1. A: . . . Yes, B . . . it was a good lesson . . . you elicited the information and completed the table on the . . . blackboard . . . to elicit and . . . build up . . . the . . . production model . . . you also used your . . . voice . . . to . . . indicate mistakes.

2. B: Thank you.

3. A: I . . . noticed that . . . you were . . . keeping yourself . . . er . . . aligned to the . . . row near the door . . . rather than . . . moving to the . . . other side of the . . . classroom.

4. B: Oho!

5. A: What do you think?

6. B: My movement . . . actually not always . . . I think . . . this is the . . . least movement . . . that I have done in . . . this lesson. I usually move around . . . keep moving . . . running actually and I . . . it is interesting . . . you know . . . you raised this point . . . because it gives me a . . . chance of considering myself . . . and really what I feel . . . during this . . . stage of the . . . lesson . . . at the production model . . . I am always trying . . . to be at the front . . . of the class.

---

7. A: What do you think about . . . your . . . voice, B?

8. B: I think . . . well . . . I think . . . it is quite . . . loud, sometimes . . . but . . . mm . . . that is a . . . habit of mine . . . Have you got any . . . point which is . . . you know.

9. A: I don't . . . know . . . you see . . . my voice and your voice . . . are far different . . .

10. B: In tune . . . you mean?

11. A: Yes . . . your voice is very loud and . . . my voice is very . . . weak.

12. B: It is not weak . . . but . . . I must confess . . . and really I'm glad you . . . raised that point . . . I feel of myself I'm . . . a bit loud . . . I agree with you . . . and . . . it caused . . . tiredness to the vocal cords . . . of . . . and always . . . I try hard to . . . keep . . . my . . . (voice) down a bit . . . but I could not. I feel my voice . . . is not . . . clear when I am trying to . . . a bit . . . quieter . . .

13. A: However, B, you spoke very . . . confidently to the . . . students . . . Your instructions were . . . very . . . clear.

14. B: Thank you.

© Cambridge University Press 2001

Session 2

(A: Teacher; B: Observer/mentor)

1. B: Well A . . . before I say my opinion of the lesson I want you to . . . tell me . . . how it went in . . . general.

2. A: Well . . . I did what I . . . expected (planned) to do. I . . . worked through steps by . . . or following the notes . . . in the teacher's book and adding something . . . but in general . . . I saw it . . . or . . . I did it . . . well.

3. B: What about . . . the . . . aims of this lesson, the linguistic aims and . . . the skills?

4. A: The aim . . . as written in the book is to . . . practise the use of . . . 'can' and 'can't' and how to . . . join two sentences with one word like . . . 'or', 'and', 'also' . . . these words . . . this is my aim of the lesson . . . and I think I . . . covered all the skills . . . listening, speaking and writing . . . and reading.

5. B: You see . . . one of the aims of this lesson . . . is to . . . use . . . connective words 'or', 'also' and 'and' but do you think . . . the students have understood . . . the use of these words?

6. A: During the lesson . . . yes . . . but after the lesson . . . they do not . . . remember . . . but I did not explain . . .

7. B: Yes . . . I think . . . you should have given the students more examples to . . . clarify the use of these words.

8. A: Well . . . I . . . forgot to do this . . . and . . . the teacher's book suggested this . . . because I had to . . . relate this to the . . . time of the lesson.

9. B: I agree with you about the . . . time . . . but it would . . . have been better if you . . . had thrown some . . . short . . . examples.

10. A: (Nodding his head with no verbal reply.)

---

11. B: You used drawing to . . . clarify the . . . meaning of 'can't' on the board . . . you did this by drawing on the . . . blackboard. This was good . . . because I see this . . . as . . . an . . . additional aid to the aids . . . suggested by the teacher's book . . . but you . . . did not give more examples . . . and . . . did not . . . explain the opposite of 'can't' . . . 'can'.

12. A: No . . . I . . . thought the . . . students know from the word 'no' . . . it is the opposite . . . of 'yes'.

13. B: Anyway . . . I don't think these words are new words . . . What do you think?

14. A: No . . . they were not new words.

© Cambridge University Press 2001

Photocopiable resource 24 (Task 6.1, page 193)

Sketch 1

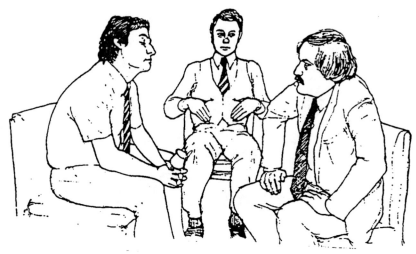

From Pease, A. (1981) *Body Language*. Sheldon Press

Sketch 2

From Pease, A. (1981) *Body Language*. Sheldon Press

Sketch 3

From Pease, A. (1981) *Body Language*. Sheldon Press

Sketch 4

From Pease, A. (1981) *Body Language*. Sheldon Press

Photocopiable resource 25 (Task 6.1, page 193)

Sketch 1
The man on the left is using superiority gestures and appears to have an arrogant attitude towards the man sitting opposite. He is using the eye block signal as his brain attempts to block the other man from sight and his head is tilted back to 'look down his nose' at him. Defensiveness is evident as his knees are held tightly together and he is holding a wine glass with both hands to form a barrier. The man in the middle has been excluded from the conversation as the other two men have not formed a triangle to include him. He does, however, seem quite aloof as shown by his thumbs-in-waistcoat gesture (superiority), he is leaning back on his chair and is sitting with his legs apart. His head is in the neutral position. The man on the right has heard enough and has taken the starter's position (ready to leave) and his foot and body are pointed toward the nearest exit. His eyebrows and the corners of his mouth are turned down, and his head is slightly down, all of which demonstrates disapproval.

Sketch 2
The man on the left is using an excellent gesture cluster to convey openness and honesty – exposed palms, foot forward, head up, coat unbuttoned, arms and legs apart, leaning forward and smiling gestures. Unfortunately for him, however, his story is not going across. The woman is sitting back in her chair with her legs crossed away (defensive), she has a partial arm-barrier (defensive), a clenched fist (hostile), head down and is using the critical evaluation gesture (hand to face). The man in the middle is using the raised steeple gesture, indicating that he feels confident or superior, and he is sitting in the figure 4 leg position, showing that his attitude is competitive or argumentative. We assume that his overall attitude is negative. As he is sitting back, his head is down.

Sketch 3
This sequence also shows a tense atmosphere. All three men are sitting back in their chairs to keep the maximum distance from each other. The man on the right is causing the problem because of his negative gesture cluster. As he is speaking, he is using the nose touch gesture (deceit) and his right arm has crossed his body to make a partial arm barrier (defensive). His lack of concern about the other men's opinions is shown by the leg-over-chair gesture and his body is pointed away from them. The man on the left disapproves of what the man on the right has to say as he is using the lint-picking gesture (disapproval), his legs are crossed (defensive) and pointed away (uninterested). The man in the middle would like to say something but is holding back his opinion, shown by his self-restraint gesture of gripping the arms of the chair and locked ankles. He has also issued a non-verbal challenge to the man on the right by pointing his body at him.

Sketch 4
In this scene the man on the left and the woman have mirrored each other's gestures and are forming 'bookends' on the couch. The couple are very interested in each other and have positioned their heads in such a way that they can expose their wrists and they have crossed their legs towards one another. The man in the middle has a tight-lipped smile which can make him appear interested in what the other man has to say but it is not consistent with his other facial and body gestures. His head is down (disapproval) his eyebrows are also down (anger) and he is giving the other man a sideways glance. In addition to this, his arms and legs are tightly crossed (defensive), all indicating that he has a very negative attitude.

Pease 1981: 140–146

© Cambridge University Press 2001

Photocopiable resource 26 (Task 6.2, page 194)

Role play 1

A	B	C
Tell B about the most difficult lesson you have ever taught. Describe it in some detail. At times, stop to think what to say next.	Be very interested in what A is saying. If A hesitates, prompt A to continue. You want A to tell you everything.	Make a note of the way B behaves. Note particularly: ■ eye contact ■ body posture ■ anything B says

Role play 2

A	B	C
Tell B about a novel you have read recently. Describe in detail the characters, the plot and the things you liked or didn't like about it.	Listen to what A is saying, but generally do not make eye contact with A. As A is speaking, make careful notes about what is being said, but do not ask A to repeat.	Make a note of the way B behaves. Note particularly: ■ eye contact ■ body posture ■ anything B says

Role play 3

A	B	C
Tell B about the most interesting or enjoyable day you have spent in the last two years. Describe it in some detail. At times stop to think what to say next.	Appear to be interested in what A is saying, but also try to hear what the next group is talking about.	Make a note of the way B behaves. Note particularly: ■ eye contact ■ body posture ■ anything B says

Role play 4

A	B	C
Tell B about your ideal house. Describe it in some detail, outlining how many rooms you would want in it, what furniture you would want in it and how you would want to decorate it.	You are not interested in the slightest degree in what A is saying and you want A to stop as soon as possible, but you must not say so openly.	Make a note of the way B behaves. Note particularly: ■ eye contact ■ body posture ■ anything B says

Role play 5

A	B	C
Tell B about a problem you once had as an advisor. Describe it in some detail. At times stop to think what to say next.	You are much more interested in talking than you are listening. Make sure you tell A about your own experiences in this area.	Make a note of the way B behaves. Note particularly: ■ eye contact ■ body posture ■ anything B says

Photocopiable resource 27 (Task 6.3, page 195)

The extract below is the complete text of a pre-lesson chat. The observer has not watched this particular teacher before.

1.   O: OK, T. Would you like to carry this conversation in Czech or in English?
2.   T: I would like carry it in English.
3.   O: Fine, can you tell me a little bit about the class?
4.   T: It isn't a special class, but it's a small-sized class, but I think rather weak. They are weak not only in English, but in other subjects too.
5.   O: And are there any difficult children?
6.   T: I think you could notice the boy by the window. He is not very interested and he is very weak so he cannot understand very much. I get his friend to help him.
7.   O: How important is English for them because they are a technical school?
8.   T: I think they like English but they are a bit lazy but to my mind English shouldn't be a big problem for them at the technical school. I think there are other problems. English is something different for them. It's more relaxed than technical subjects.
9.   O: You mean 'relaxed' by the methods, by the way English is taught in contrast with more traditional subjects?
10.   T: Yes, I mean the methods and the atmosphere, I think it's completely different. If you try to prepare the lesson for them, I think they appreciate it. A bit.
11.   O: So, this is their second year of English. Which textbook do you use?
12.   T: We use Cambridge Course Number I and we do Unit 23 now.
13.   O: Will you try to do every exercise in the book or do you choose because you know this is not the academic study where maybe they need more practical things?
14.   T: Yes, I make a choice. I will do exercise . . . and . . . today.
15.   O: And do you think they can do all this? Can you see anything that you think maybe will be difficult for them?
16.   T: Well, they are shy and maybe they are nervous from being observed.
17.   O: This is their first time?
18.   T: Yes and this is the reason I try to introduce pair and group work because they encourage each other and are more self-confident when they work in a group. I have noticed that they have really changed completely when they stopped sitting behind their desks and came into groups. They liven up and become increasingly interested in what they are doing.
19.   O: I can see only one problem. Maybe they start to speak Czech.
20.   T: Yes, if the rules of their work are not speak Czech, they follow rules, but if there is a space for speaking Czech, if they discuss some problem, well then I can't avoid it.
21.   O: Will you react in any way? Or will you just leave them?
22.   T: No, I won't leave them. Every lesson I tell them 'Don't speak Czech – try to speak English as much as you can.'

23. O: What about the mistakes they make?
24. T: I think a teacher should be patient, because mistakes at this level of learning English are something natural.
25. O: Yes, it's a kind of learning to make mistakes. Do you ever mark them, if they make all these mistakes, do you ever examine them?
26. T: No, I don't give them marks in these situations, but if I hear one mistake a lot of times, after finishing the game or the competition, I tell them. For example, they often use present progressive instead of simple, then I tell them.
27. O: I think it's a very good thing not to discourage them. So how do you get your marks?
28. T: I wanted to say something about the latest problem – they speak Czech, but when I want to finish the activity, they say 'no no let us finish' – they are involved even though they speak some Czech.
29. O: Yes, this is what happens sometimes. My question was about marking because there is this report. How do you decide about marks?
30. T: Well, we write tests, short tests and longer tests after finishing each unit, but I evaluate their work at every lesson, too. They know that a part of their mark is not only their written tests and work but also their oral work in every lesson.
31. O: And will you give them any extra writing?
32. T: No, I didn't plan to do this. Oh dear, maybe I should because in this lesson it is all speaking and listening. Do you think I should give them writing?
33. O: No, no not in the lesson. I like this homework you are giving them to write dos and don'ts to teachers. Is this the way you always choose to make it interesting for them?
34. T: Sometimes, when it suits me and when it is suitable. I can see they are very happy to do something like that.
35. O: Is there anything special you want me to notice when I am observing you?
36. T: Sorry?
37. O: Is there anything you want me to look for in particular when I am watching you?
38. T: No, no.
39. O: Is there anything else you would like to say?
40. T: Only that I teach at this school for four months, so my experience is very short. As for my subject, I can't see a lot of problems. My biggest problem is that students don't pay a lot of attention to English. They enjoy the work at the lesson but to do something at home is a big problem.
41. O: Yes, this is a problem perhaps of all the technical schools. Do you think that teaching at basic school was more rewarding and pupils were more interested?
42. T: I wouldn't say this. I think it's harder work at the basic school because children are smaller and they aren't able to concentrate. I think the work at secondary school is easier.

Photocopiable resource 28[1] (Task 6.4, page 197)

The two extracts form part of two different post-lesson discussions which took place in a secondary school outside Britain. In Extract A, the teacher is at the end of the first year of a four-year pre-service training course.

Extract A
The students were asked to read three short texts dealing with overpopulation and summarise each in one sentence.

1. S: Okay, so after you'd got them to read the texts what happened next?
2. T: I asked them to answer the questions on page 48 summarising the main point of each extract. Yes, I know that was a mess.
3. S: What makes you say that?
4. T: Well, none of them could answer. I think maybe it was just too difficult for them.
5. S: Do you really think that is why?
6. T: Well, it might have been because you were there . . . They're not used to visitors.
7. S: Do you think so? But they weren't too bad on the bit before, were they? *(He means on the introductory phase of the lesson.)* I mean some of them were answering. But they were OK before then weren't they? . . . while you were doing the warm-up? They were answering OK then.
8. T: Yeah *(laughs)* I don't know then – maybe it was just too difficult.
9. S: What was too difficult?
10. T: The level of the texts. I could have made sure they knew all the difficult words beforehand.
11. S: So it was the text itself . . . But what about the girl at the back – who said nuclear weapons?
12. T: Yes I felt a bit bad about that.
13. S: Why? Was that right or wrong?
14. T: Wrong . . .
15. S: Well . . .
16. T: Maybe she would have gone on to say something else.
17. S: And the answer you wanted was 'Overpopulation might cause nuclear war' or something like that? . . . was it?
18. T: Yes, maybe I should have probed, you know, or maybe the way the coursebook did it wasn't the best way?
19. S: What might have been better do you think?
20. T: Just to ask about one text at a time – and maybe it was too general for the beginning.
21. S: What?
22. T: Maybe the question was too general – you know – they needed to understand everything, well . . . not everything. Maybe the question was too broad, you know. They had to understand everything – extensive reading.
23. S: Maybe.
24. T: They had to understand and they had to tell everything . . . three times. *(laughs)*
25. S: Yes maybe it was a bit much.
26. T: Maybe if I'd asked them to match the sentence to the text.
27. S: Yes or match text to titles.

© Cambridge University Press 2001

[1] We would like to thank Teresa McConlogue for providing an earlier version of this transcript.

Photocopiable resource 29 (Task 6.4, page 197)

In Extract B, the students are at the end of their second block of teaching practice on a four-year pre-service training programme. The discussion again takes place in a secondary school. The trainee's supervisor is a non-native English speaker.

Extract B

The two extracts form part of two different post-lesson discussions which took place in a secondary school outside Britain.

1. S: You said that you started off with something serious and you got them to answer some questions which were questions on the book they had read. First of all there were some questions like give reasons why and so on and ended up with some vocabulary work. Can I ask you about this? Why did you decide that they should write answers to the questions?

2. T: This was to make sure that everyone did something because when we set them homework, some of them didn't do it, so if we made sure they did it in class time we could help them because probably they don't want to do it because they don't understand the questions. If we are here we could probably help them.

3. S: Where did they get the questions from? I saw that you had got them written and offered me a photocopy but where had *they* got the questions from?

4. T: Yesterday's session we asked them to write down questions.

5. S: How did you give them questions? Did you dictate?

6. T: I wrote earlier on the board and also I said that if they don't have time to finish it I would stick a photocopy on the board.

7. S: So, it was a copying exercise. Do you think that was valuable?

8. T: I think so because people checked the spelling.

9. S: Did you think about dictating the questions?

10. T: No. Even with the questions they wrote and I asked them to copy down, one or two of them said they didn't understand what they wrote and it would have been more difficult if we had just dictated.

11. S: So you think that copying from the board was a useful exercise and they have got them for reference?

12. T: Yes, I would prefer to photocopy the questions and give it to them. I did that before the homework on Tuesday. I photocopied the questions and gave each of them a copy but some of them lost the questions.

13. S: So they copied them into their exercise book and they had them to think about.

14. T: They didn't seem to appreciate that I had photocopied the questions and the problem is that we have to limit our photocopying.

15. S: Would you use copying a lot? You have seen the value of it and as you do point out, it can be a valid exercise. Would you use it a lot – copying from the board?

16. T: If I can avoid it, no, because I am much more keen on having the photocopied questions.

17. S: Ask yourself if this is the best way of doing it. Am I using time? It must have taken quite a long time to write them down.

18. T: I didn't ask them to finish copying in the session. You can come in the class any time and finish it.

Photocopiable resource 30 (Task 8.1, page 199)

Teacher Role Card A
You are in a feedback session after teaching a lesson. Here are things you feel about the lesson you have just taught and what you said to the advisor about the lesson. Read out what is on your card and then write down under a) exactly what the advisor says to you in reply .

1. I feel really happy with his class as I know the language and don't make any mistakes.
   a) ....
   b) ....
2. I'm worried about how to involve the pupils in the lesson.
   a) ....
   b) ....
3. The class showed that they can read. They read all the sentences I put on the blackboard.
   a) ....
   b) ....
4. It's impossible for me not to use their mother tongue. If I don't they won't understand.
   a) ....
   b) ....

When you have completed all four, discuss your reaction to what the advisor said.
Say what *you* thought the advisor thought of the lesson.
Get your advisor to say what they really did think of the lesson.
Did the real opinion of the advisor come across? Why / why not?

Then discuss together with your partner alternative responses which they could have made and write them under b).

Advisor Role Card A
The following represents your thoughts on the lesson you have just watched the teacher teach. Listen to what the teacher has to say about the lesson, and then make an immediate response to the teacher. When you have made that response, write it down under a). Do not at this point show your sheet to the teacher.

1. The teacher made several elementary mistakes in the language presented to the class.
   a) ....
   b) ....
2. You felt that only some of the pupils were involved but that it was not a very serious problem. There are much more serious aspects of the lesson you want to focus on.
   a) ....
   b) ....
3. In fact, in your opinion, the pupils merely repeated the sentences after the teacher and never did any real reading.
   a) ....
   b) ....
4. You are not opposed to the use of the mother tongue in the classroom, you felt it was being used too much.
   a) ....
   b) ....

When you have completed all four, listen to what the teacher thought you were saying and what the teacher felt about what you said.
Tell the teacher what you really thought (from the role notes above).
Were your feelings about the lesson conveyed accurately? Why / why not?

Then discuss together with your partner alternative responses which you could have made and write them under b).

Photocopiable resource 31 (Task 8.1, page 199)

Teacher Role Card B

You are in a feedback session after teaching a lesson. Here are things you feel about the lesson you have just taught and what you said to the advisor about the lesson. Read out what is on your card and then write down under a) exactly what the advisor says to you in reply.

1. The class is progressing well and they like learning English.
   a) ....
   b) ....
2. This is an easy lesson to introduce because I find it easy to teach the colours.
   a) ....
   b) ....
3. They all wrote the letters I wanted them to very well. They are good at writing.
   a) ....
   b) ....
4. They need grammatical terms; it helps them to understand the lesson.
   a) ....
   b) ....

When you have completed all four, discuss your reaction to what the advisor said.
Say what *you* thought the advisor thought of the lesson.
Get your advisor to say what they really did think of the lesson.
Did the real opinion of the advisor come across? Why / why not?

Then discuss together with your partner alternative responses which they could have made and write them under b).

Advisor Role Card B

The following represents your thoughts on the lesson you have just watched the teacher teach. Listen to what the teacher has to say about the lesson, and then make an immediate response to the teacher. When you have made that response, write it down under a). Do not at this point show your card to the teacher.

1. You thought the class was rather quiet.
   a) ....
   b) ....
2. You felt that the teacher did not have enough examples of the different colours to effectively introduce them.
   a) ....
   b) ....
3. You saw many children forming the letters wrongly and the teacher did not seem to pay any attention to the way letters were formed.
   a) ....
   b) ....
4. Although you are not against the use of some grammatical terms you thought the teacher used too many.
   a) ....
   b) ....

When you have completed all four, listen to what the teacher thought you were saying and what the teacher felt about what you said.
Tell the teacher what you really thought (from the role notes above).
Were your feelings about the lesson conveyed accurately? Why / why not?

Then discuss together with your partner alternative responses which you could have made and write them under b).

Photocopiable resource 32 (Task 8.2, page 200)

Part A

OBSERVATION SHEET

Teacher   Date 6.03.97.

Class VIII   Topic   someone had taken it – Past Perfect. Grade (1st
  11 pupils.   Handbook New Discoveries III

Description of the Classroom a small classroom with desks/chairs
    arranged in rows, some posters, and display of pupils' works.

Objectives / as written on the lesson plan, stated by the
teacher or based on observation /
      to describe past activities using Past Perfect Tense.
      to develop listening skills

1/ To what extent were these achieved?
      the listening passage was too difficult and pupils had problems when
      answering questions
      they didn't really know how to do some of the exercises on their own

2/ Skills practised? reading aloud / listening / speaking

3/ Materials / audio-visuals – their appropriacy for the aims,
for the Ss.
sets of scrambled sentences, cassette

8.50.	T asks pupils to present the dialogues (no comment on their performance).	SS → C T → C
8.52.	T asks pupils to open their books, and asks pupils to read the text one by one and them explains new words (lecturer, luggage).	S → C T → S
8.59.	T explains how to form Past Perfect tense and its usage. T writes on the board. "I went for a walk when I had finished my work". T asks us to find examples of Past Perfect in the passage. then draws an axis on the board and explains. Past Past NOW Perfect Simple	T → C
9.07	T puts subject + had+ past participle Pupils copy the sentences and the rule. T asks pupils to open their workbooks and do an exercise on the 2 tenses. Pupils read sentences one by one. T prompts the pupils and finally gives the correct form. Someone had locked the door and we couldn't leave the classroom T: When we got to the cinema they had went in already. T elicits the correct form of go – GONE, and gets them to repeat it.	T → S

9.15.	T hands out jumbled sentences and the pupils are to put them together to form a story. Pupils work in pairs putting the sentences together. Then T asks the to read the story	T → C
		S → C
9.20.	T tells ss they are going to listen to a story and they must answer some questions. Then T plays the tape.	T → C
9.25.	After playing the tape for the second time, T explains some vocab. (bury, atube, wrap up, escalator, set off) using definitions and putting them on board. listening with	
9.30.	T asks questions from the book to check/ understanding. T reads out the questions and nominates pupils to answer them (helps with the words) Pupils have difficulties, so the T provides them some words, finally gives the answer.	T → C
9.34.	T suggests preparing a dialogue (2 mins. left.)	

COMMENTS AND SUGGESTIONS
Reading – checking comprehension – remember was reading aloud necessary?
Praise the pupils for good performance
Plan the tasks more carefully and prepare examples beforehand

© Cambridge University Press 2001

Photocopiable resource 33 (Task 8.2, page 200)

Part B

1. The best thing about the lesson was putting the jumbled story together.
2. Another thing I enjoyed was the introduction of new vocabulary (techniques)
3. As a result of the lesson I now see only the best students grasped the meaning and usage of Past Perfect Tense
4. The teacher really planned too many things for one lesson
5. The students were obedient, yet not really involved in the lesson.
6. There was a lot of repetition of instructions and
7. I would have liked to see a more solid lesson.
8. The hardest thing for me as an observer was to follow the grammatical presentation and explanation
9. The next time I observe this teacher I would like to see much better presentation, timing and organisation of activities.

© Cambridge University Press 2001

Photocopiable resource 34 (Task 8.3, page 202)

Report 1

<u>2nd Preparatory (Science)</u>   <u>Steps 75/76</u>   <u>7.1.88</u>

— Good Role play — It was a good warming up exercise. But be a bit
cautious about your price tags — a gold ring 100 baisa and a book 100
rials — not usual.

— You played just a few lines and stopped the player. Why didn't you
continue. It doesn't matter how simple it is, you should remember to
give them an assignment/task before you get them to listen.

— You tried different pairs for the dialogue. But all the time they
were reading off the page. You should get them to say the lines —
this should be your aim.

— The mark you can you use for 'opposite' is 'x' . light x heavy/
cheap x expensive/big x small, etc. You put about 15 such pairs on
the bb. Get them to copy them down in their exercise books. They'll
come in handy later.

— I liked the way you reminded them of the grammatical classes — adj.
and nouns. But don't overdo it.

— Make it a point to stop them and ask them to read/say sentences again
if they don't stop at the end of a sentence.

General Points:

1. Considering their ability, they need more group/chorus practice.
   Small dialogues are meant to be said not read out.

2. Get one/two brighter pairs to say the dialogue before the others
   start practising.

3. Don't write full sentences on bb. They'll read if you do that. Write
   just the key word phrase.

Report 2

<u>1st Preparatory</u>   <u>EFO 4 85–88</u>   <u>2.1.88</u>
   <u>(Revision lesson)</u>

1. This revision lesson moved along very briskly with a good response
   from pupils.

2. I think you did the right thing to spend the last 15 minutes of the
   lesson checking the work in WBs. The long pieces of written work in
   WB 89 (p.44) need special preparation before setting the pupils on to
   them, and in any case it is better to catch up on the marking left
   during absence before taking in any more.

3. The written work had been done fairly well on the whole: the first
   part of WB86, 87 and 88 were mainly excellent. However, there was
   some confusion and some mistakes in the 6 sentences of WB 86 second
   half: these were mainly the use of a (glasses) <u>is</u>, and has (got) or
   wears. Don't give too many sentence patterns at once in an exercise
   like this — they will be doing free writing at the end of the Unit on
   WB p.44.

4. Nevertheless, the girls are responding well.

Report 3
<u>1st Secondary</u>

1. Your lesson notes were good. You linked the present part of the lesson with the past through W/A. You talked about the picture. You also handled the reading passage in chunks. The Qs you asked about the passage were nicely worded.

2. Suggestions:

   i) The first Q about the picture should have been an open one, eg. Tell me about the picture. This type of Q can encourage even the weaker lot to say something about the picture.

   ii) Before you ask the boys to read something please give them a reason (a task to do).

   iii) Please don't make things too easy for your boys. For example: You asked, 'What's the man's nationality?' A moment later you added, 'My nationality is Egyptian, yours is Omani, how about this man?' This is what I call to make things a bit too easy for our students. Give them challenges and give them time to think.

   iv) Reading aloud by a student towards the end of the lesson was unnecessary.

   v) Please take care of your pronunciation. I would like you to look up these words in the dictionary for pronunciation: wearing, cupboard, were, clothes, injured.

   vi) You also stressed last sounds in words like pain, think, some, mark, man etc. which are understressed.

   vii) How about the noun clause e.g. you said, 'Do you remember What is his name?'

   viii) Some of the students got more chances to speak. The Qs should have been fairly distributed.

3. WBs: I went through them and I realised that this was the area where your attention was most needed.
   a) Please see to it that the boys write their tasks regularly.
   b) I noticed that sometimes the ticks had been put where they shouldn't have been.
   c) Watch for their writing habits, HW problems etc.

Happy New Year and good teaching. Thanks.

Report 4

1st Preparatory   2.12.87

The teacher has obviously overcome the class management problems
mentioned in his visit report of 3.1. 87 (Temporary Visit form). This
class was well-behaved, well-motivated and clearly had respect for and
confidence in the teacher. He is a resourceful teacher who adapts the TB
very freely to suit local difficulties but he must be careful not to lose
sight of the aim of the course plan altogether. In the reading passage
section of this lesson, selected pupils showed a reasonable level of
attainment for this point in the year, though they need more guidance in
the <u>sense group</u> patterns of English. The teacher controlled the class
well in the general sense but I would like to see more movement around the
class in future -- checking and advising pupils who were in some cases
apathetic and in some cases not fully aware of what was required of them.
At present he holds too insistently to the front of class central
position. The standard of work in the copybooks was quite good, where the
pupils have lines to guide their writing, but I'm afraid the workbooks
showed a rather poor standard of free writing and were not all corrected
carefully enough. I have suggested he review them and insist on
corrections where necessary. He has assured me he will attend to this. He
seems to be doing a much better job than before and with attention to the
points mentioned will I am sure do an even better one in future.

Report 5

6th Elementary/3   Sad Sam and the   27.1.88
                          Orange Balloon

The lesson is on the Reader.

1. Brief introduction of the story through the pictures on the cover
   done as a warm up,
   — I recommend that at the beginning of every reading lesson
     before you ask them to read make the Ps guess from pictures
     what they are going to read about and discuss with them what
     is the story going to be about and is going to happen before
     they start reading.
   — Try to include everyone in the lesson and make the lesson
     interesting.

2. This is a reading lesson for the pupils <u>not</u> for the teacher. You
   should have allowed the Ps to read themselves not you reading for
   them.

3. Give the Ps a purpose for reading e.g.
        a) pre questions before reading
        b) looking for missing information while reading
   Because you just told the Ps to read silently they did not read
   properly and when you gave them questions they were not able to
   answer them. Obviously they did not understand what they read.

4. Try to devise a technique to help them read without your assistance,
   so they can read alone at home!
   Thanks.

Report 6

<u>6th Elementary</u>   <u>Unit 14</u>   <u>10.4.88</u>

What I have seen completely stunned me . . . the teacher is the sole factor in the process of teaching while the pupils are sitting passively unwilling to participate in spite of the incessant attempts of the teacher to arouse their interest. However, if you follow all the instructions you will certainly get better results. Resort to pair work, group work, chorus and not let them to look at you only, keep them always busy doing something. Whatever the results you expect, it will be better than this stagnant state.

If you encourage your pupils to read silently helping them to understand and then retell the story, you can write a good summary on the BB. You can change this summary into a very nice exercise. The exercise you wrote on the BB was a bit difficult.

The only merit I observed was acting the scene.

Pupils should be encouraged to read and then answer without looking at their books.

Pupils should be encouraged to write short paragraphs, according to the circular you received.

This class is in dire need for a remedy work.

Photocopiable resource 35 (Task 8.4, page 204)

University of Leicester • School of Education
Modern Languages/TESOL

Individual Action Plan on Teaching Practice

1. PROFILE QUESTIONNAIRE

Indicate how confident you feel about: low   high

Subject Knowledge

- your knowledge of the subject and its contribution to the curriculum   1 ② 3 4 5
- your understanding of National Curriculum: NCATs and PoS   ① 2 3 4 5

Subject Application and Planning

- setting clear objectives for the lesson   1 ② 3 4 5
- planning lessons in line with NCATs (where applicable)   ① 2 3 4 5
- presenting new language/content   1 ② 3 4 5
- communicating ideas clearly   1 2 ③ 4 5
- pacing lessons appropriately   1 ② 3 4 5
- timing the stages of a lesson   1←② 3 4 5
- using questions in the target language   1 2 3 ④ 5
- giving clear instructions   1 2 ③ 4 5
- providing for a balance of skills (LSRW)   1 ② 3 4 5

Planning and Using Resources

- producing appropriate materials   1 2 3 ④ 5
- using visual aids excluding boards, OHP   1 2 3 ④ 5
- using the chalkboard/OHP effectively   1 2 3 4 ⑤
- use of a textbook or resource packs   1 2 3 ④ 5
- use of computers to assist learning   ① 2 3 4 5

Class Management

- organising pair work   1 2 ③ 4 5
- organising co-operative group work   ① 2 3 4 5
- generating interest and enthusiasm   1 ② 3 4 5
- giving appropriate and genuine praise   1 ② 3 4 5
- providing equal opportunities for learners of all abilities   ①→2 3 4 5
- controlling the class   ① 2 3 4 5

Assessment and Recording of Pupils' Progress

- marking pupils' work   1 2 3 ④ 5
- evaluating pupil progress   1 2 ③ 4 5
- identifying individual learning differences   1 ② 3 4 5
- helping pupils to learn   1 2 ③ 4 5

Relationships

- getting on with pupils   1 2 ③ 4 5
- getting on with colleagues   1 2 3 4 ⑤

2. AREAS FOR DEVELOPMENT

a) Which skill areas do you feel you most wish or need to develop?

 *Presenting new material / Developing rapport with students / Controlling the
 class / Generating interest and enthusiasm.*

b) Which skills do you feel most confident about?

© Cambridge University Press 2001

Teaching Practice First Review (2nd Page)

At first, I was a little uncertain about teaching. I didn't like the fact that there was no coursebook. However, I find I have been able to find quite interesting materials from a series of coursebooks. I have also enjoyed making my own materials

General Classroom Issues

I must learn to relax with the children more
I need to be more definite about being in charge

Language Specific Issues

I need to plan the new material I am going to introduce more carefully
I must try to cover a more reasonable amount in the lesson
I need to make sure my instructions are not too long and convoluted

Tutor Support Required (if any)

How do I come across to the students? How does my body language appear? Is there anything I can do to appear more confident?

Praise – am I praising students for the right things in the right way? Am I praising enough?

General Review

I think I am being more focused in my praise – praising both individuals and class for work which is truly well done.

I think I am being more realistic about what can actually be covered within a lesson

General Classroom Issues

Still need to be more relaxed and more myself with the class.
I still need to show more enthusiasm for what I am doing
I need to act promptly and firmly to control (name of student)
Although I am getting better at not trying to cover too much, I still need to concentrate on the pace and flow of the lesson overall

Language Specific Issues

I still need to focus on keeping instructions short and clear
I need to modify my level of English more to make sure that all can understand ....and do this, without distorting the pronunciation.

End of Practice Review

Self Evaluation

Before I started teaching, I was most worried about planning lessons without a book which would be well sequenced both within the lesson and from one lesson to another and which would fit in with the time of the lesson. During the course of the teaching practice, I feel I have managed to achieve this, although I do still need to work at making my lessons more interesting.

I think I still need to relax more so that I become more confident and increasingly enjoy what I am doing

Controlling the class is still sometimes quite difficult, but again this is improving and will improve even more as I relax more.

Targets for Future Development

Course

I would like to have more specific techniques for controlling a difficult class.
Also more about designing and making worksheets particularly for a particular grammar point. In fact, I would like more advice on different ways of teaching grammar, in particular ways which will generate the interest of the students.

Also differentiating activities to cater for the mixed levels within the class

Spring / Summer Teaching Practice

In the next teaching practice, I need to work on:

- Maintaining discipline
- Appearing more self-confident
- Pacing my lessons better
- Giving short and clear instructions
- Dealing with the different levels within the class
- More imaginative ways of presenting and practising grammar

© Cambridge University Press 2001

We would like to thank the staff at the School of Education, University of Leicester, including Tom Whiteside, Richard Aplin and Wasyl Cajkler, for this form. The comments here reflect those typical of trainee teachers but are not from a real trainee.

Photocopiable resource 36 (Task 9.1, page 205)

A college mentor (M) is talking to two female Malaysian student teachers who have just worked with a class in an English middle school. This is their first teaching practice experience at the end of their first year of an undergraduate programme.

1. M   So it was an English lesson. How old were the children?
2. S1 12–13
3. M   And there were?
4. S2 8
5. M   Uhum
6. S2 Mixed ability,
7. M   Uhum
8. S1 26 of them.
9. S2 But some were absent. 'Cos some went on French exchange.
10. M   Yes.
11. S2 So some were absent.
12. M   Yes. OK. And it was the last lesson you had with them. We talked very briefly, yesterday and you said that you wanted it to be fun as well as doing something worthwhile, so . . .
13. S1 I think we had fun during the interview because they were allowed to do whatever they wanted. But I did tell them to be sensible about it because I went round to some groups. You expect some people to do something silly sometimes.
14. S2 I went round and told them to take the characters and the voice and everything and I think some of them did it quite well. The characters that were used in the book.
15. S1 And the voices also.
16. M   So when you thought that some might be a bit silly which were they and were they silly in the end?
17. S2 The boys at the end at the back they didn't have time to finish. So I don't know what it would have been like. I think it would have been good because they are very good workers it's just that they don't want to listen to you sometimes are difficult to pin down sometimes.
18. M   Yes, yes. It seems to me where they were being, as it were, silly they were, they got the character more and the ones that weren't serious seemed to get it over really well.
19. S1 Most of the time we had to pay attention more to be aware of what they are doing all of the time, 'cos they looked like they're doing work but they're mucking about and I liked particularly that group over there – those few boys over there – because they . . . a few of them are slow, very slow.
20. S2 They are special needs group
21. S1 Yes.
22. S2 and extremely slow. That's . . .
23. S1 But they really . . . That's why I like the group. Whatever we asked them to do they tried to do it.

24. S2   As best as they can.
25. S1   Yes, as best they can.
26. S2   We were told about that and erm we could see that for when we took them for lessons. so . . . I think it's quite easy to see them do that.
27. M   Do you think they did it specially for you because they like working with you and for you? Or do they usually do that?
28. S2   We don't know about that but Mrs Creadin did say they are a very hard-working group, even though they are very slow but they try their best all the time.
29. M   It was nice and it was about the third interview but of the three it was by far the best. The whole class appreciated what they'd done.
30. S1   Yes and they did tell Marina they didn't like to read aloud and all that because they were ashamed.
31. S2   And they feel embarrassed.
32. M   I wanted to ask you about that because you set it up as a radio interview and you set it up very clearly and now you have just said they don't like reading aloud, but in fact, you asked them to write down the questions and the answers.
33. S2   And then after that it was up to them – it was spontaneous.
34. M   So why . . . I wasn't quite sure why you asked them to write down . . .
35. S1   At first because we wanted to . . .
36. M   the dialogue.
37. S1   make it more proper like er they've got something to fall back on.
38. M   So it was a kind of reminder.
39. S2   And then after that we saw that there wasn't much time, so that's why we thought we would have a chat with you and see if we could change our plans. And it worked out quite well I mean the idea to make it more spontaneous.
40. M   On the whole if you were doing something like a radio interview and you weren't short of time do you think it is a good idea to get down the script as you said as you pointed out. You said to them, 'Write down the script.'
41. S1   Yes that is if we concentrate the whole lesson on the radio, . . . so why need to . . . it is better to ask them to write down the script so that it will involve writing skills as well.
42. M   Yes.
43. S2   And we can include details of events that they are talking about.
44. M   Erm . . . Do you think that if there is a real radio interview they do write the script?
45. S2   It's going to be like notes on what they are going to ask.
46. S1   It depends on whether the person doing the interviewing is very experienced, but it would be more competent to do it without a script, but I think you would need some notes.
47. M   Do you think it makes any difference to the voice if you read something or speak spontaneously?
48. S2   It does, but I think even if you have a script if you work on it and really work bringing over the character it can help as well, I think.

49. M It can help because you have written it down and you have focused your attention.

50. S1 But we don't want them to just read the script because it's like, you know, you alter your voice to reading tone . . .

51. M Yes, but that's exactly the first two pairs. It was very . . . The first two pairs were very much reading and you noticed didn't you, and said don't just read, get your head up. 'Cos that's the danger that they do alter to a reading tone and you lose the feeling that it is an oral interview.

52. S1 Mm . . .
  & 2

53. S2 Probably if we had more time and we asked them to really get into these characters and probably eliminate them from reading. If they can memorise what they say then it's fine.

54. M Or another thing is to have some questions written down and some prepared and some questions written down which the other person does not know about.

55. S2 Yes, I told the group at the back after a question if they would like to pop in some questions which they weren't expecting, then it would be much more interesting to see what they have to say.

56. M Yes, because usually, if you are speaking to someone they don't know how they are going to answer, so in that way you have both – you have the safety of starting off with something prepared and then you've got the . . .

57. S1 and then you have the spontaneous part.

58. S2 It was also difficult because when I went around asking them to be more spontaneous like just write down the question and some of them were a bit insecure and said but I don't know what to say and I said OK just write down some notes on what you might say when this question is asked.

59. M It was very pleasing that some did answer in character, didn't they? It was really pleasing that they did that. Good. Do you feel that that was a good way to finish up all your lessons with them? Are you pleased with it?

60. S2 Yes, because we started off with something serious and they had to do individual work . . . which needed a lot of concentration so this is why they were . . .

61. S1 You feel like . . . in a way it is like er not summarising.

62. S2 It's like putting it all together.

63. S1 In a nutshell.

64. S2 In a nutshell.

65. S1 You choose important events, incidents and feelings, we don't we don't say from this chapter and that chapter, it's just from any chapter.

66. M I thought it was a really good way of finishing.

Photocopiable resource 37 (Task 9.2, page 207)

Teacher role cards

Teacher 1

You are rather shy and diffident and are really worried about your teaching. You have come on the teacher training course because you really want to know about how to teach and you consider the trainer to be really experienced and want to learn from her.

Teacher 2

You are a self-assured, assertive teacher and you think that the lesson was very good indeed. You consider yourself to be the best trainee on the teacher training course.

Teacher 3

You have been teaching for some time and have done this lesson before many times. You have a lot of well-established routines which you are reluctant to change because these routines are based on a strong experiential base.

Photocopiable resource 38 (Task 9.3, page 209)

The following are problems to do with giving advice to teachers, which have been raised by various advisor teachers on different advisor training programmes. Discuss in groups the possible course(s) of action which you might take in each situation.

Problem	Course(s) of action
Advisors:	
1. You need to have a person who is ready to accept advice. Some people are not ready to accept any advice.	
2. There are some trainee teachers who appear to be listening, but who I know have no intention of following the advice I am giving.	
3. It's all very well to ask the teacher to analyse their own problem, but that assumes a certain level of competence in the teacher. Many trainees do not know what their problems are.	
4. I get a lot of trainee teachers who do not want to work things out for themselves. They just want to be told the answer. What should I do?	
5. I have this trainee teacher who thinks he knows it all. He's actually a very poor teacher. Whenever I make any criticism of his lesson he just becomes defensive and I know he's not listening to what I say.	
6. I have real problems with the older teachers. They feel that as I am younger than them I don't have the experience to help them, yet I can see that their teaching techniques really need to be modernised as there is almost no real communication taking place in their classes.	
7. I had a situation in which a teacher was so upset about one incident in the lesson she had just taught, and was so tense about teaching, that she just burst into tears and it was impossible for me to get her to look at the lesson in any way.	

© Cambridge University Press 2001

Photocopiable resource 39 (Task 9.3, page 209)

The following are solutions which different groups have come up with when faced with the problems on the previous page. Are they the solutions you came up with? How do yours differ?

1. It is true that not everyone is ready to accept advice. What you need to establish is the reason for not accepting advice. Is the person being defensive because of the situation they are in? In this case you need to work hard on instilling a supportive and relaxed atmosphere. Is the person someone who refuses to listen to other people because they are convinced of their own point of view, or are convinced that they are correct? In this case, confronting the person with their behaviour in order to make them aware of what is happening may be necessary. However, it should be noted that even the second person may actually be putting up a defensive wall around themselves because they are, at bottom, worried and defensive about the situation.

2. In this case, the problem may well lie in the way that you are giving the advice. Are you really involving the student in jointly structuring and exploring the answers to the problems you have identified? Is the student convinced that there is a problem? Advice is accepted better if the student 'owns' the problem and the solution i.e. accepts that there is a problem and has played a part in negotiating the resolution. Once this agreement has been reached between the supervisor and the student, it is important to draw up an action plan to remind both sides of the results of the discussion and the action to be taken.

3. The advice offered should be carefully tailored to the needs and the point of development of the teacher. At the early stages of development of a teacher more prescriptive interventions (e.g. offering a model, giving direct advice) may be more appropriate than with a mature teacher. However, it is important to guide the teacher to a new awareness of the teaching process rather than simply giving the solution. Solutions to problems should be evolved in cooperation with the teacher rather than imposed from the outside.

4. It is true that different people are at different stages of development and these need to be taken into account when giving advice. Young trainee students have probably come from a learning environment in which the teacher always gave them the answer. As trainee teachers they must be developed to a point in which they can work things out for themselves. It is important to guide them to make this difficult transformation from a passive receiver of information to a more reflective practitioner. Thus, you should create a collaborative atmosphere in which the students are aware, both of the reasons for the approach you are using and of the way which you want them to think about their teaching. Establishing restricted tasks (such as analysis of small sections of lessons, asking specific or directed questions about the lesson) which will lead to more reflection on the lesson

are probably useful. These tasks should be signalled in the action plan at the end of the session and followed up in the next session.

5. Confrontation with such a teacher may be the only way to get through to him. But be careful. The confrontation should be aimed at making him aware of his behaviour in the classroom, not about his personality. Criticism should be owned by you and should be non-punitive. The intention should be to raise the teacher's awareness of his behaviour, not to punish him for being a 'bad teacher'.

6. This is a really difficult problem and one which we have all faced at one time or another. It is often magnified in societies which have a lot of respect for age. It is important that we all empathise with older teachers and value what they have to say. They have, after all, been teaching for a long time and have a lot of experience of the classroom. This experience should be recognised and it is important that as the younger, less experienced observer, we do not become defensive ourselves by 'attacking' the teacher, laying down rules and prescriptive solutions which finish up with both parties being bound in by defensive 'walls'; one firing out salvos of directions and the other defending by refusing to listen and retreating even further behind the defence of their experience. Empathy and a collaborative approach is the only way to deal with such a situation. Confrontation will only make things worse.

7. In this case it is important to let the teacher discharge her emotions and to allow her to 'get it out of her system' before trying to continue with the feedback. It is important to listen to her account and to try to understand the problem(s) she is having. She will need reassuring and she will need supportive interventions and made to feel valued. Her problems may not be that different from many others and interventions such as personal disclosure may well help her to put her problems into perspective. However, it is also important to try to get to the root of her problems. They may lie outside teaching and it is important to explore this area, to establish the agenda on which you are talking to the teacher.

References

Adams, K. and Markiewicz, M. (1995) 'Cross-cultural problems in teacher training', paper given at the Polish Teacher Training Conference, Krakow.

Agar, M. (1994) 'The intercultural frame', *International Journal of Intercultural Relations*, **18**, 2, 221–237.

Allwright, D. (1988) *Observation in the Language Classroom*, London: Longman.

Anderson, E. M. and Shannon, S. L. (1988) 'Toward a conceptualisation of mentoring', *Journal of Teacher Education* **39**, 1, 43–45.

Anderson, J. R. (1983) *The Architecture of Cognition*, Harvard: Harvard University Press.

Argyle, M. (1988) *Bodily Communication (2nd Ed.)*, London: Routledge.

Atkinson, T. and Claxton, G. (eds.) (2000) *The Intuitive Practitioner: on the value of not always knowing what one is doing*, Buckingham: Open University Press.

Bailey, F. (1996) 'The role of collaborative dialogue in Teacher Education', in Freeman, D. and Rogers, J. (eds.) (1996).

Bampfield, A. (1997) *Looking at Language Classrooms Video*, Cambridge: Cambridge University Press.

Beck, A. (1976) *Cognitive Theory and the Emotional Disorders*, New York: International Universities Press.

Bennett, N. & Carre, C. (1993) *Learning to Teach*, London: Routledge.

Berliner, D. (1987) 'Ways of thinking about students and classrooms by more and less experienced teachers', in Calderhead, J. (ed.) (1987) *Exploring Teachers' Thinking* London: Cassell.

Berne, E. (1964) *Games People Play*. Grove Press.

Bolitho, R. (1979) 'On demonstration lessons', in Holden (ed.) (1979) *Teacher Training*, Modern English Publications.

Bowers, R. (1987) IATEFL

Brand, C. (1984) 'Personality dimensions; an overview of modern trait psychology', in Nicholson, J. & Beloff, H. (eds.) *Psychological Survey 5*, 175–209.

Breen, M. P. (1991) 'Understanding the language teacher', in Phillipson, R., Kellerman, E., Selinker, J. K., Sharwood Smith, M., and Swains, M. (eds.) *Foreign/Second Language Pedagogy Research*, Clevedon: Multilingual Matters.

Britten, D. (1985) 'Teacher Training in ELT (Part 1)'. *Language Teaching*, **2**, 112–128.

Brookfield, S. (1987) *Developing Critical Thinkers: Challenging adults to explore alternative ways*. Milton Keynes: Open University.

Brookfield, S. D. (1995) *Becoming a Critically Reflective Teacher*, San Francisco: Jossey-Bass Wiley.

Bruner, J. (1990) *Acts of Meaning*, Cambridge, Mass: Harvard University Press.

Burns, A. (1996) 'Starting all over again: From teaching adults to teaching beginners,' in Freeman, D. & Richards, J. C. (eds.) *Teacher Learning in Language Teaching*, Cambridge: Cambridge University Press.

Calderhead, J. (ed.) (1987) *Teacher's Professional Learning*, London: Cassell.

Calvert, M. and Fletcher, S. (1994) *Working with your Student Teacher*, Cheltenham: Nelson Thornes.

CDELT (1992) *Peer Coaching Handbook*, Cairo, Egypt: Ain Shams University, Centre for the Development of English Language Teaching.

Chambers, J. (1993) *The Mentor's Guide*, UBI.

Cheetham, M. (ed.) (1993) *The First Year of Teaching*, Apple Pie Publications.

Clutterbuck, D. (1992) *Mentoring*, Henley Distance Learning.

Collins, E. and Scott, P. (1978) 'Everyone who makes it has a mentor', *Harvard Business Review*, 56, 4, 89–101.

Cramer, D. (1992) *Personality and Psychotherapy*, Buckingham: Open University Press.

Cullen, R. (1994) 'Incorporating a language improvement component in teacher training programmes', *ELT Journal* 48, 2, 162–172.

DfE (1992) *Initial Teacher Training (Secondary Phase)*, Circular 9/92, London: Department for Education.

Daniels, H. (ed.) (1993) *Charting the Agenda: Educational Activity after Vygotsky*, London: Routledge.

Dreyfus, H. L. & Dreyfus, S. E. (1986) *Mind over Machine: The Power of Human Intuition and Enterprise in the Era of the Computer*, New York: Macmillan.

Earley, P. and Kinder, K. (1994) *Initiation Rights: Effective induction practice for new teachers*, Windsor: NFER-Nelson.

Edge, J. (1992) *Co-operative Development: Professional Self-development through Co-operation with Colleagues*, Harlow: Longman.

Egan, G. (1994) *The Skilled Helper* 5th Edition, Pacific Grove California: Brooks/Cole Publishing Co.

El Naggar, Z. (1986) 'Egyptian EFL Student Teachers' Evaluation of their Pre-Service Program, *CDELT Occasional Papers*, 7 74–99. Cairo, Egypt: Ain Shams University, Centre for the Development of English Language Teaching.

Ellis, A. (1990) *Reason and Emotion in Psychotherapy*, New York: Citadel Press.

Ellis, G. and Sinclair, B. (1989) *Learning to Learn English: A course in learner training*, Cambridge: Cambridge University Press.

Faerch, C. and Kasper, G. (1987) *Introspection in Second Language Research*, Clevedon: Multilingual Matters.

Fairclough, N. (1992) *Critical Language Awareness*, Harlow: Longman.

Fish, D. (1995) *Quality Mentoring for Student Teachers*, London: David Fulton Publishers.

Freeman, D. (1982) 'Observing teachers: Three approaches to In-service Training and Development', *TESOL Quarterly*, 16, 1, 21–8.

Freeman, D. (1990) 'Intervening in practice teaching', in Richards, J. C. & Nunan, D. (1990) *Second Language Teacher Education*, Cambridge: Cambridge University Press.

Freeman, D. (1994) 'Educational linguistics and the education of second language teaching, in Alatis, J. (ed.) *Proceedings of the 1994 Georgetown University Roundtable on Languages and Linguistics*, Washington, D.C.: Georgetown University Press.

Freeman, D. (1996) 'The "unstudied problem": Research on teacher learning', in Freeman, D. and Rogers, J. (eds.) (1996) *Teacher Learning in Language Teaching*, Cambridge: Cambridge University Press.

Freeman, D. and Richards, J. (1993) 'Conceptions of Teaching and the Education of Second Language Teachers', *TESOL Quarterly*, 27, 2, 193–216.

Freeman, D. and Rogers, J. (eds.) (1996) *Teacher Learning in Language Teaching*, Cambridge: Cambridge University Press.

Freud, S. (1986) *The Essentials of Psychoanalysis* (Collection of writings, selected by Anna Freud), London: Penguin Books.

Garry, A. and Cowan, J. (1986) *Continuing professional development: a learner-centred strategy*, London: FEU/PICKUP

Gibbs, G. (1981) *Teaching Students to Learn: A student-centred approach*, Milton Keynes: Open University Press.

Gieve, S. (1995) 'Discourses of rationality: Argumentation in EAP and teacher education across cultures', in Blue, G. and Mitchell, R. (eds.) *Language and Education. British Studies in Applied Linguistics, 11*, Clevedon: Multilingual Matters.

Gebhard, J. and Oprandy, R. (1999) *Language Teaching Awareness: a guide to exploring beliefs and practices*, New York: Cambridge University Press.

Gebhard, J. (1984) 'Models of supervision; choices', *TESOL Quarterly*, **18**, 3.

Goleman, D. (1996) *Emotional Intelligence: Why it can matter more than IQ*, London: Bloomsbury.

Graddol, D., Cheshire, J. and Swann, J. (1987) *Describing Language*, Milton Keynes, Open University Press.

Griffiths and Sheen (1992) 'Disembodied figures in the landscape: A reappraisal of L2 research on field dependence/independence', *Applied Linguistics* **13**, 2.

Grossman, P. L. (1992) 'Why models matter: An alternative view of professional growth in teaching', *Review of Educational Research* **62**, 2, 171–80.

HMI (1988) *The New Teacher in School*, London: HMSO.

Habermas, J. (1984) *The Theory of Communicative Action Vol. 1: Reason and the Rationalisation of Society*, London: Heinemann.

Hancock, R. & Settle, D. (1990) *Teacher Appraisal and Self-evaluation: A practical Approach*, Oxford: Blackwell.

Haste, H. (1987) 'Growing into rules', in Bruner, J. and Haste, H. (eds.) *Making Sense*, London: Methuen.

Heron, J. (1990) *Helping the Client: A Creative Practical Guide*, London: Sage Publications.

Hofstede, G. (1986) 'Cultural differences in teaching and learning', *International Journal of Intercultural Relations* **10**, 301–320.

Hofstede, G. (1991) *Cultures and Organizations: Intercultural Co-operation and its Importance for Survival*, McGraw-Hill International: London.

Holliday, A. (1994) *Appropriate Methodology and Social Context*, Cambridge, Cambridge University Press.

Holliday. A. (1995) *Appropriate Methodology and Social Context*, Cambridge, Cambridge University Press.

Honey, P. and Mumford, A. (1986) *Manual of Learning Styles*, Maidenhead: Peter Honey.

Honey, P. and Mumford, A. (2000) *The Learning Styles Questionnaire and Helper's Guide*, Maidenhead: Peter Honey Publications.

Horwitz, E. and Young, D. (1991) *Language Anxiety*, Englewood Cliffs, NJ: Prentice Hall.

Hutchinson, T. and Torres, E. (1994) 'The textbook as Agent of Change', *ELT Journal* **48**, 4.

Jarvis, J. (1991) 'Perspectives on the in-service training needs of nns teachers of English to young learners' *The Teacher Trainer*, 5, 1, 5–9.

Jarvis, J. (1992) 'Using diaries for teacher reflection on in-service courses', *ELT Journal* **46**, 2, 133–143.

Jeffrey, H. and Ferguson, S. (1992) *The Mentoring Guidebook*. The Mentor Programme: North London College.

Johnson, K. E. (1996) 'The vision versus the reality: The tensions of the TESOL practicum', in Freeman, D. and Rogers, J. (eds.) (1996) *Teacher Learning in Language Teaching*, Cambridge: Cambridge University Press.

Jung, C. (1923) *Psychological Types*, Princetown, Princetown University Press.

Kagan (1992) 'Professional growth among preservice and beginning teachers', *Review of Educational Research*, **62**, 2.

Kelly, G. A. (1955) *The Psychology of Personal Constructs*, New York: Norton.

Kemmis, S. (1985) 'Action Research and the politics of reflection', in Boud, D., Keogh, R. and Walker, D. (eds.) (1985).

Kennedy, C. (1987) 'Innovating for a change: teacher development and innovation', *ELT Journal* **41**, 3, 163–170.

Khalfan, R. (1987) 'A survey of inspection visit forms', Advanced Diploma in ELT Administration assignment, University College Chichester.

Knowles, M. (1983) 'Andragogy: An emerging technology for adult learning', in Tight, M. (ed.) *Adult Education and Learning*, Beckenham: Croom Helm.

Krashen, S. (1982) *Principles and Practice in Second Language Acquisition*, Oxford: Pergamon.

Kirkham, G. (1993) 'Mentoring and headteachers', in Smith, P. and West-Burnham, J. (1993) *Mentoring in the Effective School*, Harlow: Longman.

Kolb, D. A. (1984) *Experiential Learning: Experience as the source of learning and development*, New Jersey: Prentice Hall.

Lago, C. and Thompson, J. (1997) *Race, Culture and Counselling*, Buckingham: Open University Press.

Lantolf, J. P. & Appel, G. (eds.) (1994) *Vygotskian Approaches to Second Language Research*, Norwood, NJ: Ablex Publishing Corporation.

Lee, C. C. (1991) 'Issues in counseling 1.5 generation Korean Americans'. In Lee, C. C. and Richardson, B. L. (eds.) *Multicultural Issues in Counseling* (1991), American Association for Counseling and Development.

Mace, S. (1996) 'Developing personal theory in pre-service education: A Romanian case study', paper delivered at the IALS Symposium, Edinburgh, Nov. 1996.

MacLeod, G. & McIntyre, D. (1977) 'Towards a model for micro-teaching', in McIntyre, D., MacLeod, G. and Griffiths, R. (eds.) *Investigations of Microteaching*, London: Croom Helm.

Malamah-Thomas, A. (1987) *Classroom Interaction*, Oxford: Oxford University Press.

Malderez, A. and Bodóczky, C. (1999) *Mentor Courses: A resource book for trainer-trainers*, Cambridge: Cambridge University Press.

Martin, T. (1995) 'Giving feedback after a lesson observation', *Mentoring and Tutoring*, **3**, 2, 8–12.

Maslow, A. H. (1970) *Motivation and Personality*, 2nd Edition, New York: Harper and Row.

McDonough, J. (1994) 'A teacher looks at teacher diaries', *ELT Journal* **48**, 1, 243–252.

McIntyre, D. (1988) 'Designing a teacher education curriculum from research and theory on teacher knowledge', in Calderhead, J. (ed.) *Teacher's Professional Learning*, 97–115.

McIntyre, D. and Hagger, H. (1994) in McIntyre, D., Hagger, H. and Wilkin, M. (eds.) *Mentoring: Perspectives on School Based Teacher Education*, London: Kogan Page.

McIntyre, P. D. and Gardner, R. C. (1991) 'Methods and Results in the Study of Anxiety and Language Learning: A Review of the Literature', *Language Learning* **41**, 85–117.

Mercer, N. (1995) *The Guided Construction of Knowledge: Talk amongst teachers and learners*, Clevedon: Multilingual Matters.

Miller, A. (1991) 'Personality types, learning styles and educational goals', *Educational Psychology*, **11**, 3 & 4, 217–238.

Miller, G. A. (1956) 'The magic number seven, plus or minus two: Some limits on our capacity for processing information', *Psychological Review*, **63**, 81–93.

Montgomery, D. (1999) *Positive Teacher Appraisal Through Classroom Observation*, London: David Fulton Publishers.

Murdoch, G. (1994) 'Language development provision in teacher training curricula', *ELT Journal* **48**, 3, 253–265.

Myers, I. and McCaulley, M. (1985) *Manual: a guide to the development and use of the Myers-Briggs Type Indicator*, Palo Alto, CA: Consulting Psychologists Press.

Nicolson, D. and Ayers, H. (1995) *Individual Counselling Theory and Practice: A Reference Guide*, London: David Fulton Publishers.

Nyiro, Z. Nemeth, D. and Grof, S. (1995) 'Mentor Role in long-term teaching practice', paper given at IATEFL York.

Nunan, D. (1990) 'Action research in the language classroom', in Richards, J. C. and Nunan, D. (eds.) (1990) *Second Language Teacher Education*, Cambridge: Cambridge University Press.

Nunan, D. (1992) *Collaborative Learning and Teaching*, Cambridge: Cambridge University Press.

Oxford, R. (1991) 'Style Orientation Survey', Tuscaloosa, AL: University of Alabama.

Oxford, R. L., Holloway, M. E. and Horton-Murillo, D. (1992) 'Language learning styles: Research and practical considerations for teaching in the multicultural tertiary ESL/EFL classroom', *System*, **20**, 4, 439–456.

Parsloe, E. (1992) *Coaching, Mentoring and Assessing*, London: Kogan Page.

Pease, A. (1981) *Body Language*, London: Sheldon Press.

Pease, A. (1997) *Body Language (3rd Edition)*, London: Sheldon Press.

Phillips-Jones, L. (1982) *Mentors and Protegees*, Arbor House.

Pollard, A. (1993) 'Learning in primary schools', in Daniels, H. (ed.) (1993) *Charting the Agenda: Educational Activity after Vygotsky*, London: Routledge.

Pope, M. L. and Keen, T. R. (1981) *Personal Construct Psychology and Education*, London and New York: Academic Press.

Porter, P. A., Goldstein, L. M., Leatheram, J. and Conrad, S. (1990) An on-going dialogue: Learning logs for teacher preparation in Richards and Nunan (eds.) (1990).

Pusey, M. (1987) *Jurgen Habermas*, London: Tavistock Publishers.

Ramani, E. (1987) 'Theorising from the classroom', *ELT Journal* **41**, 1, 3–11.

Randall, M. and Lavender, S. (1997) 'Personality, Task or Culture?', paper presented at Cross-cultural Convergence Conference, Leeds Metropolitan University, 1997.

Rees, A. L. W. (1980) 'The teacher observed – but how?', *ELT Journal* **35**, 1.

Richards, J. C. (1998) *Beyond Training*, Cambridge: Cambridge University Press.

Richards, J. C., Ho, B. and Giblin, K. (1996) 'Learning how to teach in the RSA Cert', in Freeman, D. and Richards, J. C. (eds.) *Teacher Learning in Language Teaching*, Cambridge: Cambridge University Press.

Richards, J. C. and Nunan, D. (eds.) (1990) *Second Language Teacher Education*, Cambridge, Cambridge University Press.

Richards, J. C. and Rodgers, T. S. (1986) *Approaches and Methods in Language Teaching*, Cambridge: Cambridge University Press.

Riding, R. (1991) *Cognitive Styles Analysis*, Birmingham: Learning and Training Technology.

Riding R. and Rayner, S. (1994) *Personal Style and Teacher Effectiveness: A staff development programme*, Birmingham: Learning and Training Technology.

Rogers, C. (1969) *On Becoming a Person: A Therapist's View of Psychotherapy*, London: Constable.

Rogers, C. (1983) *Freedom to Learn for the 80s*, Columbus Ohio: Charles E. Merrill.

Rogers, C. (1992) *Client-centred Therapy*, London: Constable.

Rybak-Dryniak, I. (1995) 'How much do trainees really learn from lessons?', *The Polish Teacher Trainer*, **4**, 1.

Schön, D. A. (1984) *The Reflective Practioner: How Professionals Think in Action*, London: Temple Smith.

Schön, D. A. (1987) *Educating the Reflective Practioner*, London: Jossey-Bass Wiley.

Sergiovanni, T. J. (1977) 'Reforming teacher evaluation: naturalistic alternatives', *Education Leadership*, **34**, 8, 602–7.

Shea, G. F. (1992) *Mentoring*, London: Kogan Page.

Sheldon, L. (1989) *ELT Textbooks and Materials; Problems in Evaluation and Development*, London: Longman.

Shulman L. S. (1987) 'Knowledge and Teaching: foundations of the new reforms', *Harvard Educational Review*, **57**, 1–22.

Sinclair, J. M. and Coulthard, R. M. (1975) *Towards an Analysis of Discourse: the English Used by Teachers and Pupils*, London: Oxford University Press.

Skehan, P. (1989) *Individual Differences in Second Language Learning*, London: Edward Arnold.

Skinner B. F. (1993) *About Behaviourism*, Harmondsworth: Penguin Books.

Smith, F. (1985) *Reading 2nd Edition*, Cambridge: Cambridge University Press.

Smith, P. and West-Burnham, J. (1993) *Mentoring in the Effective School*, Harlow: Longman.

Smith, R. M. (1983) *Learning How to Learn*, Buckingham: Open University Press.

Spratt, M. (1994) *English for Teachers: A Language Development Course*, Cambridge: Cambridge University Press.

Stephenson, H. (1994) 'Management and participation in ELT Projects', *ELT Journal* **48**, 3, 225–232.

Steil, L. K., Barker, L. L. and Watson, K. W. (1983) *Effective Listening: Key to your success*. Reading, Mass: Addison Wesley.

Stones, E. (1984) *Supervision in Teacher Education*, London: Routledge.

TTA (1997) *Notes for Guidance on Newly Qualified Teachers*, London: DfE.

Thornbury, S. (1991) 'Watching the whites of their eyes: the use of teaching practice logs', *ELT Journal* **45**, 2, 140–146.

Tomlinson, B. (1990) 'Managing Change in Indonesian High Schools', *ELT Journal* **44**, 1, 25–37.

Tomlinson, P. (1995) *Understanding Mentoring: reflective strategies for school-based teacher preparation*, Buckingham: Open University Press.

Turner, J. M. and Hiraga, M. K. (1996) 'Elaborating elaboration in academic tutorials: Changing cultural assumptions', in *Change and Language. British Studies in Applied Lingusitics* 10, Clevedon: BAAL and Multilingual Matters.

Turney, C., Cairns, L. G., Ettis, K. J., Hatton, N., Thew, D. M.,Towler, J. and Wright, R. (1982) *Supervisor Development Programmes*, Sydney: Sydney University Press.

Underwood, M. (1987) *Effective Classroom Management*, London: Longman.

Vygotsky, L. S. (1978) *Mind in Society*. Cambridge, Mass: Harvard University Press.

Wallace, M. (1991) *Training Foreign Language Teachers – A reflective approach*, Cambridge: Cambridge University Press.

Wallace, M. (1998) *Action Research for Language Teachers*, Cambridge: Cambridge University Press.

Wajnryb, R. (1993) *Classroom Observation Tasks*, Cambridge: Cambridge University Press.

Wertsch, J. V. (ed.) (1985) *Culture, Communication and Cognition: Vygotskian Perspectives*, Cambridge: Cambridge University Press.

Wertsch, J. V. and Smolka, A. L. B. (1993) 'Continuing the dialogue: Vygotsky, Bakhtin and Lotman', in Daniels, H. (ed.) (1993) *Charting the Agenda: Educational Activity after Vygotsky*, London: Routledge.

White, J. M. (1988) 'English for Yemen Textbook Project, Yemeni Arab Republic', *Evaluation Report EV403*, London: ODA.

White, R. V. (1987) 'Managing Innovation', *ELT Journal* **41**, 3, 211–218.

White, R. V. (1988) *The ELT Curriculum – Design, Innovation and Management*, London: Blackwell.

Woods, D. (1996) *Teacher Cognition in Language Teaching*, Cambridge: Cambridge University Press.
Wragg, E. (1990) *Teacher Appraisal. Macmillan School Management Project*, Basingstoke: Macmillan.
Wright, T. (1987) *Roles of Teachers and Learners*, Oxford: Oxford University Press.
Young, R. E. (1996) *Intercultural Communication*, Clevedon: Multilingual Matters.

List of figures

Index

NOTE: Tasks are in **bold** print. Worksheets are in *italics*.

Lightning Source UK Ltd.
Milton Keynes UK
09 March 2011

168963UK00001B/12/A